TRANSNATIONAL DEMOCRACY IN CRITICAL AND COMPARATIVE PERSPECTIVE

The International Political Economy of New Regionalisms Series

The International Political Economy of New Regionalisms Series presents innovative analyses of a range of novel regional relations and institutions. Going beyond established, formal, interstate economic organizations, this essential series provides informed interdisciplinary and international research and debate about myriad heterogeneous intermediate level interactions.

Reflective of its cosmopolitan and creative orientation, this series is developed by an international editorial team of established and emerging scholars in both the South and North. It reinforces ongoing networks of analysts in both academia and think-tanks as well as international agencies concerned with micro-, meso- and macro-level regionalisms.

Transnational Democracy in Critical and Comparative Perspective

Democracy's Range Reconsidered

Edited by
BRUCE MORRISON
University of Western Ontario, Canada

ASHGATE

Published by
Ashgate Publishing Limited
Gower House
Croft Road
Aldershot
Hants GU11 3HR
England

Ashgate Publishing Company
Suite 420
101 Cherry Street
Burlington, VT 05401-4405
USA

Ashgate website: http://www.ashgate.com

British Library Cataloguing in Publication Data
Transnational Democracy - Lessons from the Nation-State?
(2002 : London, Ont .)
    Transnational democracy in critical and comparative
    perspective : democracy's range reconsidered. - (The
    international political economy of new regionalisms series)
    1. Democracy - Congresses 2. Globalization - Political
    aspects - Congresses 3. International relations - Congresses
    I. Title II. Morrison, Bruce
    321.8

Library of Congress Cataloging-in-Publication Data
Transnational democracy in critical and comparative perspective : democracy's range
    reconsidered / edited by Bruce Morrison.
        p. cm. -- (The international political economy of new regionalisms series)
    Includes bibliographical references and index.
    ISBN 0-7546-3524-4
    1. Democracy. 2. World politics. 3. Globalization. 4. International organization. 5.
    International relations. I. Morrison, Bruce, 1962- II. Series.
    JC423. T662 2003
    321.8--dc21

2003052053

ISBN 0 7546 3524 4

Printed and bound in Great Britain by MPG Books Ltd, Bodmin, Cornwall

Contents

List of Tables, Figure and Appendix

Tables

Figure

Appendix

List of Abbreviations

CIA	Central Intelligence Agency (USA)
CLRAE	Congress of Local and Regional Authorities of Europe
COE	Council of Europe
COR	Committee of the Regions (EU)
CRIC	Centre for Research and Information on Canada
EAC	East African Community
ECHR	European Court of Human Rights
ECOSOC	Economic and Social Council (UN)
EU	European Union
FTC	Free Trade Commission (NAFTA)
G7	Group of Seven Wealthiest Countries (United States, Canada, United Kingdom, France, Germany, Italy, and Japan)
G8	G7 and Russia
GATT	General Agreement on Tariffs and Trade
GDP	Gross Domestic Product
GLR	Great Lakes Region (Africa)
HIPC	Heavily Indebted Poor Country
ICBL	International Campaign to Ban Landmines
ICC	International Criminal Court
ICISS	International Commission on Intervention and State Sovereignty
ICJ	International Court of Justice
IDEA	International Institute for Democracy and Electoral Assistance
IDRC	International Development Research Centre (Canada)
IFAD	International Fund for Agricultural Development (UN)
IFI	International Financial Institution
IGO	Intergovernmental Organization
IMF	International Monetary Fund (UN)
INGO	International Non-Governmental Organization
ITO	International Trade Organization
MNC	Multinational Corporation
NAFTA	North American Free Trade Agreement
NATO	North Atlantic Treaty Organization
NEPAD	New Partnership for Africa's Development
NFIO	National Firms with International Operations
NORAID	Irish Northern Aid
NRM	National Resistance Movement (Uganda)

PEAP	Poverty Eradication Action Plan (UNCTAD)
PFP	Policy Framework Paper
PMA	Peoples Millennium Assembly
PRSP	Poverty Reduction Strategy Paper (UNCTAD)
SADCC	Southern African Development Coordination Conference
SAP	Structural Adjustment Programme (IMF)
TNC	Transnational Corporation
TSM	Transnational Social Movement
TSMI	Transnational Social Movements Industry
TSMO	Transnational Social Movement Organization
UDN	Uganda Debt Network
UK	United Kingdom
UN	United Nations
UNCHS (Habitat)	United Nations Centre for Human Settlements
UNCTAD	Untied National Conference on Trade and Development
UNDP	United Nations Development Programme
UNESCO	United Nations Educational, Scientific and Cultural Organization
UNO	United Nations Organization
UNU	United Nations University
US	United States of America
WACLAC	World Assembly of Cities and Local Authorities Council
WMO	World Meterological Organization (UN)
WTO	World Trade Organization

List of Contributors

Chadwick F. Alger is Mershon Professor of Political Science and Public Policy, Emeritus, at The Ohio State University. His research and teaching is focused on the UN system of organizations, with special interest in the roles of Non-Governmental Organizations (NGOs), the world relations of people in local communities, and the development of long-term strategies for peacebuilding. He is the editor of *The Future of the UN System: Potential for the Twenty-First Century*, UNU Press, 1998, and has written numerous recent articles on NGOs and the UN. He served as President of the International Studies Association (1978-79), and Secretary General of the International Peace Research Association (1983-87).

Daniele Archibugi is a Director at the Italian National Research Council and Professor of International Organization at the University of Rome, "La Sapienza". He has written extensively on the question of democracy beyond the nation-state. Among his works in English, he edited or co-edited *Cosmopolitan Democracy: An Agenda for a New World Order*, Polity Press, 1995; *Re-Imagining Political Community: Studies in Cosmopolitan Democracy*, Polity Press and Stanford University Press, 1998; and *Debating Cosmopolitics*, Verso, forthcoming.

David Beetham is Professor Emeritus at the University of Leeds, specializing in democratic theory. He also serves as a consultant to many international organizations on democracy and human rights assessment. His publication credits include *Democracy and Human Rights*, Polity Press, 1999; and the co-authored books *Legitimacy and the EU,* Longman, 1998, and, most recently, *Democracy Under Blair*, Politicos, 2002.

Katherine Fierlbeck is Associate Professor of Political Science at Dalhousie University in Halifax, Nova Scotia. She is the author of *Globalizing Democracy: Power, Legitimacy, and the Interpretation of Democratic Ideas*, Manchester University Press, 1998, and is currently working on issues of accountability in health-care governance.

John A. Hall is James McGill Professor in the Department of Sociology at McGill University in Montreal. Recent books include *International Orders*, Polity Press, 1996, and, with Charles Lindblom, *Is America Breaking Apart?*, Princeton, 1999. He is currently completing a biography of Ernest Gellner.

Patti Lenard is a D.Phil. candidate in political theory at Nuffield College, Oxford University. Her doctoral thesis focuses on the importance of trust in democracies, in particular those with high levels of ethnic diversity. Her other research interests include minority nationalism, ethnicity and constitutionalism, and liberal nationalist theory.

John Markoff is Professor of Sociology at the University of Pittsburgh. His research interests include historical sociology, social movements, and the historically based analysis of democracy. In addition to numerous articles, he has written *Waves of Democracy: Social Movements and Political Change*, Pine Forge Press, 1996; and *The Great Wave of Democracy in Historical Perspective*, Cornell University Press, 1995.

John N. McDougall is Professor of Political Science at the University of Western Ontario. He teaches courses on globalization and national sovereignty, as well as North American political economy, and he has published extensively on North American integration and the American impact on Canadian public policy. He is currently completing a book on the effects of the NAFTA on Canadian-American relations.

Glyn Morgan is Associate Professor of Government at Harvard University. He is the author of *Justifying European Integration*, Princeton University Press, 2004. He is currently working on a book on liberal theories of progress.

Bruce Morrison is Assistant Professor of Political Science at the University of Western Ontario. His research and teaching interests include democratization, state formation, and social policy. He is currently completing a manuscript with the title *Democracy by Default: States, Regimes, and the Process of Reform in Modern Europe*.

Timothy M. Shaw is the Director of the Institute of Commonwealth Studies and Professor of Commonwealth Governance and Development at the School of Advanced Study of the University of London, as well as Professor of Political Science at Dalhousie University, Halifax, Nova Scotia. His primary research focus is African politics. He has researched and written extensively on globalization, regionalism, and the changing character of relations between states, civil societies, and the private sector in Africa and elsewhere.

Luc Turgeon is a Doctoral candidate in the Department of Political Science, University of Toronto. His main fields of research are urban politics, Canadian and British politics, and theories of federalism and constitutionalism. He has published in *Revue internationale d'études sur le Québec* and *Commonwealth and Comparative Politics*.

Preface

This volume grew out of a series of conversations among scholars associated with the Nationalism and Ethnic Conflict Research Group at the University of Western Ontario. Talk turned to conference plans, and, after a few intellectual and organizational struggles – some won, some lost – a gathering of international scholars convened in March of 2002 in London, Ontario, Canada. The conference – 'Transnational Democracy: Lessons from the Nation-State?' – was intended to extend beyond general discussion of the political consequences of globalization into more specific consideration of the utility of the national analogy, the familiarity of which makes it all too easy to rely upon in encounters with new possibilities.

As the discussion continued after the conference, however, and as people adjusted their ideas and approaches in response to what they had seen and heard, it appeared that the papers collectively addressed in more targeted fashion the various ways, both direct and indirect, intended as well as unintended, in which contemporary developments suggest the potential for democratic change at a level above that of the nation-state. In a sense, this is simply another way of examining the same problem, since some of these developments bear a resemblance to state formation and consolidation, whereas others are best contrasted with state-like processes. In the new version, however, the emphasis is placed cleanly upon the possibility of novelty not just in outcomes, but also in the pathways leading to them. It keeps our ear to the ground for shifts in the meaning of democracy, in its institutional expressions, and also in the kinds of conflicts and constructions that can have democratic effect. The nation-state experience still compels, confines, and otherwise influences, but it must also be set against the economic, social, cultural, and other changes that serve as the new context in which institutional adaptation takes place. This work does not, however, provide cheerleading for transnational democracy in any or all its forms. Rather, it adopts a critical standpoint, one which appreciates strengths as well as weaknesses, positive prospects as well as dangers, associated with developments which may possess a democratic character.

Producing a book of this type generates a variety of new friendships as well as new obligations. I am grateful to Richard Vernon, Andrés Pérez, and Charles Jones, who participated in the initial conversations in 2001 that laid the foundation for the conference and the resultant volume. The organization and execution of the conference benefited from the assistance of Sid Noel and Richard Vernon, whose timely interventions were particularly important on the questions of funding and conceptualization, as well as that of Robert Young, Charles Jones, and Deans Peter Neary and Brian Timney. I would also like to acknowledge the crucial behind-the-scenes efforts of Nigmendra Narain, Mojtaba Mahdavi, and Samir El-Masri. The conference, as well as the book it spawned, also benefited from the generous financial support of the Social Sciences and Humanities Research Council of Canada and the Nationalism and Ethnic Conflict Research Group of the University of Western Ontario. The staff at London's Windermere Manor, meanwhile, took extremely good care of the participants.

The conference's attendees formed a brief intellectual community of remarkable cohesion and creativity, resulting in a book project that was both self-evident and (almost) self-generating. I would like to highlight the contributions of those not appearing in the book: Susanne Soederberg, whose work on international financial institutions in the context of the Asian crisis of the late 1990s provided a new case to consider and a valuable alternative approach; André Drainville, whose critical appraisal of both sociological theory as well as actor subjectivity in the globalizing world will find a deserved audience in an upcoming book; and Christian Leuprecht, whose study of minority rights and European multinational institutions shed useful light on eastern European cases. Since the conference, the authors you will read in the following pages have maintained a constructively critical conversation which helped tremendously in my evaluation of the chapter contributions and their placement in the most appropriate intellectual context. One contributor in particular, John Markoff, deserves special mention because, in spite of his unavoidable absence from the conference, he continued throughout the period of the book's gestation to provide valuable commentary on individual chapters as well as the broader themes that connect them. Chadwick Alger, John McDougall, Glyn Morgan, Adam Harmes, Katherine Fierlbeck, and Luc Turgeon provided extremely useful critical guidance regarding the introductory chapter. John McDougall was a source of helpful advice at several other points as well. James Riker and Michael Keating came through with extremely stimulating commentaries at key moments. I would also like to thank Peter Hall for his standard invaluable advice, which had application at all stages in the creation of the collected volume. Nigmendra Narain deserves a second mention for his tireless and highly capable help with the formatting and editing of the book. Wendy Gray provided support in the design and proofreading departments. Last, but certainly not least, I want to express my gratitude to the team at Ashgate Publishing, above all series editor Tim Shaw, who provided direction as well as encouragement, and Kirstin Howgate and Irene Poulton, whose editorial assistance was prompt and always on the mark.

Assembling a cast of characters for a challenging and stimulating conference, as well as a resultant book which stands as a unit rather than a mere collection of papers, is a daunting one. Once the right scholars have been found, however, things become infinitely more manageable. I hope that they, as well as the readers of this book, feel that the contributing authors' work has been introduced and presented in a way that appropriately highlights their intelligent contributions to a crucial area of analysis.

Bruce Morrison
March, 2003
London, Ontario, Canada

Chapter 1

Introduction:
Transnational Democracy
in Context and in Question

Bruce Morrison

1. The Case for Transnational Democracy

This book brings together two themes of enormous current intellectual and emotional impact: *democracy* and its institutional forms, and the *globalization* of economic, social, and cultural affairs. Their point of intersection is easily located: recognition of globalization as fact or prospect drives a growing interest in transnational versions of democracy. Even as the post-1974 'third wave' of democracy inspired hopes of a world replete with extensively democratized nation-states,[1] the simultaneous decline of the power and purchase of these nation-states – the so-called 'retreat of the state' (Strange, 1996) associated with contemporary globalization – generated great concern. What, many have asked, might be the real value of extending democracy to a greater number of states, when these states are increasingly constrained in their ability to respond to the demands of their citizens? If even the First World, 'first wave' democracies are losing their grip on their affairs, what might it mean to extend democratic governance to polities perpetually lacking in capacity? (Haynes, 2001; Held, 1998: 16) Global economics and culture, it has therefore been argued, require global politics which will be at least as responsive to popular desires as the most democratic of national states. If the nation-states that contributed crucial public goods are failing, then they must either be replaced or supplemented by broader institutions which can persist in the performance of these democratic obligations (Cerny, 1999b). The 'third wave' of democratization, in any case, seems to have stalled (Diamond, 1999), which should fuel rather than restrain interest in a democracy that is genuinely and appropriately transnational.

Transnational democracy can therefore be viewed as a response to the various weaknesses of the national democratic project in a globalizing world. This context is, however, crucial, as globalization is claimed not merely to reduce the influence of states over issues of significance to their national constituencies, but also to change the character and range of these issues, thus rendering these states less relevant. Environmental protection, for instance, is becoming ever less a national and ever more a transnational public good, at which point national governments simply do not exist on the appropriate scale for full and effective response. From finances to security, meanwhile, recognition has grown, gradually and often reluctantly, that nation-states require the assistance of either formal or informal institutional arrangements that they cannot readily control (Archibugi and Held, 1995; Elliott, 2002; Kaldor, 1998; Scholte, 2002b).

Modern politics took shape on the basis of a fit between a national economic, social, and cultural environment, on the one hand, and the institutions of national government on the other. These governing institutions helped, first, to create this environment and, second, to develop its internal forces to the point at which a democratic response was required (Mann, 1993b; Tilly, 1992; van Creveld, 1999). If, however, the economy has outgrown the state, and the society is increasingly preoccupied with matters that extend beyond the national level, then perhaps the time has arrived for the state to yield to, or rather participate in, institutions that are transnationally rather than merely nationally democratic.

A transformation in international relations has been the principal catalyst for change. The Cold War 'had a strongly hierarchic structure, with few states able to escape subordination to the overall strategy of the great powers' (Archibugi and Held, 1995: 1). A statist logic therefore prevailed, with strong states bound by structural rivalry and weak ones propped up in the service of bipolarity. Even as important international institutions such as the United Nations, the International Monetary Fund, and the World Bank grew in significance, therefore, they remained functionally limited and further inhibited by the polarization of the era. The collapse of the Soviet Union, however,

> brought to a close the era of stalemate politics within the UN and associated agencies. This created the prospect of a more active and effective international governance. It also enabled a more inclusive form of multilateralism than had been feasible in a politically and economically divided world (Held et al., 1999: 8).

The case for transnational democracy has, finally, found confirmation and support in this new inclusiveness, itself premised upon the marked increase in activism that transcends national borders. It is undoubtedly the case that transnational engagement and organization is a long-standing phenomenon, either 'as old as religion' (Florini and Simmons, 2000: 8), or at least as old as the establishment of a modern capitalist international political economy (Nimtz, 2002). However, the burst of organizational activity since the Second World War and especially during the 1990s (Anheier et al., 2001: 5; Smith, Jackie, 2000; Kidder, 2002) gives substantial credibility to Richard Falk's (1997) notion that globalization has a 'from below' component. This component does, certainly, feature a variety of organizational forms, from international professional associations to broad activist associations such as Greenpeace and Amnesty International. And these organizations possess a variety of political motivations, ranging from outright opposition to globalization through reformism to advocacy (Held et al., 1999; Anheier et al., 2001b: 7-10). Collectively, however, they are seen as cultivating the transnational interconnections that will ground and even necessitate a form of democracy beyond the nation-state. They serve as counter-weights to existing authority at the national and supranational level, with effects on both procedures and policies regarding transnational issues; they help to generate, enforce, and reinforce supportive norms at the transnational level; and, in many cases, they not only directly influence the key intergovernmental organizations that constitute current transnational governance, but also participate in a number of ways in the governance of world affairs (Scholte, 2002b: 152-9; Keck and Sikkink, 1998; Khagram et al., 2002: 4, 12-17; O'Brien et al., 2000).

The case for transnational democracy is both compelling and highly contentious. If these concerns regarding the adequacy of national democracy as well as the 'hope, visions – and illusions' (Messner and Nuscheler, 2002: 125) unleashed by recent economic, cultural, and international-political changes are not about to go away, neither is the debate they have triggered. There are, in fact, multiple debates, all of which will find a place of prominence within this volume devoted to a critical appreciation of the prospects for transnational democracy. The following discussion will gather them into two groupings, dealing, first, with the identification and evaluation of transnational democracy and, second, with the question of causation and causal agency. This treatment will begin, next, with a section devoted to the complex definitional problems associated with transnational democracy. A schematic portrait will first be offered, stressing points of commonality amongst transnational democracy's advocates, after which the significant points of disagreement in characterization will be underlined. A second section will treat the difficulties with assessing such a complex, multi-tiered phenomenon. The causal analysis, which follows, will also be divided into two parts, the first of which will examine the problems associated with the relationship between globalization and transnational democracy, with a second one exploring the complications introduced when causal agents, and in particular transnational social actors of various descriptions, are brought into view.

2. What Transnational Democracy Is, Is Not, and Might Become

2.1 The Meaning and Forms of Transnational Democracy   The first category of debates revolves around the identification and evaluation of transnational democracy. These are far from straightforward matters. First of all, transnational democracy must be distinguished from 'transitional' democracy, a slightly awkward way of referring to the process of democratization of nation-states exiting from authoritarian rule. As Daniele Archibugi points out in the book's concluding chapter, democratic states do not necessarily contribute to the pacification or democratization of the international setting, which renders this distinction particularly crucial. Transnational democracy is not, therefore, to be equated with an extension of a third or subsequent wave of democratization to completion, not least because the number of democracies does not speak to their adequacy in the face of the forces of globalization and issues that also transcend their borders.

At the other extreme, transnational democracy is generally seen as something other than a democratic form of world or global government. Although favoured by science fiction writers and a few scholars, by and large it is understood that a world state would be either unmanageable or tyrannical, and probably both at once. There are some, of course, who advance intriguing cases for the cultivation of a global parliament (Falk and Strauss, 2001), but this is offered as an element in a broader scheme of global governance which, as Latham puts it, 'conveniently allows us to avoid articulating a single vision of order for fear of being taken for naïve rationalists or, worse, ethnocentric techno-imperialists' (1999: 24). This point is especially significant since, as Archibugi suggests, some critics do tend to fall prey to the fallacy of the excluded middle and so call to account a version of transnational democracy which few seriously propose (see his engagement, later this volume and in Archibugi et al., 1998, with the work of Zolo, 1997).

So what, then, is it that lies in the middle? The first thing to note is that there is as of yet no agreement as to what constitutes transnational democracy.[2] Like the socialist post-revolutionary paradise, it is driven more by dissatisfaction with the present state of affairs, and the conviction of its unsustainability, than by singularity or finality of vision as to what should replace it. Transnational democracy is, for its advocates, that which resolves the key dilemma of our time, identified as the incompatibility between national democracy and a globalizing world. Its functional character gives it flexibility as to precise form. It is revolutionary, in the sense of involving the creation of a new organization of power and structure of legitimacy in world affairs. In the view of most proponents, however, it does not require the levelling of existing institutions and total reconstruction. It is subtle but substantial change, gradual in some respects and abrupt in others.

Above all, if transnational democracy is a plan of action, a 'project' (Archibugi, 1998: 198), it is also responsive to the emerging forms of global governance – retaining, resisting, and reforming them. It concerns itself greatly with the fact that 'there is no single organizing principle on which global governance rests, no emergent order around which communities and nations are likely to converge' (Rosenau, 1998: 12). The heightened complexity associated with globalization has called forth rules of a variety of types (Sandholtz, 1999: 89-90; Rosenau, 1998: 14), but incompletely and unsystematically. Those who call freedom the radical decentralization associated with rapid marketization and technological change, meanwhile, might be either neglectful of or simply disinterested in the absence of formal democracy in the emerging (dis)order. Transnational democracy, therefore, 'aims to engender greater public accountability in the leading processes and structural alterations of the contemporary world' (Archibugi et al., 1998: 4). It wants globalization to be governed, but most significantly according to arrangements that are consistent, lawlike, and also, crucially, democratic (Archibugi, 1998).

Consistency does not mean uniformity in every respect, however. Beginning with David Held's compelling and ambitious *Democracy and the Global Order* (1995), transnational democracy has generally been conceived of as a multi-layered phenomenon featuring different versions of democracy at different levels of governance. While transnational democracy is not, of course, confined to nation-states, and does involve some degree of erosion of state sovereignty, it is inclusive of nation-state democracy. Though buffeted by powerful external forces, the state can still provide opportunities in the form of deliberative assemblies and national judiciaries, for instance, for the cultivation of democratic citizenship as well as for democratic decision-making on issues that continue to operate at the national level (Held, 1995).

New institutions have, however, already emerged to provide governance beyond the ken of the nation-state, and these intergovernmental bodies are also crucial pieces of the transnational democracy puzzle. On the one hand, they do provide occasion for the representatives of nation-states to discuss issues of general concern, and to reach decisions or at least foster the development of norms to deal with these issues. On the other hand, these bodies suffer from serious deficiencies from the democratic point of view. In many cases, they are exclusive, as in the case of the G7 or G8 meetings and, in a different way, the International Monetary Fund and the World Bank, which respond to Third World poverty on the terms of the First World (You, 2002; Woods, 2002). In the case of the United Nations, meanwhile, a very impressive move to universalization of membership over the past fifty years has not managed to override such in-built biases as the 'superpowers of yesterday and today' permanent membership of the crucial Security Council.

Transnational democrats do not necessarily call, however, for the supplanting of these cases of imperfect intergovernmentalism. Instead, first of all, they note that these institutions do provide a degree of governance, and with at least a degree of democracy, which helps to compensate for the inadequacies in capacity and legitimacy of existing nation-states. Second, they appeal for the democratization of these IGOs, and in ways appropriate to their form and function rather than in a futile attempt to replicate nation-state democracy. Against those who sigh at the UN's apparent unreformability, for instance, Daniele Archibugi adopts the spirit of the approach by insisting that 'it is unrealistic to look for more finely tuned vehicles to achieve a democratic world order, and that we must mobilize forces to reform the UNO [Organization] democratically' (1998: 221). Transnational democracy advances, therefore, to the extent to which such changes as a broadening of the Security Council, the establishment of a more powerful Assembly of Peoples, and a reduction of the UN's financial dependence on the wealthier states and the United States in particular come into effect (Falk, 2002; Archibugi, 1995).

In the end, however, intergovernmentalism itself reaches its limits, at which point only genuinely supranational institutions – those possessing authority and powers of enforcement not confined by their origins in interstate agreements – will provide sufficiently competent and democratic coverage for issues of the breadth of environmental or military threats to humanity (Woods, 2002). Successfully and thoroughly revamped intergovernmental institutions, such as the UN, or such new creations as a fully competent International Criminal Court, could serve the purpose. The European Union is of particular interest to transnational democrats, as it stands as a hybrid, in two senses: it bears a regional character which offers a possible stepping stone between the national/international and the supranational/global; and, it features, in addition to strongly intergovernmental elements such as the Council of Ministers, also supranational elements, such as the Commission, the European Parliament, and the European Court of Justice, which have shown surprising if fitful capacity for growth in significance over the course of a series of hard-bargained interstate treaties since the 1950s.

Transnational democracy is, therefore, not national democracy, but it includes it in its orbit. Nor is it intergovernmental democracy, although it encompasses it as a crucial element and grows in significance with the democratization of these bodies. It does of course aim at the cultivation of supranational institutions which offer the ability to deliberate and/or decide, but these must be set within this broader context. Its proponents are certainly idealists, but the ideal they offer builds upon that which exists, and imagines the development of a series of interconnected democratic sites which would extend from the local level to the national, intergovernmental – regionally as well as worldwide – and, ultimately, the supranational level.

As mentioned above, however, this schematic representation conceals significant differences of emphasis amongst those who advocate democracy beyond the nation-state. For proponents of cosmopolitanism, for instance, what binds together this broad vision is the pursuit through these institutions of 'democratic public law' which 'sets down criteria for the possibility of democracy – a range of entitlement capacities for members of a democratic society' (Held, 1995: 200). In the end, therefore, it comes down to the individual, whose autonomy and self-determination are crucial to democracy's prospects, and who is therefore the bearer of a series of rights corresponding to the seven sites of power.[3]

Cosmopolitanism, with its emphasis upon 'prescrib[ing] general principles, structures, and practices necessary for a more humane order, in which people's needs come to take precedence over the interests of states and their geopolitical machinations' (McGrew, 2000: 272), constitutes a powerful influence upon all those who seek democracy beyond the state. Radical democrats, however, want to ensure that global governance be as participatory as possible. From heightened transnational social movement activity to the establishment of deliberative and ultimately legislative bodies at the broadest level, their aims make them somewhat less comfortable with the top-down character of cosmopolitanism and with content-filled rights which foreclose the results of democratic engagement and contestation (Hutchings, 1999: 166-71; McGrew, 2002: 274-5; Falk and Strauss, 2001).

Deliberative or discursive democrats, as well as liberals, are much less comfortable than both cosmopolitans and radicals with transnational democracy's 'multiplication of decision-making authorities' and the associated danger of confused or competing majorities (Thompson, D., 1999: 112-3). For the deliberative approach, the solution is to abandon the fixation upon sovereignty and territoriality, and instead find ways to fashion temporary functional communities for the consideration of particular issues. They take very seriously the cosmopolitans' concern with the all-affected principle,[4] but fail to see why the insufficiency of national discussion and decision-making justifies over-reaching with new transnational or global structures (Dryzek, 1999: 33; McGrew, 2002: 277-80; Thompson, D., 1999: 119-23). Liberals, finally, are more hesitant to innovate either territorially or functionally, preferring instead to view the extension of economic and social actors into the sphere beyond the state, as well as the emergence of institutions for the promotion of international cooperation, as an opportunity for a type of transnational pluralism. Delegation, accountability, and transparency have been the liberal watchwords (Keohane, R.O., 1998).

Not only are these ideal types, of course, imperfectly capturing the views of individual analysts, but as the debate proceeds increasing cross-fertilization seems to be the fruit of effective criticism. Thus, for instance, the liberal Keohane is increasingly concerned with institutional legitimation via 'honest communication and rational persuasion,' (2002: 340) which seems to import some of the concerns of the deliberative democrats. Michael Saward, meanwhile, seeks out such ways as enhanced interstate cooperation, reciprocal representation, and deliberative forums in order to 'go further towards institutionalizing the all-affected principle, while still recognizing the importance of the territorial basis of much political representation' (2000: 34, 35-7; 1998: 135-8). In this volume, Chadwick Alger calls for a particularly democratic multi-tiered solution, involving the creation of a series of interconnected global assemblies for the representation of cities, peoples, states, and so on. Each of these territorial – but not necessarily governmental – units would itself strengthen their democratic character as part of this plan.

It will not be the purpose of this book to try to adjudicate amongst these approaches to defining and identifying transnational democracy, although the assembled essays will indeed cast some light on these matters. Nor is the aim in this volume to settle the terminological debate, and it will happily accommodate for instance Archibugi's preference for the use of 'cosmopolitan' rather than 'transnational'. In part, however, the latter term is more generally adopted in these pages because it is less confining, and perhaps somewhat less normative, given the existence of substantial disagreement. More importantly, its usage is based on recognition that, while those interested in democratizing globalization differ in theoretical grounding as well as in their willingness to countenance the creation of new institutional arrangements, there does nonetheless seem to be fairly general agreement in practice as to what constitutes more rather than less democracy in the new context. Democratic states make a contribution, if they are less than required; intergovernmentalism should strive to be more inclusive, and 'one state, one vote' is a partial rather than fully satisfactory formula for the incorporation of a wider range of global participants; greater institutional transparency at all levels marks an improvement; and, transnational activism can enhance democracy, in accountability if not also participatory terms.

Overall, the most fascinating thing about this debate is the extent of interaction between abstraction and empirical reality, between that which should be and that which is coming into existence (Bellamy and Jones, 2000: 208-13). Revolutionary and reformist, provocative and accommodationist, visions of the future are to varying degrees mapped onto readings of recent, and more distant, history. This engagement between past, present, and future, and the possibilities for novel forms of partial and imperfect democratic advancement, mark the primary terrain of this book. 'Transnational democracy', as concept and as focal point for this volume, does an effective job of moderating between the cosmopolitan and intergovernmental features of increasingly complex proposals for change (Latham, 1999: 46-7), accommodating actors as well as institutions at all levels, and placing the emphasis upon increments as well as end results. It allows the different authors to maintain and advance more or less clear visions, while also participating in a general search for the sites and sources of change. The term will, therefore, be employed as an overarching one, in the manner of McGrew, rather than, as with Dryzek, in association with the deliberative variant.

2.2 Complex Democracy, Complex Assessment Evaluating this broad, utopian, nuanced, grounded, and highly contested proposal for change will be one of the book's primary challenges. In a manner appropriate to the subject matter, this will be done at all levels of analysis. David Beetham, for instance, draws upon his expertise in assessing nation-state democracy to inquire into the utility of these assessment tools at the level above the nation-state. Armed with a presumption in favour of universal democratic principles, but also a sensitivity to the complex and multi-layered institutional environment of our time, Beetham finds a 'relatively modest' basis for transnational democratic assessment. Within the states themselves, first, the prospects are strong, though 'what counts as democratic in given circumstances may be deeply controversial', especially given heightened interactions between states and intergovernmental/supranational institutions. Second, the novel and uncertain nature of institutions beyond the state makes it harder to discern whether and to what extent democratic values are finding expression. Doing so requires close attention both to institutional characteristics and to the varying influence upon them of variously democratized nation-states. Overall, Beetham is confident that the pursuit of 'good democratic practice' is possible and useful, but he acknowledges that it requires more patience, creativity, and openness to debate the further one travels up the scale of territorial governance.

Glyn Morgan derives a different lesson from the nation-state experience: just as national democracies have had to come to terms with what he calls 'the constraints of modernity' – the delegation of decision-making authority to experts is, so Morgan contends, a necessary and desirable feature of modern politics – so transnational democrats must restrain their enthusiasm for democratizing supranational institutions. Whereas Katherine Fierlbeck wants to instrumentalize democracy as the basis for settling claims of national self-determination, Morgan argues that technocratic effectiveness, a more recognizably instrumental consideration, is in some cases at least as important as democratic participation. David Beetham views such an argument as being based on a flawed analogy. For him, experts should properly make decisions only on the basis of established rules, while the setting of these rules remains the exclusive domain of democratically elected representatives (for more, see Woods, 2002: 34-7).

Patti Lenard and Luc Turgeon, for their part, focus on a particular set of nation-states, implicitly challenging the singularity of 'the' nation-state as historical experience and as model for transnational possibilities. They suggest that countries like Canada might offer particularly helpful guidance to satisfactorily democratic transnational arrangements precisely because such countries have long experienced the difficulties associated with multinationalism, and experimented with ways to overcome or minimize these difficulties. Accordingly, they recommend a 'conversational' rather than 'contract' approach to constitution-making as the basis for transnational democracy. As the European Union attempts to frame a founding document, Lenard and Turgeon's call for the kind of constitution that is more process than outcome, that places 'sustaining a conversation over time' above closure regarding the 'constitutional essentials' (Chambers, 1998: 161, 149), is particularly interesting. It also usefully reminds us that the term 'transnational' carries with it certain disquieting assumptions regarding the 'national' character of the states which 'transnational democracy' proposes to incorporate and transcend. Finally, it invites exploration of cases in which multinationalism does not co-exist with Canadian-style order, the implications of which for constitutionalism and the mapping of transnational democracy might prove to be quite different (Keating, 2001).

The nation-state, whether narrowly or more broadly construed, remains highly relevant to consideration of transnational democracy, as both source and analogy, the exploration of which will constitute one of the book's primary purposes. The authors in this volume, however, go beyond merely relating nation-states to intergovernmentalism and transnationalism. John McDougall, for instance, provides a careful evaluation of regionalism as cause or template for transnational democracy, and finds in the end that the European Union, to the extent that it offers the possibility for growth in both transnational and democratic terms, is the beneficiary of postwar European circumstances that have not and will not likely be reproduced in North America or, indeed, elsewhere in the world. The implication is that the EU's role in the transnational project is and will remain a special one, and that in general trade, increasingly organized on a regional level, will not offer possibilities for the extension of democracy beyond the nation-state.

Interestingly, Morgan agrees with McDougall regarding the distinctiveness of the European project. Nonetheless, he maintains that the success of the American state should encourage Europeans to pursue further political integration for the express purpose of providing a counterweight to American hegemony. This will also allow Europeans to pursue the possibilities associated with American statism. McDougall, having examined Europe in North American comparison, turns back to the nation-state with hopes of strengthening its democratic character. Morgan, however, sees the United States as the single best argument in favour of the continued relevance of the nation-state, and turns to Europe to reproduce some of the beneficial effects of the American state in the interest of maintaining a degree of balance in the world. John Hall shares a somewhat similar view. Tim Shaw, in contrast, is much more hopeful that regionalism in Africa and elsewhere constitutes one important part of the emerging and expanding web of interconnections amongst economic, social, and political actors, and that much of democratic import will derive from these developments. For him, the regional is crucially connected to the domestic. Chad Alger completes the multi-layered picture with his portrayal of the way in which local authorities are extending into regional, intergovernmental, and supranational spaces, and his insistence that local democracy now depends upon a form of transnational democracy which it also makes possible and meaningful.

3. Transnational Democracy: Causal Considerations

3.1 The Meaning and Democratic Implications of Globalization The second set of key debates emphasizes the causal question, and in particular the claims made on behalf of globalization and its consequences. In definitional terms, first, there is wide disagreement as to the meaning of globalization, a term Nye and Donahue find to be 'at once a rallying cry, a riddle, and a Rohrshach test' (2000: xi). Held et al. (1999: 2-10) begin by emphasizing 'a real or perceived intensification of global interconnectedness' in a number of realms of human activity, after which they feel the need to divide the discussion into three approaches: that of the hyperglobalizers, who emphasize the increasing homogenization of human activity and experience; the skeptics, for whom globalization is an overstatement if not a myth; and the transformationalists, who see it as 'an essentially contingent historical process replete with contradictions' (Held et al., 7). In this volume, the meaning of globalization itself will not be the object of serious contention, except insofar as the definitional question connects up with that involving its implications for the state.

This is, of course, a connection that can only with great difficulty be avoided in any case. So, for instance, if globalization is unreal or strongly exaggerated, then the need for a compensatory political response is of course either much reduced or eliminated. Perhaps we have seen it all before, particularly in the late nineteenth and early twentieth centuries, a time of intensive cross-border movements of capital, goods, people, as well as significant cultural influences (O'Rourke and Williamson, 1999; Hirst and Thompson, 1999). This was, of course, very much a geographically concentrated episode of globalization, but this does not in itself set it thoroughly apart from today's uneven and differentiated pattern of integration. Amongst our authors, John Hall certainly embraces this position, concluding on these and other bases that the day of the nation-state is not yet done. John McDougall, though attentive to the deepening of economic integration and the emergence of regional institutional arrangements as significant novelties, nonetheless holds that only nation-states, rather than structurally limited trading apparatuses, are equipped to offer democratic accountability in today's context. Earlier instances of globalization hardly forestalled the growth in scale and rise to global prominence of the twentieth-century state. International conflict, and the strengthening of industrial capitalism in the core, combined with its extension to new places, contributed to these outcomes. There is, then, a case to be made for continued reliance upon the state, on the view that its reserves have neither been fully depleted by the possibly temporary challenges of our day, nor its potential for democratic response exhausted (Weiss, L., 1998; Thompson, D., 1999: 118-9; Nayyar, 2002: 380-2). Intriguingly, McDougall builds his case upon foundations which include the work of Ian Clark (1999), for whom globalization is essentially a form of state transformation.

Others remain impressed by globalization in spite of its imperfections. The world has changed substantially, and will continue to do so, which for Archibugi necessitates an incorporation of infinitely less capable states within a broader architecture of democratic transnational governance. As Tim Shaw and his colleagues have elsewhere written, however, these changes will continue to be 'profoundly contradictory, combining both "a fundamental shift towards an integrated and coordinated division of labor in production and trade" and a simultaneous fractionalization of social order, widening of economic disparities and multiplying political disintegrations' (Quadir et al., 2001: 7). It is this blend of 'integration and fragmentation' (Landau, 2001:1), along with its multifaceted character, that interests Shaw and others in pluralizing globalization (Held et al., 1999). These elements also interest Shaw in a broad and novel consideration of the actors involved in shaping the new world in political as well as other respects. Shaw therefore adopts the notion of a 'governance triangle' in order to underscore his point that, especially but not exclusively in the African context, there is no longer reason to privilege the state over business and civil-societal actors. This framework allows him more clearly to sketch out the oppositions and interconnections amongst these participants in a broadened political process (see also Shaw, T., 1999: 3-5; Callaghy, Latham, and Kassimir, 2001; Woods, 2002: 31-4). Chadwick Alger's comprehensive portrait of current institutional and civil-societal developments at the local and intergovernmental levels serves a related purpose, exposing us to new sources of democratic potential, albeit without attempting to settle the relationship between his transnational social movements and local authorities on the one hand and firms and states on the other. Whereas for both contributors, globalization's tendency toward 'fragmentation' provokes a democratizing response from the excluded and those active on their behalf, it also generates through 'integration' a series of opportunities for either direct or indirect transnational democratic impact. Daniele Archibugi draws upon both of these strains in setting out the terms for his justification of the cosmopolitan democracy project. For him, this dictates an emphasis upon a spatial or territorial continuum from the local to the global, as well as upon the 'communities of stake-holders' which are not merely national in character and therefore merit a transnational political and financial response.

3.2 Transnational Democracy and Social Agency If the status of the state is very much in question in the pages to follow, so also is that of the proposed substitutes or supplements for state agency. What does seem entirely convincing is that we no longer inhabit – if we ever did – the world of exclusive and separate interacting states as set out by stricter readings of realist international relations theory. Actually existing states, properly considered much more porous and much less in control of their fates and environment, share the stage with economic, social, and political actors at the domestic and transnational levels, as well as with institutional bases of cooperation such as the norms and regimes generated in part by the efforts of these new actors. What remains in dispute is how to characterize these actors as well as how seriously to take them. Some analysts are attached to the fact, or at least the prospect, of a global civil society as the form or foundation for transnational democracy (Scholte, 2002a). Given, however, that international non-governmental organizations (INGOs) are still largely concentrated in the North, especially Europe and North America, are still heavily dependent upon Northern resources, and still devote a disproportionate amount of their energies to lobbying the most internationally influential national governments – the United States in particular – then the term 'global' remains more than a bit ambitious (Sikkink and Smith, 2002: 35-9).

Anheier et al. (2001) nonetheless find 'global' superior to the increasingly commonly used 'transnational civil society', but perhaps for the wrong reasons. Certainly, as they contend, 'all one needs to be transnational is a single border-crossing', and so 'transnational' runs the danger of underplaying the arguably 'revolutionary' changes in social organization in recent decades. 'Global', however, is an overstatement, as Anheier et al. acknowledge. It might also be the case, meanwhile, that we need less reminding in our day of globalization hype of how much has changed than how little (Hirst and Thompson, 1999; Williamson, 1996). John Markoff, in his essay in this book, provides the historical perspective required for the evaluation of some of the more expansive claims made regarding the novelty of today's social actors (see also Nimtz, 2002). John Hall, in his chapter, goes further, to the point of offering the transatlantic experience as evidence that transnational connections and identities have at least experienced setbacks over time as well as surges.

Anheier et al. are also attached to 'global civil society' as a source of 'normative aspiration' which can more appropriately and effectively be set against other global processes as a counterweight. It remains open to question, however, whether there can be a civil society properly understood at the global or transnational level. 'Civil society' remains a deeply contested concept, but there is at least fairly general agreement that it emerged responsively with the development of the modern state (Gellner, 1994a; Cohen and Arato, 1994). As noted by Anheier et al., in fact, 'there is doubt about the very existence of such a society without the presence of an effective state' (2001: 11). This is not to deny that conditions might come to favour the emergence of a transnational sphere with ever more civil-societal characteristics. The deepening of integration might present ever-increasing organizational opportunities, or the development of an ever more elaborate transnational governance structure might generate greater degrees of organizational concentration. The authors in a recent volume edited by Ougaard and Higgott (2002) make the intriguing if ambitious case that these developments point to the formation of a 'global polity' which is less than a global state but far more than lightly governed anarchy. Markoff, in asking 'who will construct the global order?' and exploring how key contenders emerge, and with what strength and inclinations, sets the tone for related inquiries in the essays of Archibugi, Morgan, Alger, as well as my own, and to a lesser degree throughout the book.

The abstractions of 'global civil society' aside, however, the task of characterizing these contenders remains. One way to proceed is by referring primarily to INGOs, those actors not directly bound to states which 'are organized to advance their members' international goals and provide services to citizens of other states through routine transactions with states, private actors, and international institutions' (Tarrow, 2001: 12). Alger's pursuit of democratic potential within global governance, however, draws him to focus upon the narrower group of 'those INGOs actively seeking social change' and, Tarrow adds, 'more clearly rooted within social networks and engaged in contentious, sustained interaction' (2001: 11). These are transnational social movements, and they are key actors in Alger's account.

Other scholars respond by undercutting the relevance of these transnational actors. In this volume, this view comes above all from Glyn Morgan, with his insistence that these movements suffer intractable problems of representativeness, accountability, as well as effectiveness, and are therefore subject to question as legitimate participants in the cultivation of democratic transnational authority. Kathryn Sikkink, for her part, notes the irony that efforts to rectify the 'democratic deficit' of INGOs 'may mean more bureaucratized professional organizations' which have lost the efficacy rooted in 'their flexibility to respond rapidly, their gadfly quality, and the informality of the global networks' (2002: 315).

There are also signs, however, that 'transnational social movements' might be losing ground in the literature to 'transnational advocacy networks' as an acknowledgement that these collective actors tend to be much more loosely affiliated than traditional social movements, bound largely by a common orientation towards changing discourses and the values embedded in them (Keck and Sikkink, 1998; Khagram, Riker, and Sikkink, 2002: 6-10). Otherwise put, networks 'contain' (Tarrow, 2001: 13) social movements, extending them beyond their normal reach into the rarefied transnational air. In these terms, both could be seen as offering strengths and weaknesses:

> [N]ew organizing is done in networks because of the capability of networks to integrate and interpret new information, and to transfer knowledge and 'know-how' between interdependent actors. Networks seem to be particularly effective at empowering people, transforming their views and identities (frames), and encouraging member participation. Networks seem to do less well at maintaining communication between large numbers of members and coordinating financial resources, which hierarchical organizations may do better (Kidder, 2002: 291).

Our aim in this volume is not to foreclose the conceptual question but to invite discussion of it, and therefore Alger and Shaw make reference to transnational social movements while Markoff and I tend to favour the network terminology.

No less important an aim is to invite debate about the implications of these choices. In my essay, as well as in Markoff's, the link is offered between the absence of concentrated institutions at the transnational level and the absence of concentrated movements at that level. To the extent that transnational forms of democracy will depend upon movement activism, therefore, I suggest that it may have to await the emergence of a denser institutional environment, the product of the interested actions of governmental, business, and other actors. Markoff cautions that, thus far, 'the structures of transnational governance...often lack some of the important features of the states that tied the histories of national movements and national democratizations together'. Kidder's conclusion, meanwhile, is that 'the effective transnational campaigns tend to skillfully combine the strengths of both networks and hierarchical organizations' (2002: 291).

Even those who employ the term 'global civil society' do not necessarily ascribe to it all the characteristics of national societies, especially their cohesion, except perhaps by projection or extrapolation. At present, however, the absence of a supportive community – as opposed to a series of organized agents acting on its behalf – is one of the strongest arguments against the possibility of a transnational democracy. Democracy, it is claimed, requires a *demos*, or at least a substantial degree of solidarity and shared understandings as preconditions for the kind of behaviour that makes democracy work (Offe, 2000: 63-9). For John Hall, an earlier sense of transatlantic community has long been on the wane, and the United States, certainly, will continue to be an engine for making Americans.

Fierlbeck is also impressed by the resilience of the nation-state, although the cultivation of consent is of more interest to her than the cultivation of identity. Lenard and Turgeon take identity more seriously, and view it more fundamentally, disagreeing therefore with Fierlbeck's refusal to give cultural identity primacy of place. Fierlbeck denies that either sovereignty or democracy make sense on the basis of 'culturally-oriented self-determination', whereas Lenard and Turgeon are much more appreciative of arguments stressing 'the intercultural nature of dialogue'.

The intensity of Lenard and Turgeon's attachment to this approach does not, interestingly, lead them to follow communitarians in their resistance to an overwhelming and ultimately stifling democratization beyond the zone of comfort and control of human communities (Miller, D., 2000; Coates, 2000: 92-3). John Markoff points to migration and the resultant ethnocultural dilemmas as deeply problematic for the future of national democracy. Lenard and Turgeon, however, argue that the success of transnational democracy might depend upon the selection of the very institutional arrangements – the aforementioned 'conversational' constitution – which made a virtue of necessity in multicultural Canada. Archibugi, finally, argues on the basis of a belief, given some limited additional support in Markoff's essay and my own, that the process by which national communities developed can reproduce itself after a fashion at the global level, and thus serve as the basis for a well-functioning transnational or cosmopolitan democracy (see also Newman, 2000: 29).

4. Conclusion

These are fascinating debates, and they will receive extensive treatment in the pages to follow. They are also highly interconnected – for instance, one's preferred form of democratic institutions is very much related to one's understanding of the character of globalization – and these interconnections will be highlighted. More central still to the purposes of this volume, however, will be the pursuit of the sources of democratic potential at the transnational level. To a very great extent, this task depends upon a critical examination of the history of nation-state formation and democratization in various regions of the world. This was and remains a highly complex and poorly predictable process. Attempts to fashion an overarching theory of democratic change have produced great insight but ultimate frustration. Meanwhile, recognition is growing that democracy need not emerge in complete and lasting fashion; rather, democratic partiality seems not only conceivable but also sustainable in many parts of the world. We are, therefore, growing in our appreciation of the complexity of democracy, sometimes structurally derived, sometimes fashioned by democrats, and sometimes the by-product of conflict at, between, or beyond key institutional sites (Diamond, 1999; Collier and Levitsky, 1997).

It is in this spirit that the authors in this volume have taken up the task of evaluating transnational democracy. They want to discuss preconditions and prodding into existence, certainly, but they are no less interested in analyzing existing institutions and relations in order to determine their democratic possibilities, immediate or otherwise, intended or unintended. They understand that the path to broader democratic arrangements may but need not be direct, and so they are inclined to explore a number of possible sources of the democratic impulse, from local governmental processes to national and transnational social movements through to such high-level processes as new trade and financial arrangements at the international and even supranational level. As a result, the authors in this volume find themselves drawn into intellectual and geographic territories as diverse as Viennese municipal government, Canadian constitutionalism, North American as well as European trade agreements, Ugandan state-society relations, and the United Naitons. While, therefore, the coverage is global in its attention to transnational institutions and transnational collective actors, for instance, it is also genuinely regional, and even local, with the emphasis upon the pursuit of the potential building blocks for a more appropriately democratic future in the varied forms that the institutionalization of globalization assumes around the world.

Therefore, just as the debate rages on over the relative contribution of mass and elite actors – pact-makers or deal-breakers – as well as socioeconomic and institutional factors, to national democratization, so also must we continue to explore the varied springs of conflict and cooperation, at all levels, of possibly democratic effect. It is John Markoff who establishes most explicitly the connection between democratization theory and transnational democracy in this collection, but the connection extends more broadly, and in a way that illuminates its limitations as well as its value. Overall, as Chadwick Alger rightly specifies in his chapter, 'it is in the loam of complexity that the roots of democracy are to be found!' This is not at all to suggest, however, that the authors in this volume are merely seeking out democratic impulses. Rather, the analysis is highly critical in nature, with some authors reporting democratic dead-ends and others suggesting that institutions that bear international and even transnational status might not ideally be designed in democratic fashion or to democratic effect. The general result is a comprehensive portrait of the bases for dissatisfaction with present arrangements, in which the reach of popular control seems increasingly to exceed its grasp, as well as a portrayal of the prospects, direct and indirect, for overcoming this growing sense of frustration with the limitations of nation-state democracy.

Notes

1   The use of 'national' or 'nation-states' is not intended to imply the existence of any strongly national unity or identity in the states in question, many of which are deeply divided on ethnic and cultural lines. Similarly, 'supranational' is meant to refer to that which exists above the level of the nation-state broadly defined, but which is not merely international or intergovernmental in character. These distinctions, and their relationship with the term 'transnational democracy' will become clearer as the text proceeds.
2   Nor, as we will see, is there agreement on the term itself.
3   The body, for instance, is a site of power which stipulates the existence of physical, environmental, and reproductive health rights; social rights, to education, community services, and the like, emerge in association with the 'welfare' site; rights to freedom of belief and expression stand in association with culture as a power site; civic associations give rise to associational rights; the economy as a site suggests the existence of rights linked both to economic activity and individual protection against its consequences; collective coercion is a site which dictates the existence of pacific rights both within and beyond states; and, finally, the institutions of law and regulation call forth political rights which support participation in setting the public agenda and discussing public outcomes. See Held (1995: 190-216).
4   This principle holds that all those affected by an issue, regardless of their location, should acquire some influence over decisions concerning it.

Part I

Transnational Democracy
and the Nation-State:
History, Identity, and Sovereignty

Chapter 2

Who Will Construct the Global Order?

John Markoff

1. Globalization as a Challenge to National Democracies

Toward the end of the twentieth century, as the democratization of the national states embraced many more states and citizens than ever before, some were suggesting that an emerging global order was challenging the authority of those states, including their capacity to provide satisfactory democracy. Consider Adam Przeworski's (1997: 11) warning:

> We know very little and understand next to nothing about "globalization". All we have so far is slogans and anecdotes. But we do know that the supra-national question is alarming from the point of view of democratic theory.

What are the arenas of social life to which 'democratic theory' pertains? Is democratic theory restricted to the democracy of the national states and the conditions that favour, enhance, deform, prevent, or destroy that democracy? If so, I believe that the supranational question is indeed disturbing. Just as the redeployment of power over past centuries away from villages and towns and towards the national state made national structures of power far more important to the lives of most people, so we are probably near the beginning of a similarly epochal redeployment of power towards transnational structures as yet to be created. But whether such new structures present new opportunities as well as new threats will be a question increasingly likely to capture the imagination of anyone concerned with the future of democracy. We need a shift in what it is that political theory needs to be a theory of.

Let us begin by addressing Przeworski's concerns about the democracy of the states in a global era. His alarm is in very considerable contrast to the confident and triumphal note of many just a short while before. Francis Fukuyama's 1992 book had told us it was now *The End of History*, dropping the cautious question mark with which he had ended the title of an earlier article (Fukuyama, 1989, 1992). But a decade later, democracy was confronting very troubling issues, some quite novel. We can appreciate the novelty by contrasting an earlier moment of democratic triumph and concern captured in James Bryce's *Modern Democracies* of 1921.

Let us locate that moment within the history of democratization. On the eve of World War I a significant transnational current of democratic reformism brought forth an effective secret ballot in France, women's suffrage in Norway, expanded male suffrage in Italy, limitation of the authority of the British House of Lords, and direct election of Senators in the US. Acknowledging and reinforcing that transnational current, Argentina's president announced that his country's distinctive contribution would be mandatory voting (Sáenz Peña, 1915: 44-5). This significant reform current coincided with a cluster of revolutionary upheavals directed against autocratic rule and in favour of republicanism, constitutionalism and liberalism that moved from Russia in 1905 to its southern neighbors Iran, the Ottoman Empire, and China (and probably we should include the contemporaneous upheavals in Mexico and Portugal as well) (Sohrabi, 1995; Kurzman, 1998). A classic content analysis of leading newspapers in some half-dozen Great Powers informs us that the decade beginning in 1910 saw a tremendous upsurge in discussion of democracy, pro and con (de Sola Pool, 1952: 67). When only the democracies emerged from the Great War's slaughter with their political systems intact, a cluster of new states, formed on the ruins of Hohenzollern, Habsburg, Romanov, and Ottoman empires, endowed themselves with democratic constitutions.

At that moment, Bryce (1921: 4-5) writes:

> Four great empires in Europe – as well as a fifth in Asia – all ruled by ancient dynasties, crash to the ground, and we see efforts made to build up out of the ruins new States, each of which is enacting for itself a democratic constitution. China, India, and Russia contain, taken together, one half or more of the population of the globe, so the problem of providing free government for them is the largest problem statesmanship has ever had to solve.

Note Bryce's mix of hope and hesitation. The big challenge could be summed up as further geographic extension: how to successfully bring new countries into the democratic fold. Over the next decade and a half Europe's democracies were challenged by a variety of monarchs, militaries, and mass movements, often successfully, an experience that demonstrated that a newly democratized constitution was no guarantee that democracy had any depth or strength. Today's analysts of our even greater wave of democratization do sometimes express similar concerns by questioning the 'quality' of the new democracies or employing adjectives to distinguish 'illiberal' or 'broken back' democracy from the real thing, or even wondering if some of the new 'democracies' are not better described as 'plebiscitarian authoritarianisms' (Diamond, 1999: 24-63; Linz, 2000 [1975], 34; Rose et al., 1998: 200-1, 217-23).

Weighty as such questions are, we confront new issues as well. Survey research enables us to identify some of the specific discontents of publics in countries that have participated in the great wave of democratization. We can examine a Brazilian public appalled at the incapacity of the state to control violent criminality, an Argentine public persuaded that the police are among the major criminals, or various post-Communist European concerns about the disintegration of social safety nets. But observation of such data points to something I consider more striking: that the voicing of doubts about central political institutions is not merely a feature of post-Communist Europe or post-military Latin America, but of the wealthy and allegedly well-established democracies as well. We are getting works with titles like *Disaffected Democracies: What's Troubling the Trilateral Countries?; Critical Citizens; Why People Don't Trust Government;* and *Absent Mandate* (Pharr and Putnam, 2000; Norris 1999; Nye et al., 1997; Clarke et al., 1995). Among the wealthy democracies, the US seems to have been in the temporal lead in disaffection.[1] Comparativists for a while debated whether this was perhaps a new form of American exceptionalism, but the data from the 1990s make it pretty clear that something of the same sort is characterizing Western Europe as well. There is some generic dissatisfaction pretty much everywhere, not just in illiberal, broken back or dubious democracies.

I want to venture a simple hypothesis: the democracy of the states at the turn of the twenty-first century cannot meet what it is that many people expect from democratic government. Important aspects of democratic politics are deeply challenged by the thickening web of transnational connection that was emerging at the same time as many of the states were democratizing – 'globalization', in short. What is in question is the meaningfulness of the democracy of states in general in a global age – not just the newly democratized or redemocratized.

By the contentious word 'globalization' I simply mean the web of significant social interaction – economic, cultural, and political – that crosses national frontiers. At the cost of bypassing a very rich debate,[2] I want to just postulate here that such interaction has been increasing, and I will briefly spell out some of the consequences that constitute challenges to the democracy of the states under four rubrics.

1.1 The Declining Political Weight of Labour   Although falling union membership is particularly marked in the United States, comparative survey evidence shows considerable decline in confidence in labour unions in many countries (Dogan, 1997: 29). Revolutionary developments in transportation and communications technologies have increased the mobility of both capital and labour, though the former far more than the latter (Overbeek, 2002). Labour migrations were increasing in the late twentieth century, but still did not rival the transatlantic migrations a century earlier. Differently put, state controls over the mobility of persons, emblematized by the passport (Torpey, 1999), remain a good deal stronger than over the mobility of capital.[3] This disparity suggests a tremendous advantage to capital in negotiations within the boundaries of national states. Precisely how this will play out politically will no doubt vary a good deal from place to place. For the richer countries at the turn of the twenty-first century, we observe some mix of downward pressure on wages, reductions in social services, rising unemployment, and importation of less expensive workers, along with an abandonment by traditional parties of the left of some of the positions that until recently were central to their identities. Since one of the engines spurring democratization over two centuries has been the mounting of working-class demands, the weakening position of labour has serious implications. Charles Tilly (1995a) titled a forceful article 'Globalization Threatens Labor's Rights' – I would add: 'and Therefore Democracy'.

Despite these very important elements of deterioration in labour's position, there may be new vulnerabilities emerging for capitalism's global elite as well. As worldwide competitive pressures induce firms to shift to global sourcing and just-in-time inventories, complex transnational flows of goods may be subject to disruptions that very quickly impose major costs on firms dependent on smooth supply flows (as Beverly Silver observes [2003]). So in addition to considering how increased transnational mobility of capital disadvantages labour, and the consequent weakening of one of the historical sources of national democratization, we need to think about the possibilities for new forms of labour action at a transnational level. It may be that an increasingly globalized economy will open new democratizing challenges to global elites even as some important sources of national democracy are seriously wounded.

1.2 New patterns of migration People may be less mobile than investment flows and the immigrant presence in some richer countries may not have reached the extent it had a century earlier, but the combination of a) people from poorer countries seeking work in wealthier ones and b) the seemingly endless flows of refugees from war and abusive regimes in tandem with globalized communications are making rich countries into multiethnic, multiracial, multicultural places, if they were not such to begin with. If impoverishment and violence help explain the supply side of immigration, there are significant elements on the demand side as well: the aging populations with shrinking families that are characteristic of all rich countries are not able to provide the next generation of workers without importing them.

All the richer countries are going to confront the politics of ethnocultural exclusion and inclusion, with its potential for further weakening the political capacities of labour and its particular challenge to welfare systems. This latter point comes from the reluctance of many to pay taxes to support those with whom they do not identify. Although global economic downturn and fear of terrorists may exacerbate these concerns in the wake of September 11 – and show up in the ready embrace of immigration as an issue by contenders for office all over western Europe (Erlanger, 2002) – there already was plenty there to be exacerbated. There is an important argument made by many political sociologists that conflicts framed in ethno/racial terms are less readily amenable to the bargaining processes of democracy than are conflicts framed in class terms (e.g., Diamond et al., 1995: 42). At an extreme, there are the threats of electoral majorities supporting deprivations of minority rights, and of minorities opting out of democratic processes, out of the existing state, or both.

1.3 The Technocratic Character of Economic Decision-Making To the extent that central decisions on economic policy are made with an eye on transnational institutions – whether these are formally constituted bodies like the IMF, World

Bank, and World Trade Organization, or *ad hoc* clusters of financiers, the meaningfulness of democratic input at the national level is challenged. To the extent, furthermore, that such decisions are made by a cosmopolitan technical elite, professionally socialized in similar viewpoints, the space for democratic debate over economic life is further constricted as economic managers of different parties and different countries agree on the principles of economic science to be applied to affairs of state (Markoff and Montecinos, 1993; Montecinos and Markoff, 2001). The actual trends of recent decades include an ascent of professional economists to positions of decision-making power in many national states. The intellectual formation of economists, moreover, is becoming more uniform, with a US degree now setting the standard in many parts of the world. Both cause and consequence of globalization, the managers of national economies readily communicate across national frontiers in part because of their common intellectual culture. These trends may in some ways seem to be good things – if one believes that economists know something about managing economies and if one believes that newer trends in economic thought are advances that quite properly are driving older ideas from the field. They are, however, challenges to the meaningfulness of the democracy of the states. And if you think the experts' expertise or their dispassion is exaggerated, then so much the worse. (For more observations on the problematic relationship between expertise and democratic accountability see Glyn Morgan's chapter in this volume; David Beetham and Daniele Archibugi also offer useful observations on these matters.)

1.4 Redeployment of power away from the states This is perhaps the most fundamental challenge. For hundreds of years political life has been organized within the container of what were conceived of as sovereign states. While that sovereignty was always an idealized exaggeration, especially for weaker players on the world stage, by the 1970s, on the crest of decolonization, most of the people of this planet were living in such entities. But in the later twentieth century power was being redeployed in ways that some political scientists summed up as three vectors: *downwards*, *upwards*, and *outwards*. Decision-making moves downwards as regional or local organs of government take on new powers or are provided with new resources. Decision-making moves upwards as transnationally organized institutions gain in significance. Decision-making moves outwards with privatization, contracting out, and deregulation.

On the level of the formal rules of democratic government none of this redeployment need have any impact at all. There is no diminution in citizens' rights against the states, no weakening of electoral processes, no formal limitation on public debate. And yet there are two very significant implications. First of all, to the extent that states are enmeshed in a world of powerful suprastate actors, state policy makers are going to be increasingly constrained by something other than the will of their citizens. And second, what it is over which the national state has authority will shrink. So incumbents may be accountable to citizens, and yet more and more of the decisions that affect the lives of those citizens are made somewhere else. The continuing discussion of the European Union's 'double democratic deficit'[4] is one important place where these issues are being thrashed out (Markoff, 1999a).

None of this remotely means that states will cease to be significant, since the states are and will surely continue to be among the major actors in the construction and reconstruction of the global political order. But it does mean that significant decision-making may become very much more removed from scrutiny by citizens, and thereby very much less accountable to them. One symptom of this particular challenge is the emerging issue of 'transparency' (Holzner, 2002).

In summary: discussion of democracy and the conditions that favour, enhance, deform, prevent, or destroy it can no longer be confined to the national states.

2. Democracy's History

In speculating about the future of democracy beyond the states, I will draw lessons from four aspects of the history of the democracy of the states – the role of elite divisions, the propensity to institutional innovation, the tension between democracy as a claim to legitimacy and democracy as a set of institutionalized procedures, and the multiplicity of paths.

2.1 Elite Divisions   It is becoming a truism among scholars of social movements that the success of challenges to established patterns is to a significant degree dependent on opportunity, including very importantly conflict among dominant elites. Two particular clusters of conflict stand out in the histories of the national states as opportunities that were critical to launching modern democracy.

First, the frequent difference of interest between a monarch at the head of a centralizing bureaucracy and local aristocratic powerholders, as well as conflicts among those aristocrats and within those bureaucracies, provided opportunities for popular forces:

- to bargain for their loyalties with warring elite claimants to power who sought their support (including taxation and military personnel) (Te Brake, 1998);
- to mobilize on their own in support of the less undesirable alternative.

At some very important times and places those popular forces could manage to go beyond backing the least noxious of the elites and put forward their own visions. The English Civil War of the seventeenth century was one such very important formative moment in the history of democracy (Linebaugh and Rediker, 2000: 104-142; Morrison, in this volume, offers a different reading of the democratic impact of elite conflicts).[5]

Second, in those states where rulership was held to be connected to some sacred source of authority there were often tensions between monarchical hope for autonomy from constraint and monarchical need for religious legitimation. This made the relationships of religious and monarchical authority very rich and complex, generating lots of interesting terminology for classifying such things on the part of Max Weber. This tension sometimes created opportunities that encouraged daringly deviant and innovative religious points of view:

- by monarchs dissatisfied with inadequate support from religious orthodoxy;
- by aristocrats challenging monarchs or each other;
- by those down below the radar screens of the powerful, for whom dissenting religious visions might sustain challenges to social hierarchies (e.g., Hill, 1972).

Thus the histories of grass-roots mobilizations and the histories of elite politics are deeply intertwined. I believe that there are some very rough analogies in the emerging global scene, with both happy and unhappy consequences for the prospects of transnational democracy.

2.2 Innovation At the tail end of the seventeenth century, a *savant* could describe the *Universal Dictionary* he had written as 'Broadly speaking, containing all French words both ancient and modern as well as the terminology of all the sciences and arts'. Antoine Furetière (1970 [1690]) needed no more than the first ten of the words devoted to the entry for 'Democracy' to define it ever so tantalizingly as: 'Form of government in which the people have all authority'. Tantalizing because there is no specification of the fashion in which authority was to be exercised, nor over what, nor even how one might know *who* were these all-powerful people let alone how one might determine what their will was. For those many political scientists of today who insist on a 'procedural' definition, Furetière's words are perhaps devoid of sense.

What Furetière has no interest in addressing is telling – democracy has no role to speak of in the national states of his day and no prospects either. There is thus no practical consequence to exploring what its institutions were or what they might be. Only on a small scale, and under long-gone circumstances at that, could democracy exist. As the author points out: 'democracy only flourished in the republics of Rome and Athens'. And a good thing, too: as the entry adds, 'seditions and turmoil happen often in Democracies'. Democracy in the modern national state, then, is neither possible nor desirable; no doubt at our own moment more than a few would say pretty much the same of democracy beyond the states (see Archibugi's development of this point later in this volume).

One hundred years after it appeared, all the many questions not worth that dictionary's troubling about were very much on the agenda of those for whom the creation of new institutions was not merely a possibility, but in some places a necessity born of social turmoil. In 1790, newly independent North Americans had just ratified their constitution, French revolutionary legislators were working on theirs, Dutch and Belgian Patriots considered how to reorganize their homelands should the French example reverse their recent defeats, and Polish aristocrats debated drastic reform under threat by rapacious neighbors. In some places reforming elites were the central participants, in others the working people of town and country mounted waves of insurrections against the privileged powerholders of old regimes – or new ones.

It was just a bit earlier that the word 'democrat' seems to have entered the vocabulary of political struggle, as some identified as democracy the broad lines of the cause for – or against – which they fought (Palmer, 1953; Conze and Koselleck, 1972-1984: 821-899). 'Democracy', as the Furetière story indicates, was a very old word, easy to define and often deride, as long as it was taken to refer to a concept that was part of a political typology that came out of a very distant past. But now, in the eighteenth century, there were 'democrats'. It is far easier to specify what those democrats were against than what they were for. The new political identity of democrat was, as identities often are, largely defined in opposition, in this case opposition to another powerful label, that of 'aristocrats'. Democrats were certainly against, for example, divinely sanctioned monarchy, against immutable hierarchy based on birth, and against self-perpetuating corporate institutions. But it was hardly obvious in the late eighteenth century what were the institutions that would be taken to embody this new democracy.

In appropriating a term associated with the republics of Rome and Athens the shapers of democracy did not on the whole follow the ancient institutions that they would have associated with that word. The assembled citizenry as decision-maker and the selection of officials by lot played little role in the institutional design of the democracy of the national states. Nor would reflection on Antiquity have suggested any fundamental incompatibility of democracy with slavery or with practices under which women, like children, were to be represented by men. It would hardly have been obvious to anyone in the 1780s that two centuries hence many would think of democracy as characterized by representative institutions, near-universal adult suffrage, secret ballots, and multiparty electoral competition, all notions that would have encountered serious principled objection by some of those who first thought about how to connect democracy with modern national states. Some of these notions, like multiparty electoral competition, would have been objected to by practically all of that first generation of modern democrats. And those revolutionary democratizations were far more likely to codify the exclusion of women from political rights than to move towards women's suffrage (Markoff, forthcoming).

So one lesson we can draw from the democratization of the national states is that the history of the democracy of the states has been less an increasingly successful approximation of some known model than an extremely conflictual series of innovations. Democracy has meant change, with the result that practices from the democratic past are at least as likely to seem oddly foreign to us as they are eerily familiar, as demonstrated in Michael Schudson's (1998) marvellous *The Good Citizen*.

This lesson may be a source for some optimism. To say that transnational democratization requires new thinking and new institutions is simply to say that democracy must be reinvented if it is to continue meaningfully – as it always has been.

2.3 Legitimation as an Invitation to Challenge As states began to claim they ruled on behalf of, in the name of, and by the will of the sovereign people, real people – not just the fictional collectivity invoked by the rulers – found their own mobilizations, dissents, and organizations profoundly encouraged. Once, for example, the English Parliament, throwing off the king, claimed a popular mandate, it found that it was not so easy to ignore all those many groups who claimed they were the people whom parliament allegedly represented. Indeed, MPs quickly discovered that petition campaigns were so powerful that they had better get in the business of orchestrating petition drives addressed to themselves so that they had ammunition in their disputes with other MPs (Morgan,1988: 227-228).

By the time we get downstream from the French Revolution, quite a variety of states were claiming a popular mandate in one form or other. Other social transformations made it easier for people to join in movements thus legitimated:

- the growing strength of parliamentary bodies, whose elections became an opportunity for mobilizations, even when suffrage was limited;
- the developing literacy that enabled distant people to feel themselves united around ideas they read – thus, for example, the followers of the People's Charter in the 1830s and 1840s in England were Chartists;
- the new social and cultural densities of an urbanizing and industrializing world.

Democracy creates conditions for movements to contest democracy as it exists, to demand new institutions and deeper democratization. The very beautiful architectural motifs of the new Washington DC, with its White House here, its Capitol there, and its Supreme Court elsewhere, in giving beautiful materiality to the idea of separation of powers, virtually invites all who do not want to limit participation to election day to come in person and demonstrate or to hire lawyers to lobby. The sovereign people may be, as Morgan (1988: 306) observes, another formula by which the few claim to rule over the many – but it is a formula that invites the many to challenge the few, too. In short, monarchical legitimation and its trappings and ceremony and connection to sacred things were displaced by democratic legitimation and its trappings and ceremonies and its own sacred things – from *vox dei* to *vox populi* – and mobilization for change became part and parcel of democracy itself.

This particular lesson from the history of the states should give one pause because analogies in the transnationalizing world are problematic, as I will develop below.

2.4 Paths The more democratic states of the early twenty-first century arrived there from somewhere else by many paths, often involving backtracking and detours, propelled by conflict – including war and revolution – with major but varying roles played by social movement mobilizations and elite reformers, with some elements of democratization advancing rapidly and others at a snail's pace (and what was fast and what was slow differing a lot from case to case). In very broad strokes we might distinguish two families of such paths: those characteristic of strong and those of weak states (McAdam et al., 2001: 264-304). In the strong-state family, the achievement of an effective and generally quite undemocratic central bureaucratic authority developed first, often at the expense of semidemocratic local institutions. In such places as France and Britain, as the result of a good deal of conflict, those effective states came to have a more democratic character. In the weak-state family (which we might represent by Switzerland or the Netherlands), existing semidemocratic local or regional institutions built up a weaker central authority that preserved their semidemocratic character – and only at a later stage was the centre dramatically strengthened.

In a world of at least nominally sovereign states and only quite limited transnational institutions, the weak-state path might at first seem the analogy to be explored, but one of the lessons of the history of the national states is that such paths were far rarer, no doubt because weak states tended to succumb to more powerful neighbors, distant colonizers able to apply coercion across great distances, or internal destruction. States tended to get significantly stronger before they got to be significantly more democratic. One of the lessons from the states, then, is that the construction of an undemocratic global order is not necessarily the end of transnational democracy but rather may be its starting point. Although a fuller delineation of imaginable futures would explore weak-state analogies and see what we learn from the few such cases, here I will only be considering the analogies from stronger states.[6]

3. Globalization as an Arena for Democratization

Decision-making beyond the state level will grow. This contention rests on the premise that diverse problems that are not resolvable by the states will impel the creation of new institutions of transnational cooperation. To briefly indicate some of these threats:

- *Proliferation of nuclear weapons*. The end of the Cold War has replaced a low but non-zero probability of destruction of civilization and perhaps human life through superpower nuclear exchange with a high probability of occasional nuking of cities by impassioned terrorists, criminal extortionists, nuclear-armed weak states about to go down to crushing non-nuclear military defeat, or the demented;
- *Environmental catastrophes*. Pollutants emitted in one place have truly global consequences beyond the control of any single state, at least until humanity manages to devise technology to control air and ocean currents;
- *Uncontrolled flows of global capital*. The new electronic media permit financial movements that are extraordinarily volatile and hard to track, all the more so when states and their economic advisors tend to be convinced of the irrationalities of state intervention and the foolishness or malice of those less

convinced than they. Calls for improving transnational mechanisms to control capital flows are straws in this particular wind;[7]

- *Transnationally organized criminal empires.* In a world united by the new electronic media, it is not only legal business enterprises that organize across borders but also illegal and often violent ones. If consumers in rich countries desire goods and services in plentiful supply in poor ones, from opium and coca derivatives to sex, criminal entrepreneurs will generate vast profits and deeply corrupt law enforcement. The transnational trade in weapons and the skills for using them may be an especially consequential symptom, product, and cause of a decline in state effectiveness. The observation by social scientists of a Weberian bent that the long-term growth of state power entailed the disarmament of those who were not the agents of states may be on its way to supersession by the capacity of a globalized arms trade to empower violent entrepreneurs. To the nuclear dangers mentioned above, the likelihood that such entrepreneurs will acquire cheaper but lethal toxins or biological weapons is great;

- *Human rights anarchy.* The flourishing of notions of human rights is one of the most interesting and in some ways hopeful of developments. Toward the beginning of the modern era of democratization the French revolutionary Declaration of the Rights of Man and Citizen wonderfully encapsulated in its title a major ambiguity. Did one have rights as a 'man' or as a 'French citizen'? Until recently most sociologists who thought about such things would have held that one could only have rights as a citizen, because rights were meaningless if there was no obligation on others to respect them, and obligations were meaningless unless backed by the coercive force of a state. We live at a moment in which one can no longer be certain that human rights are merely pretty words, in which new tribunals with real if incompletely developed teeth are being called into existence, in which judges here and there are claiming universal jurisdiction over certain crimes, and in which some states have claimed human rights as the basis for bombing others. In the absence of clearly defined and delimited institutions, the actual course of events has become deeply unpredictable. Could, say, Henry Kissinger be hauled into court somewhere by some judge? We don't know. So for the states, the current unregulated human rights anarchy may be on the verge of looming as a major problem of the new international disorder (Becker, 2002).

For such reasons (and others) it is highly likely that institutions of global coordination will continue to be created. This is not an especially optimistic premise because it makes no assumption about the depth and variety of the global turbulence that will impel sufficiently effective coordination to manage the growing crises. But on the presumption that the significance of transnational political institutions will continue to grow, the very big question we confront is whether these institutions might have a democratic character, or might be made to have a democratic character. Who are the actors creating the global political order?

4. Actors

There seem to be three classes of such actors.

4.1 The States Although some think of globalization as the antithesis of the states and foresee their relegation to the scrap heap of history, in fact the states are major players in the construction of the transnational order. Many so-called international organizations, from the United Nations to more narrowly defined but powerful bodies like the IMF, the World Bank, and the WTO, are creatures of the states themselves, and an awful lot of consequential decisions are taken by meetings of the powerful states of the world. Among organizations created by the states, none thus far has more of a suprastatal character to it than the European Union that now takes actions to which member states are bound. (On the atypicality of the EU among transnational institutions at the beginning of the twenty-first century, see John McDougall's chapter, this volume.)

In the creation of transnational institutions the states are neither equally weighty, nor homogeneous. There are important North-South differences in state interests, and important US-Europe differences in strategy (and differences in interests as well). It is partly because states have their differences, their shifting alliances, and their hesitations that it is imaginable that other players may have some influence, just as the divisions between monarchical centralizers and feudal and often feuding lords created opportunities for bold plebeians, and just as divisions between states and dissident religious forces created opportunities for the emergence of new ideas.

Nor are the institutions created by the states identical. The actual and potential conflict among these institutions may provide some opportunity for movements, particularly since some of these institutions embody some democratic elements, one of the reasons a good deal of activism is organized around the United Nations (Smith, Jackie, forthcoming a; see also Alger, this volume). Although many anti-globalization activists see international financial institutions as interchangeable, others look for differences between, for example, the World Bank and the International Monetary Fund, and take heart from the differences they see.

4.2 The Firms A second class of player is made up of the large business enterprises of transnational or even global reach. These are no more uniform or homogeneous than the states and have varied relationships with them. Some firms work hand in glove with some states; some firms squirm to be out from under constraining state authority. Giovanni Arrighi (1994) follows Fernand Braudel in usefully distinguishing for the sixteenth century the vivid contrast in firm-state relations summed up as Venice and Genoa. In Venice, the firms and the state were mutually supportive to the point of indistinction; whereas the merchants and bankers of Genoa owed it little loyalty and often regarded it as merely a nuisance, finding more profit in funding the Spanish empire than in supporting Genoa. Some of our capitalists are Venetians, some Genoese. It depends on the particular state, the particular firm, the particular opportunities of the historical moment (Sklair, 2002).

4.3 Transnational Activist Networks If the only sorts of actors involved in constructing transnational political institutions were some mix of the states and the firms, the prospects for any sort of transnational democratization would not be very brilliant, any more than would have been the prospects for democratization of the states had the only players been the monarchs and the aristocrats without the frequent challenge and occasional success of an awful lot of grass roots contention. Students of globalization are increasingly prone to direct our attention to a wide range of organized action carried out by something other than either the states or the firms, and some are speaking of 'global social movements'. But the careful and gently skeptical survey of Sidney Tarrow makes clear that this is often an extremely misleading expression, so let us use the more capacious label 'transnational activist networks' (Keck and Sikkink, 1998) to include actors who are neither states nor firms and that a) are organized across national borders and b) seek to influence the policies, forms, or even existence of national or transnational political structures. This is an extremely heterogeneous collection. If we include all international bodies we find a large and growing number of organizations. Among such transnationally organized groupings, probably none are more important for the prospects of democracy than the transnational social movements enumerated in the work of Jackie Smith (forthcoming b; also Sikkink and Smith, 2002), which also turn out to be rapidly growing. (For more see Chadwick Alger's contribution to this volume.)

Some recent studies by Roberto Patrico Korzeniewicz and William Smith (2001) are especially helpful in clarifying the variety within this sector. They propose a continuum between two polar types. At one pole are organizations that aim to develop 'links with governmental agencies and international organizations', that produce 'policy papers addressed to influential political elites', and that have had some 'success in influencing the rhetoric of policy elites'. At the other pole we find organizations forging 'ties to labor unions' and 'grass roots social movements' that develop 'confrontational strategies and oppositional identities' in relation to existing international organizations, and that attempt to mobilize collective action in public through 'teach-ins, street protests, and demonstrations'. These latter have had some 'success in mobilizing grass roots sectors' but far less in influencing official agendas (Korzeniewicz and Smith, 2001: 30).

So if we are looking for some analogies either to the reforming elites or to the social movements that were such important components of the democratization of the states, we find more than zero on either score. But how much more than zero, and with what transformative potential? Consider for a moment the vivid expression on one of the Brazilian websites that sprang up in the course of mobilizing for the World Social Forum in Porto Alegre in 2001. It spoke of 'a planetary archipelago of resistance',[8] an expression that encapsulated a sense of numerous, far-flung organizational sites that were disconnected and that may even lack any collective identity. Could these separate little islands, the very phrase almost seems to ask, become a mighty continent?

Tarrow (2001: 14) suggests three reasons to doubt the emergence of such a continent: 1) 'the weakness or absence of social networks outside people's neighborhoods, towns, cities, social groups, and political allegiances'; 2) 'the weakness or absence of transnational collective identities'; 3) 'and the absence of mechanisms to compete with the political opportunities of national polities'. These are weighty matters, but they need to be thought of dynamically. After all, a skeptical observer in 1750 might have doubted the likelihood that nationally organized grassroots movements would have emerged as a routine part of national political life by arguing from an analogous thinness of translocal networks and translocal identities. To question a bit further each of these points in turn:

*   Can the new electronic media of communication and their users form rich enough cross-border networks to facilitate social action? (Markoff, 2001). A full assessment would have to take into account the very limited and uneven geography of such networks with far greater densities in the wealthy countries than in the global South;
*   Can the weakness of transnational identities be to some degree offset by the ways in which identities are forged out of conflict itself, with transnational contexts generating transnational identities (as anti-globalization activists, for example)?
*   Will opportunity-seeking movements arise as transnational structures of decision-making become more powerful and more visible, something very strongly suggested by the history of the national movements?

With regard to this third point, however, one has to wonder if here the analogy will founder on the absence of visibility and the absence of democratizing legitimations. Some transnational institutions do indeed seem to become important sites that both attract social action and nurture it (as shown in Jackie Smith's [1995; forthcoming a] work on the UN), while others manage to constitute targets powerful enough to attract transnationally organized activism (like the World Trade Organization, the International Monetary Fund, and the World Bank, despite the shifting locales of their meetings). But the structures of transnational governance thus far often lack some of the important features of the states that tied the histories of national movements and national democratizations together (see Morgan, this volume).

4.3.1 They are secretive Their internal deliberations, and even the fact that they are deliberating, are often obscured. It is hard to see how England's nineteenth-century social mobilizations around issues from slavery to tariff policy would have come to move in tandem with parliamentary debates about those same issues (Tilly, 1997), without parliamentary debates being as public as the slogans chanted in the streets. The pervasive secrecy of many of today's transnational institutions makes this look a lot less likely as a significant path toward transnational democratization.

4.3.2 They are decentralized and fluid The democratization of the states followed the redeployment of power away from village and town toward distant centres of power. It made little sense to develop new techniques of social struggle aimed at long-term pressure on national governments until what those governments did counted a lot in village and town. Peasants angry at the new claims of some lord in fourteenth-century Europe were a lot more likely to try to bargain with the lord directly – by concealing grain, by threat, by insurrection – than hiring a lawyer to petition a central government to pass some agrarian legislation, because the government could not have cared less, and even had it cared had no effective power in the village anyway. In the more recent history of social movements, it helped that there were physically fixed, visible centres of power, with many institutions in close proximity. When twenty-first century farmers demonstrate before central institutions, they may well find elite allies down the street.

This suggests that there may be no route to a more democratic transnational order that does not pass first through a more effective, pervasive, and authoritative undemocratic one.

4.3.3 The absence of legitimation As observed earlier, claims to govern on the basis of popular consent were an invitation for social movement entrepreneurs to claim popular support for favoured causes. But most of the structures of transnational governance thus far do not claim to repose on popular consent and therefore do not implicitly invite popular mobilization. Nor do they suggest a language for the effective framing of protest. We shall see where, if anywhere, the new EU constitutional discussions go, but even if we are toward the beginning of a democratized EU, it is very hard to see anything that encourages a democratized IMF, a democratized WTO, a democratized NAFTA, a democratized G7, a democratized multinational corporation, a democratized transnational gangster network, a democratized network of terrorists with a global reach. Now it is perfectly true, as Korzeniewicz and Smith (2001) describe with great clarity, that significant transnational institutions often invite NGOs of various sorts to join them in hashing out issues. But this is very different than those institutions being accountable to those NGOs or to much of anybody else, except maybe to the states that created them, or to the banks that finance them, or, for some economic enterprises, to their stockholders.[9]

4.3.4 The conceptual vacuum I leave this issue for last, but it is surely not least. From the 1780s to the present, the entity whose democratic character might be under discussion has been first and foremost the national state. Some might speak of a family or a school or a factory or a way of life as having or as lacking the attributes of democracy, but primarily it was the state.[10] So long as we think of political life as first and foremost the political life of separate and sovereign national states, notions of transnational democracy will simply seem vacuous to many, hardly worthy of serious thought. There are many reasons for skepticism about any notion of transnational democracy, some of which we've touched on here – the weakness of transnational identities, the barriers to transnational collective action, the resistance of the existing states (not least among the resisters being the most powerful), and the very different degrees to which the states are democratic.

Let me try an analogy. In discussing political regimes, Juan Linz (2000 [1975]) famously distinguished democratic, totalitarian and authoritarian regimes (and added a few other possibilities to this typology as well). Now these adjectives are all characteristics of national states, and perhaps don't belong very well in the transnational arena in the first place. But if we can consider the possibility of transnational democracy, we need some terminology to characterize the alternative or alternatives to that democracy.

I don't think anyone would question the proposition that the transnational political order as it exists at present, and as it might exist following any trend visible today, has little of a democratic character. But it has, if anything, even less of a totalitarian one. There are too many centres of power, there is no monolithic global party, there is no globally coordinated mass mobilization, and there is far too much social action uncoordinated by those on high and often in opposition to their goals. Those who meet at the World Economic Forum may have diverse, including antipathetic, views of the anti-globalization protestors outside their hotel lobbies, but they haven't the slightest inclination to mobilize a pro-globalization mass movement. Secrecy, rather than public rituals of legitimacy, is the more important protection mechanism for global finance. On the other hand, recall the *differentia specifica* of authoritarianism for Linz. There is plenty of pluralism all right, but it is 'limited' rather than 'responsible' pluralism. The IMF and the like do indeed meet with and take into account the positions of NGOs and others – but only those they choose to listen to and only when they feel like it. They are not responsible to citizens, but neither do they come close to totally squelching citizen voices, while they do listen selectively to selected citizens. The citizens in question, moreover, are citizens of member states, not of the transnational institutions themselves, which have none.

Consider another example. With or without the intermediation of the IMF, the government of the United States has an enormous impact on the lives of people all over the planet. To say that actions of the US government only have an impact on citizens and residents of the United States would be to take leave of one's senses, yet only a rather small proportion of the people of this planet get to vote for the government of the US. But of course the US government from time to time listens to some of what some people outside its borders think. There is no democratic accountability at all, but this does not mean that opinion never prevails. If we are to credit press reports at the time, for example, the reason the US reversed course and endorsed new funds for Argentina in August 2001 was because various Latin American and European heads of state prevailed on it to do so. This hardly suggests global democracy of any sort, but it is even less suggestive of global totalitarianism.

5. Conclusion

The global order into which we appear to be heading is fragmented, dispersed, with multiple centres that have very different degrees and kinds of power, with limited but not responsible pluralism. It is likely to become stronger, more coherent, and more effective, and only then will emerging movements be likely to address with any effectiveness the structures of transnational decision-making rather than just particular decisions. Let us remember, too, that forms of social conflict, including the social movement, that emerged at the national level were profoundly different than anything that had been invented in the villages.

I have not addressed here whether the redeployment of power beyond the states will summon forth new forms of social struggle for which we lack any taxonomy, with new modes of recruitment, new ways to deploy their resources, and new forms of challenging the holders of power or whether we are looking forward to the now familiar social movements acting on new and enlarged terrain.

But the history of the national states suggests very strongly that with increasing coherence, effectiveness, and strength in transnational structures of power, the movements, too, will emerge strongly in one form or another, and with them will emerge as well the possibility of new institutions, the possibility of reinventing democracy yet again. Possibility is not certainty. By no means. But it is a lot more promising than impossibility.

Notes

1   The US was correspondingly early to generate scholarly attention on this point (Lipset and Schneider, 1983). Researchers soon noted something similar to the north (Adams and Lennon, 1992).

2   For various arguments about 'globalization', see Keohane and Milner, 1996; Held, 1995; Albrow, 1997; Appadurai, 1996; Beck, 1996; Hannerz, 1996; Kincaid and Portes, 1994; Robertson, 1992; Sassen, 1994; Weiss, L., 1997; Piven and Cloward, 1997; Wallerstein, 1991; Tilly, 1995; Schaeffer, 1997; Sklair, 1991; Wade, 1996; Ganley, 1992; Castells, 1994; Manning, 1999; McMichael, 2001; Munck and Gills, 2002.

3   As some of the states attempt to control transnational terrorism in the wake of September 11, 2001, it will be a great deal easier to retard the transborder movements of persons than of funds, and consequently controls over the mobility of people are likely to increase a good bit more than controls over the mobility of capital.

4   Critics regard the deficit as double because: a) to the extent that decisions are made at the EU rather than the national level, they are being made by decision-makers who are less democratically accountable, and b) to the extent that EU rules bind the member states they weaken the capacity of those states to respond to the will of their citizens.

5   For French instances, see Beik (1997).

6   That strong-state paths to the democratization of national states were far more common than weak-state paths does not in itself mean that a more probable future for transnational democratization will follow such paths. But it seems to me that imaginable

weak-state models are much more complex and require a correspondingly more extended discussion.

7   See, for example, Soros, 2000. This is an all the more striking symptom when considered in conjunction with a book Soros wrote a dozen years earlier in which he explains some of the tactics by which he amassed his own fortune in maneuvering in the world of transnational capital flows whose volatility was already seen as threatening (Soros, 1987). See also Frankman, 2002.

8   It may be a consequence of the evanescent character of much on the web that I am now unable to find a proper reference.

9   The Enron spectacle shows that responsibility to stockholders is not to be taken for granted.

10 In reconceiving democracy as a description of a social totality and not just the rules of government, de Tocqueville's portrait of the early nineteenth-century United States (1990 [1835-1840]) may prove an important resource for thinking about democracy beyond the states.

Chapter 3

Transnational Democracy:
The Pursuit of a Usable Past

Bruce Morrison

1. Introduction: Sites of Protest

A criticism frequently levelled at anti-globalization protesters concerns the adequacy or appropriateness of the selected targets of their activism.[1] What is the point or value, it is asked, of railing against the World Bank, the International Monetary Fund, the World Trade Organization, or the meetings of G7 or G8 leaders? Even if, in the best case, the ills in question are coherent and more or less consensually expressed,[2] on what basis is responsibility to be determined and accountability to be insisted upon? So when World Bank or WTO officials, for instance, surface after the storm in Seattle or elsewhere to insist that their organization is not only free from responsibility for the negative effects of powerful transnational economic and other processes, but is in fact doing its best to counteract them by taming the beast of globalization, while also becoming increasingly engaged with 'global civil society', the point is deeply controversial but not easily overcome in a final sense. Certainly, national governments remain more in charge than is assumed in some quarters. There does, however, seem to be ever more that they cannot control, at which point it ceases to be clear who can. If this induces some to pursue a distinctly subnational solution through the expansion of democratic local or even individual space, it triggers in others an interest in some form of democracy beyond the nation-state.[3] Crucially, however, it is asked,

> Is it possible for democratic renewal and representative forms of political accountability to survive within the new political culture characterized by decentralization, mixed with a profound revision of traditional politics? What are the capabilities of citizens to revise the traditional vision of democracy, once captured by the nation-states' extant obligation to guarantee the rights of citizens, in the face of new and rising global economic actors and institutions such as the World Bank or IMF? ... [S]ocial movements have had little choice but to adapt to the new global paradigm of collective action (Hamel et al., 2001a: 13).

Undoubtedly, social movements played a role in initiating and extending democratic change at the level of the nation-state, and in so doing they participated in the creation from the eighteenth century onwards of a world in which expectations of the democratization of lines of political authority have come to predominate. Social movements, however, emerged and developed very much in response to the growth in power and significance of the modern state, gaining their own power and motive force from the recognition that the state could legitimately and effectively be held responsible for society's major grievances. These states were, of course, far from omnipotent, but they grew substantially in scale and capacity as they mobilized domestic resources for military competition and established the ability to control and regulate increasingly sophisticated and far-reaching economic, cultural, and social developments. Relatively speaking, therefore, the case for state responsibility for the pain associated with economic and social change as well as political abuses in the early industrial era was a model of clarity and coherence. Democratizing the nation-state was not the only available answer in these circumstances, of course, but it was the one which most often managed to balance state, elite, and popular demands in sustainable fashion (see van Creveld, 1999; Collier, R., 1999; Markoff, this volume).

Globalization has muddied the waters substantially, generating a situation in which those wanting to give expression to their frustrated democratic desires find themselves all dressed up but with nowhere – at least nowhere specific and unquestionable – to go. For some, this sense of frustration supports the case for establishing institutions of transparency, accountability, and perhaps also participation at the level of today's most advanced economic and other actors. Globalization of economic, social, and cultural life, it is argued, compels the creation of democratic institutions on a comparable scale. If nation-states are no longer up to the task of providing key public goods – none less significant, to many, than the encouragement of broad societal bargains which capital is seen no longer to require at the national level – then they must be either supplanted or supplemented by institutions more capable of meeting these fundamental democratic responsibilities.

A wide range of creative proposals has already surfaced, from a form of world government to governance regimes which coordinate a variety of actors and agencies without necessarily replicating the hierarchical character of the nation-state. According to some, in fact, globalization is fashioning a new environment featuring 'multiple, interlaced competitors to the singular authority of the state' (Kobrin, 1999: 174), the result of which is best characterized as 'neo-medieval':

> A medieval lord dealt with multiple authorities – emperor and sovereign, sacred and secular – as the norm. It is the modern era, where political authority is defined in terms of unambiguous territoriality, which may be the outlier. The postmodern may well have to learn to accept a heteronomous world of interlaced regional, national, local, supra-national, institutional and non-governmental authorities (Kobrin, 1999: 175).

Writing in this vein has usefully pressed us to reconsider our options, from redemocratizing enduring national states (see McDougall, this volume) to their rearticulation within broader structures (as is Archibugi's case, chapter 12) or even ultimate disappearance. The plight of the protesters should, however, point us to the past as well as the future. In particular, it should serve as a reminder of the power of the historical connection between the nation-state and liberal democracy. This is not to suggest that these are necessarily or permanently bound; highly persuasive arguments have, indeed, been advanced which point to the extension of Western-generated institutions and practices to the transnational sphere (Held, 1995). Alternatively, a convincing case has been made that democracy has changed in meaning over the course of its history and will continue to do so in response to the novel circumstances of our day (Markoff, this volume and 1996).

As this important debate continues, a sense of historical perspective will not lose its value. We should thus remain aware of the degree to which, in addition to economic and cultural factors, for instance, the state was itself a central and crucial contributor to the establishment of national democratic politics. The literature on both historical and contemporary passages to democracy is coming increasingly to acknowledge the influence of prior institutional forms in shaping the forces which strive to open relatively closed regimes, while also determining their prospects for lasting success (see Downing, 1992; Ertman, 1997; Linz and Stepan, 1996). In fact, the very opportunity to force democratic change generally comes as undemocratic or incompletely democratic states themselves become sites of conflict over how to maintain control while adapting to changing circumstances. Very often, it is this internal tension, and the resultant pursuit of relegitimation of a troubled political order, which facilitates the emergence or rise to coherence of popular groups, often with democratic implications (Schmitter and O'Donnell, 1986; Casper and Taylor, 1996). As the French case will demonstrate, however, the point of departure may be problems related not merely to the popularity of the regime, but also to its ability to govern effectively, as filtered through the dominant formula for evaluating and legitimating authority, with democracy as the surprising by-product.

What we know of democracy, at the least, is that it has in the past been tightly interwoven with concentrated political authority. This is not to say that there is no foundation in history for the development of democracy in the context of more loosely integrated compound states, an alternative path which is just beginning to receive welcome attention (Keating, 2001; McAdam et al., 2001). However, in spite of the suggestiveness of the weak-state analogy (McAdam et al., pp. 269-90; Markoff, 1999b and previous chapter) for a transnational democracy it might more closely resemble, the commonness and centrality of the strong-state path argue in favour of its continued consideration. Meanwhile, some of the best recent work plays off of the strong-state story in order to clarify lines of differentiation and lay the bases for a more complete understanding of notably different cases (Centeno, 2002). Either way, the lessons of strong-state institutionalism are far from exhausted, as will be demonstrated in this essay. And, at the broadest level, there is simply no historical support for institutions created for the purpose of being democratic. According to Jytte Klausen and Louise Tilly (1997a, 16),

> Looking back at the history of codificaiton and institutionalization of various rights (protective as well as representational ones), rights and representation have flowed from the mobilization of state power and regulatory authority, not the other way around. In

that sense, it is appropriate to talk about a 'democratic deficit' as endemic in state building. The concentration of power and authority precedes, rather than succeeds, the granting of rights and representation.

There is no argument here against making any emerging supranational institutions as democratic as possible.[4] This is, however, not the way things have happened in the past, nor will it necessarily be the way they happen in the future. History does, nonetheless, allow us a degree of hope that the very insecurities and imperfections of institutions beyond the state may prove to be the source of their democratization through the need to reform and, in the process, to legitimate these reforms. On the transnational as the national level, therefore, institutions which have come into existence on the basis of compelling interest may indeed find themselves amenable to democratic change, thus overcoming the well-established association between the nation-state and democracy even while following the national example.

2. Democracy and the Nation-State: Contemporary and Historical Linkages

The aspiration for transnational democracy is rooted in a fundamental critique of the democratic character of the contemporary nation-state. According to David Held, for instance, the inadequacy of nation-state democracy lies in a lack of fit between the group involved in making decisions and that affected by them. 'National communities,' he writes, 'by no means exclusively make and determine decisions and policies for themselves, and governments by no means determine what is appropriate exclusively for their own citizens' (Held, 1995: 16-17). Globalization, in one version or another, is usually held to be the culprit. But Held rightly points out that globalization has not suddenly made states powerless; rather, they have always been porous, claiming sovereignty over territories better conceived of as 'overlapping networks of interaction' (Held, 1995: 19) of a variety of sites and sources of social power.[5] What is new is the expansion and intensification of such interaction, with the ironic result of substantially weakening the connection between the nation-state and democracy at the precise moment of the latter's greatest international pre-eminence. The possession by national citizens of democratic rights does not, and should not, therefore, forestall the search for 'the proper "home" of politics and democracy' (Held, 2000: 24).

Our old democratic 'home,' in short, now lets in the elements to an unacceptable degree, and it is on that basis that many scholars have turned their minds to the task of recasting these living arrangements. What is, therefore, to be done? Very little, insist some writers, since the forces currently buffeting our nation-states have been significantly exaggerated. In many respects, it is claimed, the world is no more integrated today than it was in the pre-World War I Gold Standard era. Economic and cultural flows, migratory patterns, and the like, are accordingly seen to have been at least as significant in the earlier period (Hirst and Thompson, 1999; Stirkwerda, 1997: 53-61). As importantly, nation-states have reserves of strength upon which to draw, as revealed by the persistence of fundamental differences in national approaches to political economy (Gilpin, 2001: 148-73; Hirst and Thompson, 1999: 189). The analytical upshot is not, however, to deny outright that globalization has meaning but rather to set in perspective its extent as well as its ability to compel specific political responses (Garrett, 1998: 2, 5-11). If there is not enough in this to console the François Mitterrand of 1982-3, forced to shift policy rightward in the face of capital flight, the democratic players of the early twenty-first century are advised that their options extend beyond merely bringing their polities into line with a globalizing economy.

For others, the power of globalization as a force for either homogenization (Williamson, 1996: 277-279) or, alternatively, differentiation (Rosenau, 1998; Cerny, 1999b) is undeniable. Either way, the uncontrollability and even unpredictability (Perraton, 2000: 64-70) of this phenomenon are seen as rendering futile the hopes of the new, more sophisticated nation-state democrats like Ian Clark and John McDougall, for whom globalization's negative consequences are premised upon the inadequacy of domestic democracy and need to be answered through its enhancement (Clark, I., 1999: 162-6; McDougall, chapter 8, this volume). Instead, attention is riveted by new nonstate and suprastate actors as well as emerging forms of order either spontaneously or deliberately generated in the new circumstances (Sandholtz, 1999: 84-90). While some have confidence that the eclipse of the territorial state and its replacement by neo-medieval layered multiplicity will bring new forms of cooperation, the great danger is that these new institutional forms and practices will be less than fully democratic in character. Held (1995: 138) takes this up as his very challenge:

> [I]s there any reason for thinking that a system of overlapping authority structures, even where it already exists, could be more accountable than traditional models of democracy.... [T]he dilemma of how to secure the sovereign power of the state while ensuring strict limits upon that power can be resolved, liberal democrats have always argued, by recognizing the political equality of mature individuals and empowering them with a vote. But what, if anything, would be the equivalent mechanism in a system of divided sovereignty?

From such concerns springs the interest of Held and others in a new democratic project oriented above all towards establishing a common structure of political action that would be explicitly if innovatively democratic (Held, 1995: 216; Archibugi, 1998: 198, 216, and this volume). If the nation-state is not exhausted, and retains significant authority, it will nonetheless only sustain its democratic character to the extent that it finds itself 'relocated' within voluntarily established overarching democratic public law. If 'it is increasingly difficult to be internally democratic in an increasingly interdependent world' (Archibugi, 1998: 203), the broad acceptance of a framework of cosmopolitan law and democracy will permit the democratization not only of transnational but also national and even local space. The other building blocks of this new order include those very institutions which have received more exclusive scrutiny from other scholars in the debate: the European Union, which is offered as the possible template for other regional associations, if more fully integrated and democratized; the United Nations, but with simultaneously more global balance and more teeth; and finally, a framework-providing assembly of democratic nations (Held, 1995: 234-5, 272-3).

But how do we get there from here? Spontaneously generated order might reveal new democratic possibilities, but it might also fall far short of the standards of the most open-minded democrat. Transnational democracy as a 'project' (Archibugi, 1998: 198), meanwhile, has understandably been longer on experimentation and exhortation than on the provision of ways to overcome the various hindrances to democratic advancement. Answering the 'what is to be done' question, I would suggest, requires addressing another one: can democracy and the nation-state can be de-linked, even partially, as is suggested by the advocates of transnational democracy? The standard view is that the absence of established communities above the level of the nation-state makes this extremely unlikely. Historically, Weberian states sealed off populations one from another and, in the process of establishing clarity of authority, forged identity, even loyalty, on the part of those who were so territorially bound. Thus established, this sense of community supported the foundation as well as consolidation of democratic institutions and processes (Mann, 1993b). Even in the most favourable of conditions, however, such as the relative cultural homogeneity of the countries of the European Union, transnational democracy has not been able to benefit from the weak growth in transnational self-identification (Offe, 2000: 64-9, 77-9; Axtmann, 2001a, 43-6; Green, 2000: 297-9, 310-20). By and large, the response has been that community on the broader level can be generated in the same gradual and piecemeal fashion as in the transformation of initial diversity into national unity, though perhaps more quickly with the assistance of the communications revolution (Weinstock, 2001: 54-6; Archibugi, chapter 12 in this collection).

This sort of exchange sets the debate on a solid foundation, one that militates against Rosenau's contention that the 'established territorial democracies' should not serve as the basis for evaluating the prospects of democracy within 'Globalized Space' (1998: 40). Rosenau's view is understandable, but premature. We are, clearly, still in the process of disentangling the old from the new in the globalization and transnational democracy debate, as in the case of the dispute over the relationship between contemporary changes and those of the 1870-1914 period. The degree of novelty, and thus incomparability, of the new world-in-formation remains very much at issue. Meanwhile, the national past remains almost exclusively our source for information on the conditions for democratic change. Democracy at the nation-state level has been problematic, certainly, and agreement as to what creates and sustains it has been difficult to come by. Nonetheless, no institution at the level above the nation-state has acquired a similar degree of democracy: the European Union is frustratingly stuck between the international and the incompletely democratized supranational; the United Nations is a decision-making body that welcomes democracies and non-democracies alike to participate in a less than fully equal fashion; and the transnational corporations and international non-governmental organizations (INGOs) which play so important a role in fashioning 'Globalized Space', as well as the international financial institutions (IFIs) to which they often appeal, have little basis for claiming the status of representative or accountable institutions. What we know about what makes democracy possible derives from the nation-state experience. So also does what we only think we know, as this same information set has encouraged an overweening confidence in the extent and durability of democratic change around the world, even as so many recent transitions have hollowed out into pseudo-democracy.[6] A reconsideration of democracy's past can remind us of its difficulty, its fragility, as well as its insufficiency. Above all, however, it can help by drawing our attention to the centrality of the state in the generation of modern democracy, and thus give us a clearer sense of the institutional circumstances in which it might conceivably surpass the nation-state.

3. States and Social Democratizations

As Michael Mann, upon whom Held greatly relies, understands very well, modern democracy emerged in response to the sovereign, territorial state that was its necessary precondition. In good Weberian fashion, he says, 'people became trapped within national cages and so sought to change the conditions within those cages' (Mann, 1993b: 251). Although Mann gives justifiable attention to such factors as class and ideology, war, as the late medieval and early modern state's crucial and most expensive task, stood at the root of this development. According to Charles Tilly, 'war makes states' (1985: 170), particularly in terms of the administration of military power and domestic resource extraction. Meanwhile, as the state grew in size and functional differentiation, it was required to refine its relationship with its population. The state's war fixation made it needy, and ultimately 'through struggle, negotiation, and sustained interaction with the holders of essential resources, states came to reflect the class structures of their subject populations' (Tilly, 1992: 102). State strategies, therefore, had economic roots. Cities are particularly important for Tilly: where capital-rich urban centres were few on the ground, states were required to rely on the fuller development of their coercive capacities in order to mobilize resources and so keep pace with their competitors, with obviously undemocratic implications; territories with high levels of capital concentration, meanwhile, favoured smaller states and the emergence of elite bargaining, leading to the establishment of representative bodies, property rights, and other bases for a liberal, if not yet democratic polity (Tilly, 1992: 86, 96). However, the fact that capital-intensive states could nonetheless fall in a harshly competitive geopolitical environment argued in favour of the superiority of British-style state-building, involving 'a conjunction of capital and coercion that from very early on gave any monarch access to immense means of warmaking', if 'only at the price of large concessions to the country's merchants and bankers' (Tilly, 1992: 159).

Scholarship in this vein has made a number of important contributions. First of all, it has told us economics surely matters, but not at all in unmediated fashion. Analyses of twentieth-century democratic change have, indeed, confirmed the substantial correlation between economic development and democracy, but no success has been achieved in attaching causation to correlation.[7] Some authors have in fact stopped trying, accepting that good economics simply provides a cushion for democracy otherwise achieved (Przeworski et al., 2000). Similarly, writers on democracy have by and large stopped trying to argue straightforwardly that changes in economy and society required eventual compensatory adjustments in the political sphere. Ralf Dahrendorf has, in short, been replaced by Blackbourn and Eley.[8]

Thus, Mann and Tilly's work helps us to transcend progressive assumptions as to the naturalness of demands for liberal democratic gains. For them, states are born and remain necessary evils, and well into the modern period the common impulse of most people is for freedom understood as distance from rather than access to the state. It was the failure of the struggle for autonomy which induced societal actors to exert themselves upon the encroaching state and demand some form of representation (Mann, 1993b: 85). In Britain, for instance, the eighteenth century saw an extraordinary growth in the size and capacity of the state, as the revolutionary processes of the previous century had laid the institutional foundations for the generally highly successful but deeply and increasingly expensive wars of the period up to 1815. This 'fiscal-military' state was felt to be an imposing presence in a number of respects, usurping economic resources, cowing and crowding out societal actors (Brewer, 1990; Harling and Mandler, 1993; Mann, 1993b: 115). This 'increasingly powerful and demanding state called forth a new form of politics', as localized and particularistic activism was gradually replaced by the social movement, with its altered repertoire of action (Tilly, 1995b: 13-16, 49-51, 124-145).

The state thus made the social movement as a national vehicle for collective action, or at least made it possible and necessary, by clarifying the extent to which problems either derived from the state's intrusions or at least admitted of a national political solution. As parliament had also grown in significance within the structure of the state during this period, it is not surprising that, by the 1830s, a democratic reform of this legislative body was broadly seen as the way to resolve difficulties ranging from corruption, electoral abuse, and impoverishment to perceived irrationalities in currency policy and even excesses in the toleration of non-Anglicans (Flick, 1978: 17-31; Hilton, 1977: 59-61; Brock, 1973: 77; Cannon, 1973; Tilly, 1995b: 134-15, 247-9). Certainly, part of the story of British democratization from the early nineteenth century onwards involved organization on the basis of the belief that changing parliament could change the state, the aggravating and threatening growth of which had made broad-based popular organization come about in the first instance. Meanwhile, it was less as class actors that people were drawn into organization than as participants in an economy whose dynamism was being framed by the state and turned towards its ends – a *national* economy, in short (Joyce, 1991: 3-15, 65-74; Jones, G.S., 1983: 102-19).

The social movement, clearly, born in association with the appearance of institutional and socioeconomic modernity, does not require reinvention, and its emergence at the transnational level is arguably underway.[9] However, it is still worth noting that we live in the era of the decline of the broad, overarching movements which mirrored the continued expansion of national states and distinctly national industrial economies through the middle decades of the twentieth century. Economics no longer encourages the creation of, for instance, more or less encompassing labour movements, as industrial concentration passes into post-industrial fragmentation (Melucci, 1989). The state, meanwhile, no longer participates in cultivating the organization of labour, for instance, to anywhere near the same extent, particularly as capital's greater mobility renders ever more remote the prospect of societal concertation (Cousins, 1999: 47-70, 97-113; Price, 2001: 88-104; Hall, P., 1999: 151-6). Finally, as time draws us further and further away from the totalizing wars of the twentieth century, wars which conferred upon labour political advantages in proportion to the state's demands upon its human resource base, the disappearance of the policy and organizational benefits thereby derived further reinforce labour's decline (Klausen, 1998: 277-81).

Arguably, these developments may have the effect of dimming the democratic character of advanced industrial democracies. They may indicate even greater difficulties for other countries attempting to map democracy directly onto a post-industrial economy which by-passed the full flowering of industrialism and so also its social-structural effects.[10] More to the point, they suggest limits to the growth of a transnational civil society with democratic import. Not only is the fragmented character of the globalizing economy well established, but the institutional apparatus which would support, even compel, the responsive organization of transnational society in concentrated, effective fashion remains underdeveloped. Increasingly common, therefore, is the scholarly characterization of transnational environmental, human rights, and debt relief organizations as networks rather than social movements, or in other words as decentralized, loosely affiliated groups of activists who nonetheless manage to achieve a degree of influence through a combination of external pressure and adaptation to the imperfectly realized global institutional environment (Sikkink and Keck, 1998; Khagram, Riker, and Sikkink, 2002).

Nonetheless, for some, our democratic moment understandably encourages the design of transnational institutions on an explicitly democratic foundation. For others, however, the very unstructured, disaggregated character of the transnational sphere constitutes the basis for, if not formal democracy, a new kind of freedom made more accessible and enjoyable by its ability to outpace the state more often than not. Alternatively, and intriguingly, according to Rosenau, these circumstances can provide for the emergence of some 'functional equivalents' of domestic control mechanisms as counterweights to supranational power structures (1998: 38-47). These are all genuine possibilities, and the matter can hardly be settled at this stage. However, to the extent that the past can serve as our guide, the establishment of transnational, as national, institutions will not occur primarily on the basis of democracy. The European integration process thus far, featuring the essential supranational thrust of the European Court of Justice and the European Commission (Tsebelis and Garrett, 2001: 358-66, 374), two undemocratic institutions, reminds us of the enduring truth of this. Democratization will likely have to come after the fact.

In the European case, even with the help of powerful security in addition to economic motives, intergovernmental origins have led only to a partial set of democratic structures. There are several reasons for this, and in part it has to do with the uncertainty as to the form democracy should assume within an institutional apparatus of an entirely new type. The past, therefore, offers incomplete guidance. It is nonetheless important to note that democracy's gains at the European level, in the form for instance of the post-1979 elections to the increasingly significant European Parliament, have not been matched by the growth of genuinely European parties appealing to genuinely enthusiastic voters on the basis of distinctively European issues (Smith, Julie, 2001: 280-3, 286-8; Hix and Lord, 1997: 59-61). Even interest organization and lobbying efforts are only gradually acquiring a European cast, particularly outside of the business domain (Axtmann, 2001a: 50). There is, meanwhile, cause to wonder just how knowledgeable the citizens of EU nations are with respect to the impact of this entity on their daily lives (Scully, 2000: 240-2). In sum, there is no evidence to date that, à la Mann, Europeans feel trapped within this particular transnational cage and therefore driven to alter the conditions within it. More Europe might be a precondition for more European democracy.

Looking beyond the EU, not all possess Wayne Sandholtz's confidence that a direct line runs from globalization to 'the expansion of transnational rules' and onwards over time to the development of institutions capable of generating rules and settling disputes over their terms (1999: 89-90). This is, however, precisely what transnational democracy in Europe and beyond might require. It is, of course, not to be denied that the associations, networks, and movements we might place under the rubric of 'global civil society' have of late made important strides. INGOs have grown substantially in number in recent decades (Sikkink and Smith, 2002: 24-35), as well as in influence, if more in the new politics of environmentalism, for instance, than in the associational advancement of more traditional labour concerns (O'Brien et al., 2000: 77-84, 119-26). These developments cannot, however, be dissociated from the emergence and growth of the new postwar intergovernmental organizations (IGOs) intended to manage international capitalism: the World Bank, the IMF, and the GATT/WTO. On the one hand, many INGOs have adapted themselves to the task of enhancing the accountability and transparency of the IGOs in their area of interest. To the extent that expanded INGO access and influence have been the result (O'Brien et al., 2000: 115-22), international commercial and financial institutions may have begun the very process of policy accommodation and attempted cooptation of key social interests that was characteristic of the process of democratizing the nation-state.

There are, on the other hand, two crucial areas of difficulty. First, it remains the case that 'the structures and mechanisms of international regulatory policy making – such as IGO's – are … more advanced than the institutions for their democratic control' (Axtmann, 2001a: 46). Redressing this imbalance, paradoxically, might require more rather than less in the way of institutional concentration and clarification, perhaps more than is possible in the short to medium term in a world characterized by the existence of well-established states and a very unevenly integrated international economy (see John Hall, this volume). Second, therefore, the IGOs which inhabit this complex institutional environment are not now nor will become much like nation-states. Instead of encouraging the formation of ever more transnational social movements, ever more organizationally concentrated, functionally specified bodies like the World Bank, the IMF, and the WTO, as component parts of globalization's institutional fragmentation, present a 'multilayered opportunity structure' (Khagram, Riker, and Sikkink, 2002: 18) promoting rather the formation of transnational networks which compensate for their structural weakness by stressing the provision of information and the power of moral claims.

'Global civil society' will, therefore, remain multiple, varied, and incompletely mobilized, and thus forced to pick its policy battles at specific levels of authority. These sites of struggle, meanwhile, will often remain national rather than inter- or transnational, as in the case of the centrality of the US Congress to the pursuit of Third World debt relief (Donnelly, 2002: 167, 172-7; Nelson, 2002a: 134-5), a factor which further complicates the development of truly transnational social movements. This is not a story of failure, but rather of substantial and surprising success in difficult circumstances for actors within networks pressing their cause both at and above the level of the nation-state. There will, however, be limits to the openness of the key intergovernmental organizations, and limits to the degree to which relative closure can be overcome by transnational networks, at least in the foreseeable future. Conditioned by their fragmented institutional environment, in fact increasingly forming part of the very structure of global governance, these increasingly prominent transnational bodies nonetheless lack the institutional concentration as well as the potential for concerted opposition that has often been required to win more complete democratic gains from nation states. As we will now see, however, they may be acquiring precisely the kind of positional and ideational influence that will pay off handsomely as the crucial institutions of the transnational sphere develop and, more pointedly, adjust to their rapidly changing environment.

4. Transitions to Transnationalism: 'Old' Medievalism and the Democratic Impact of French State Reform

If transnational institutions that are 'born democratic' are perhaps less to be expected than those that become democratic over time, this is not merely because of the priority of institutions from the point of view of concentrated and effective social movement activity. Nation-state democracy, certainly, has not come about solely, and often not primarily, as a result of the organized expression of popular demands relative to the state. According to contemporary democratization theory, in fact, while liberalization, as the first step in the process of change, and later democratization, may indeed come in response to pressure 'from below', they are more commonly seen as deriving mainly from the state elite as it grapples with its fears of declining legitimacy. The result is a split into 'hard-liners' and 'soft-liners' based upon their openness, first to liberalization and, ultimately, to the 'electoral legitimation' of a troubled state (O'Donnell and Schmitter, 1986: 16; Zoubir, 1995: 110-17, 127-9). Attention has also recently been drawn to the institutional character of the pre-existing authoritarian state as one of the primary influences upon the social, economic, ideological, and political materials available for democratic reconstruction (Linz and Stepan, 1996). This is helpful, but incomplete, as it involves an overemphasis upon the transitional moment combined with a reification of the institutional regime that precedes it. States, as institutions more generally, are dynamic, sites of both conflict and continuing attempts at adaptation to a changing environment (Breuilly, 1982: 7). When these processes intensify, more is at stake than the mere maintenance of institutional control. In addition, conceptions of governance and the appropriate use of power also come into play, the contestation over which can produce significant if unintended democratic effects. In this light, social actors can bear influence extending beyond their structural capacity as producers of meaning. This speaks directly to the situation of transnational networks.

Late eighteenth-century France provides us with an excellent and revealing example, one which highlights the role of ideas and institutional readjustment in democratic causation while offering a substantial degree of comparability as well. Pre-revolutionary France, as Tocqueville understood, remained very much an *ancien régime*, characterized by a complex blend of feudal and non-feudal elements. Institutional legitimacy, in particular, was very broadly understood in terms of the medieval constitution, which conferred upon the crown an extensive prerogative while also providing ideological support for the privileges of aristocrats and fortunate others as a source of balance within the polity (Keohane, N.O., 1980: 3-17; Downing, 1992: 113-8). The pattern of authority – or system of rules – was thus complex, multiple, and overlapping, by now a recognizable set of terms. One need not be a neo-medievalist to appreciate the contemporary echoes.

The French crown had, however, long laid the foundations for the endangerment of this traditional constitutional order. Out of a desire for a less effective and consequential form of political balance, French kings had since the late Middle Ages made sparing appeal to the country's main representative body, the Estates General. But if not by constitutionalist negotiation, the militarily ambitious French monarchy needed nonetheless to extract societal resources, which it did increasingly through the conferral of 'public' privileges and responsibilities upon private actors. Taxation in Bourbon France involved not just clerics, municipal governments, and provincial Estates, but also, and crucially, a series of financiers operating on their own rather than the state's behalf, and eventually acquiring near-complete independence as paid private officeholders. In effect, the French crown drew advances on the basis of tax prospects it thereby alienated, allowing a tidy profit to those who had bought the privilege of collection. France's kings compensated by selling and then taxing financial as well as judicial and administrative offices, but this strategy had its limits, and came at the price of reinforcing the standing of an expanding body of proprietary officeholders. The Bourbon monarchs also borrowed even more extensively from a variety of individual and collective corporate actors, whose credit was better than that of a monarchy lacking the support of national representation and inclined to default on its loans. This move, however, further enmeshed the crown within the structure of feudal and proprietary privilege (Bosher, 1970: 6-13, 43, 91-105; Bien, 1994: 45-9; Doyle, W., 1996; Ertman, 1997: 134-7).

Gradually, a state financing system constructed in order to avoid conflict while freeing the hands of monarchs became more deeply and dangerously conflictual. The less successful but certainly no less expensive wars of the late seventeenth and eighteenth centuries did nothing to weaken France's continental and colonial aspirations (Stone, B., 1994). The attempt to finance these military aims, however, clarified the extent of incompatibility that existed between state aims and the structure of privilege. Beginning in the 1690s, therefore, French kings began overriding aristocratic exemptions from direct taxation, thereby unleashing the more bureaucratic *intendants* on an increasingly resentful privileged class. The crown also grew increasingly unwilling to accommodate the loss of tax revenue to social actors, and even more frustrated at its inability to control, access, or even take stock of the flow of funds in the context of the privately held accounts or *caisses* of the financiers. Finally, the near saturation of the officeholding class as a source of venal taxation, and the expense involved in purging and repaying officeholders, was an ongoing source of difficulty (Kwass, 2000; Bosher, 1970: 15-25; Doyle, W., 1996).

Privilege, which had been the solution to the monarchy's problems, became increasingly part of the problem, and it is in this context that the Revolution makes sense. This is certainly not to lay claim to the inevitability of the overturning of the old order as of 1789. A number of things could have deterred the Revolution, not least a deferral of the crown's military ambitions. Given that this did not occur, however, it is important that the French state's expanding revenue needs generated a zero-sum conflict between the monarchy on the one hand and feudal and proprietary privilege on the other. Simply put, French state formation had generated a situation in which successful reform required the transcendence of the very privileged arrangements upon which the monarchy had grown dependent. However, in the absence of effective national representation, this would involve the elimination of the central loci of opposition to the monarchical regime, in the form of the judicial and financial officeholders, the provincial Estates, the guilds, and so on, and of the *parlements*[11] as quasi-political defenders of this structure of privilege, and therefore the prospect invited fears of a resurgence of arbitrary power even as the French state seemed momentarily so frail. It was, therefore, not merely selfishness which triggered the elite conflict over state reform and brought about the collapse of the *ancien-régime* state. In fact, a study of the developing crown-*parlement* relationship over the course of the eighteenth century reveals an opposition that built up gradually, responsively to monarchical innovation, and in a manner which demonstrated a profound attachment to the traditional guidelines of their relationship to the crown as they understood them. In addition to grasping onto their privileges, they also aimed at the preservation of a monarchy with at least limited constitutional checks – until, that is, the monarchy strayed beyond the reach of such an arrangement. The briefly radicalized *parlementaires* of the summer of 1788 had a basis in the institutions as well as the ideals of constitutional balance for their concern that they alone preserved France from despotism (Stone, B., 1981, 1986; Egret, 1970; Swann, 1995; Rogister, 1995).

Ultimately, the success of the privileged resistance to the liberalizing and rationalizing efforts of the great late eighteenth-century reforming ministers – Turgot, Necker, and so on – produced consequences as unwelcome to the participants in the *parlements*, the Assembly of Notables, and even, in the end, the Estates General, as they were unforeseen. Certainly, new identities were in the process of emerging in response to the changed circumstances, and social action on these new grounds remains a significant part of the story.[12] Only gradually, however, did the new and innovative supplant the old in identity and action. At first, even the revolutionaries themselves were interested above all in remaking the state in a way that did not enhance the prospects of despotic political authority. A constitutionally safe process of reform, rather than a republic, was the initial aspiration. What this meant, however, was a reform of the state which did not feed monarchical power, which meant in turn that the new political order could not be monarchical at root. The king was welcome to travel along, but the carriage of state would have to find a new motive force.[13] Traditional constitutionalism, in its association with fundamentally irrational financial and administrative institutions, had become unsustainable, and corporate France indeed became the Revolution's first victim. The logic of the French state reform process thus made room for, even necessitated, new notions of popular sovereignty and democratic legitimation of national institutions.

The substantial, if not necessarily stable, democratic consequences of the collapse of the French *ancien régime* can therefore be seen as the consequence of an elite struggle to confer new legitimacy upon the troubled French state. Again, therefore, institutionalization stands as a precondition for change in a democratic direction. This was so precisely because of the fact that, while state formation involves imposing order upon diversity, it achieves this only to a degree, leaving room for manoeuvre, even within absolutist France, for counter-elites who might fall out of sympathy not with the overarching principles of the existing order, but with their particular application in the course of a project to reform and relegitimate the state. It is this conflict, fully comprehensible only in terms of these general principles, which creates the space for more fully oppositional groups to have their day. Democracy is thus the indirect result of conflict-driven institutional change, and both elite and popular forces play a role. Without institutions, however, this cannot occur. These conflicts played out differently in different national settings, but at root modern European democratization occurred at the point of intersection between traditional institutions, meaning both formal organizations and conceptions of a properly arranged political order, on the one hand, and the militarily and economically driven need to rationalize the financial and administrative structure of the state on the other.

This merits further examination in connection with the globalization debate, although in some respects it represents the mirror-image rather than a rehearsal of our current circumstances. Whereas today the state remains a significant – in fact the most significant – player in an environment characterized by strong signs of fragmentation and disaggregation, the point of arrival of European modernity was characterized by the growth to prominence of states which had not yet managed to shirk the alternative sources of social and political legitimacy which fragmented their otherwise ordered universe. Meanwhile, it was above all the competitive dynamic of the states system that drew these states into liberalizing and democratizing compromises with old and new holders of social power (Marks, 1997: 32-3).

It seems, nonetheless, much too early to suggest that little of value could come from an exploration of the similarities as well as differences between the periods of emergence of national and transnational institutions. Instead, for instance, of following Held in his placement of regional associations in the context of an anticipated multi-level democratization from localities all the way up to an assembly of nations, it might be useful to focus on the competitive character of economic regionalization as a force for both the development of institutions and, possibly, the reinforcement of these institutions through democratization. That said, of course it should not be ignored that these are different intensities of conflict. 'Rulers who failed to meet the demands of war making and resource extraction faced coercive removal from office. European integration appears less constrained' (Marks, 1997: 39-40).

Nonetheless, it is worth noting that one of the developments which drew the French state into difficulty was its enmeshment with the actors and organizations within French society. Ideas mattered greatly here, as constitutionalism conferred substantial legitimacy upon the act of resistance to state aggrandizement and especially rationalization, thus expanding the influence of those standing opposed to the reform of a still powerful state structure. The manner of French state formation had, meanwhile, through its particular arrangements of proprietary administration and corporate-based borrowing, heightened the degree of its vulnerability to the individual and collective actors of the *ancien régime*. It is, similarly, quite possible that the enlargement of access of transnational networks and movements to IGOs will cultivate a mutual dependence, and one which will give these social actors a surprising degree of influence over the character of these institutions at key moments of required adaptation.

Finally, for those concerned about the existence of community as a precondition for transnational democratization, the revolutionary period is also highly suggestive in this regard. As the constitutional conflict over state rationalization played itself out, it became clear that neither monarchical absolutism nor privileged particularism would prevail as the basis for political organization in France. Instead, the reform process redounded to the benefit not just of democracy but of a strongly national conception of it. First, the new National Assembly replaced 'privileged corporatism' with 'a new ideal of the polity', the essence of which was 'a conception of the nation itself as a source of equity' in the form of 'laws common to all' (Fitzsimmons, 1994: xii). The new source of sovereignty, revealingly, was according to the *Declaration of the Rights of Man and the Citizen* to be the nation rather than the people, and much of the reform project was oriented to recasting the country as a singular and cohesive community rather than an assemblage of provinces and privileged segments. When the king, meanwhile, demonstrated his incompatibility with this new national vision, he too was excised from the French nation in decisive fashion. The Revolution, therefore, which was the product of a state reform project disrupted by elite conflict, contributed mightily, if not finally and completely, to the making of the French national community. Of course, the experience of war, particularly with the expanded participatory base made possible by the *levée en masse*, added significantly to this transition; even before the war, however, the process was well underway (Fitzsimmons, 1994: 77-87, 97-108; Woloch, 1994: 40, 245; Ertman, 1997: 151-2). Looking to the future, it may well be the case that increased contact, as favoured by globalization's many components, can over time generate community as the basis for transnational democracy – Daniel Weinstock argues quite convincingly against the reasons to believe otherwise (Weinstock, 2001: 54-6). It is not necessarily the only way, however, and Lenard and Turgeon's essay (this volume) suggests an alternative linkage between a state's constitutional foundations and transnational democracy, one which emphasizes accommodatng the absence of unity over the forging of it.

5. Conclusion: Constituting National and Transnational Power

Claus Offe has recently suggested that Europe today finds itself in the position of having 'a *pouvoir constitué*, limited in its ability to govern and weak in its legitimation, ... without a corresponding *pouvoir constituant*' (Offe, 2000: 74). In his suggestion (2000: 74-5),

> The only remedy for this situation is the development of a widespread predisposition toward a European internationalism.... The development of relations of trust and solidarity on the European level is contingent upon good governance, and this means that Europe's first priority must be to establish a legitimate, transparent, and effective European governmental authority that cannot be 'negatively' politicized as a form of supranational foreign rule.

Offe may well be right in this. However, the National Assembly – that earlier *constituant* – did not so much emerge in order to bring democracy as a new and transformed state to France. Democracy was a by-product, made necessary above all by the near simultaneous lapse of both monarchy and corporate constitutionalism as formulae for political legitimacy. And this was not a by-product which made those in possession of this new state so very comfortable, as revealed by the introduction of citizenship distinctions, censitary limitations, indirect elections and other means by which the complex recasting of France's institutional apparatus could be preserved from the full impact of a untutored, potentially volatile electorate (Crook, 1996: 34-6; Gueniffey, 1993: 40-60, 77-92, 319, 331). Nonetheless, if the launching of French democracy in the revolutionary years was stunted and eventually overrun, it also utterly transformed the political landscape of the country in the short to medium term – no French regime would thereafter be able to rule without taking seriously the need to demonstrate its connection to the people – and over the long haul laid the foundations for the establishment of liberal democracy in the late nineteenth and twentieth centuries.[14] What this suggests is that, while we should of course concern ourselves with ways to confer greater degrees of democracy upon the European integration project, for instance, it may be that its democratic impulse will come less directly, through an attempt to resolve particularly knotty problems of managing and extending integration, through the resultant divisions within the European elite and the resultant search for new bases of legitimacy. Clearly, the expansion in recent years of the responsibilities of the European Parliament has not in itself provided EU institutions with a sufficient degree of democratic legitimacy (Scully, 2000: 244). As a pre-democratic or only partially democratic set of institutions, therefore, the grounds for the generation of such consequential elite conflicts is greater, except to the extent that multi-tracking, the result of opting out, serves as a pressure valve, albeit one that could exist at substantial ultimate cost to the integration project.

More broadly, while democracy may indeed come to the transnational setting in brand new ways, or even in brand new forms, this analysis suggests that we should also remain open to the instruction of the experience of the nation-state. This is not to claim that transnational democracy will be conditional upon the unlikely appearance of an overarching set of sovereign institutions on the model of the post-medieval European state, or to contend that there is a single nation-state model upon which to draw in any case. Rather, the aim is to point to the ways in which institutions that emerge to manage economic, cultural, and social globalization can produce unintended democratic effects both immediately and through the mediation of thereby strengthened social organizations, particularly as they become increasingly intertwined with transnational associations of various types and organizational intensities. History does not bind us, certainly, especially in the context of a world that is changing so very rapidly; neither, however, should we close our minds to the notion that democracy beyond the nation-state might result from processes that are by now recognizable to us.

Notes

1   Examples include the editorials 'March Madness' in *The New Republic* May 1 (2000), and 'The New Trade War' in *The Economist* December 4 (1999).
2   This is subject to question in the context of 'an unholy alliance of environmentalists and human rights advocates, protectionist trade unions, and ultraconservative neoisolationists,' at least in some recent instances of protest, as reported by Robert

Gilpin (2001: 229). The variety of activists and motivations, of course, does not in itself undermine any specific aspect of the critical assault against globalization.

3   Chadwick Alger, in this volume, demonstrates the ways in which this is not necessarily an either/or proposition, as the projects of locally active democrats are becoming increasingly dependent upon those of the transnational democrats, and vice versa.

4   This is not to suggest that 'more' rather than 'less' democratic is the least bit unproblematic in this connection. It is not at all clear, for instance, whether the empowerment of the European Parliament, as opposed to functional associations, the Council, or even a softly democratized Commission, represents a step in the democratic direction.

5   The indirect reference is to Michael Mann, whose thus far two volume collection, *The Sources of Social Power*, has influenced Held's thinking about the varied forms assumed by power and the need, therefore, to integrate strictly political power within a much broader array. Held, however, extends beyond Mann in setting out seven sites of power – the body, welfare institutions, culture, civic associations, the economy, the state's security apparatus, and the institutions of law and regulation – at which human beings can find their autonomy threatened (Held, 1995: 176-201).

6   This is only coming now to receive theoretical adjustment. See Diamond (1999).

7   For an instructive overview see Rueschemeyer et al. (1992: 13-19, 27-9).

8   David Blackbourn, for instance, established that the Imperial German bourgeoisie could support a substantial recasting of the economic and social sphere without necessitating a move toward a liberal democratic political order often seen as crucial to the fulfilment of its class aims (Blackbourn and Eley, 1984: especially 176-205). Dahrendorf's views are laid out in, *Society and Democracy in Germany* (1967).

9   Smith, Jackie, 1997: 46-9; Catherine Eschle concurs, but adds a stimulating critique of the notion of a global civil society, expressing her dissatissfaction with assumptions of unidimensionality and of the firmness in the contemporary context of the distinctions between the state, society, and the economic sphere; see Eschle (2001: 68-75).

10 This is the intriguing suggestion made by James Kurth (1993).

11 The parlements were part of the structure of sovereign courts in ancien-régime France. Although, unlike the British Parliament, they never developed from judicial origins into a fully-fledged legislature, they did retain secondary political influence through their traditional right to remonstrate against and then register royal decrees. The parlementaires held their positions venally, and so were part of the proprietary arrangements they generally defended.

12 As laid out in novel terms in Doug McAdam, Sidney Tarrow, and Charles Tilly (2001: 52-9).

13 Until, that is, the king's own carriage was captured at Varennes in an escape attempt, setting in motion the series of events culminating in regicide in early 1793.

14 This move to democracy, and the supportive development of a sense of national community, was critically aided by the extended conflict with Germany, which helped to generate unity as well as institutional change in France. This point comes to me from private correspondence with Michael Keating.

Chapter 4

A Question of Identity:
Some Reflections on Empires and
Nations in the North Atlantic

John A. Hall

There is much (but not total) truth to the notion that democracy – understood here as some combination of liberalism and popular politics – depends upon shared identity. Disagreement and conflict are only accepted, and so beneficial, when they are not too serious – that is, when they are regulated by a backdrop of shared, unquestioned norms. Nowhere is this more evident, as John Stuart Mill (1975) stressed, than when considering the national question: the homogeneity of Scandinavian societies stands behind generous welfare provisions, the varied divisions within the late Tsarist empire behind the inability to make a transition to a liberal democratic polity. This consideration is raised so as to highlight a relatively unacknowledged presupposition present in the mind of those who claim that we are witnessing the birth of transnational democracy, namely that an increase in shared transnational identity is upon us. This putative development could be investigated in several arenas – most obviously including the European Union (ably discussed, to my mind, by John McDougall in this volume) and the supposed birth of global civil society. Whilst I make passing references to these cases, my attention focuses on the North Atlantic. One reason for this concentration is that of limits to my own knowledge. But there is a better reason: memories of the same civilization, vast movements of capital and people, and shared membership of international regimes surely make this a critical case. Differently put, a transatlantic identity ought to be emerging if the scholars in question are correct. It is not, so they are wrong. This should not be misunderstood. My argument is descriptive, rather than prescriptive. As it happens, I long for cosmopolitanism, but see no virtue in replacing analysis with hope.

Much of this chapter depends upon drawing a distinction between two senses of transatlantic belonging: on the one side is membership in a transatlantic political entity, whether formal or informal, whilst on the other is a sense of belonging to a society other than that of the nation-state in which one resides. Analysis will be helped by two further conceptual points. First, particular attention is paid to a broad range of social identities. The vast majority of social interaction in the historical record has been *local*; the creation of *national* patterns of interaction is accordingly quintessentially modern. Where national identity is passive, *nationalist* identity is active – especially because it has ideas about the proper conduct of geopolitics. The determination to establish that the nation has its proper 'place in the sun' can and has led to conflict with those with *internationalist* identities. In late nineteenth-century Europe, nationalists sought to control and cage foreign policy-making elites whose behaviour was held to be altogether too internationally responsible. Finally, international interaction and identity is, although this is not always appreciated, different from the truly *transnational* (Mann, 1993b). Second, a warning is in order about the celebrated notion of social construction. Everything in social life, and not just nationalism, is socially constructed. But to leave matters at this point can lead to licentious voluntarism, that is, to the implicit belief that anything can be constructed at any time. Nothing could be further from the truth: social structures limit and select ideological innovation. Attention here will certainly be given to structural as much as to ideological forces.

1. Membership in Transatlantic Entities

The broad claim to be defended here is simple: membership within transatlantic political entities has declined quite markedly in the modern world. Let us consider formal transatlantic entities to begin with, in general terms and by means of a single example, and then turn to more recent, novel informal arrangements. The latter have considerable importance but they need to be characterized properly.

Historians now pay much attention to the Atlantic society and economy of the early eighteenth century (e.g., Langley, 1996). The first British empire was, unlike its later successor, very profitable, and the same was true for the early years of French and Spanish transatlantic structures of domination. The British case is especially interesting in the key matter that concerns us. The inhabitants of the Colonies were distinctively British. One way in which this can be seen is in the cultural patterning of the United States. Bernard Bailyn has demonstrated ideological continuity, whilst David Hackett Fischer's monumental work shows the re-creation in the New World of very diverse social patterns, from architecture and familial life to political attitudes and leadership styles (Bailyn, 1968; Fischer, 1989). More importantly, rebellion occurred in large part because of colonial loyalty to the ideals of the homeland. The move from being the best Englishmen to becoming Americans took place as the result of the conflict; it was consequence not cause. The destruction of the British transatlantic empire is generally best explained in terms of the limit to the logistics of rule imposed by geography and composite construction – although the fact that Britain fought without allies played a considerable part. But the precise cause does not matter here. The analytic point is that belonging became national, nationalist and international rather than transatlantic. Bluntly, this must be true: without this development, the novels of Henry James – to take an obvious example – would simply not make sense.

This point can be made with more force and sophistication by considering the very recent history of Canada, certainly from Confederation in 1867 to the First

World War and perhaps even to the 1960s. Here was a country with a state but without a national identity of its own. This is not for a moment to say that there was no sense of identity present within Canada. If Québécois identity was in large part inward looking, the same is not true for what is now known as the Rest of Canada. Here identity had a predominantly transatlantic character, as firmly as was the case for the members of the American colonies in the early eighteenth century. The proof of loyalty was of course paid in blood, in the Boer War and still more so in two world wars. Three points are worth making here about the working of this transatlantic entity (Cannadine, 1997). First, the economic development of Canada, the shipping lines and the railways, depended upon capital provided by London. More than 70 per cent of the 500 million pounds sterling absorbed between 1900 and 1914 came from Britain. Second, Canada provided job opportunities for the highest level of the metropolitan aristocracy. One Governor-General, Lord Lorne was Queen Victoria's son-in-law; another, the Duke of Connaught, was her favourite son. Third, the imperial connection allowed for quite remarkable social mobility for colonials within the metropolis.

Three examples make this point. Let us consider first Donald Alexander Smith, who arrived in Canada, a penniless Scot in 1838. For twenty-six years he worked in the Hudson's Bay Company. He then moved to Montreal, and became a major figure in the Canadian Pacific Railway and in national politics. In 1895, when already long past seventy, he became the official representative of Canada in London, where he died in 1914 – to the considerable irritation of Sir Frederick Borden, the famous Minister of Militia and Defence, who had sought to succeed him (Miller, C., 1997). Smith piled up colossal wealth, was ennobled as Lord Strathcona and Mount Royal and lived in great state on both sides of the Atlantic. He was Chancellor of McGill University; he equipped at his own cost a troop of horses during the Boer War; he presided in London at an annual banquet each July 1st to celebrate Canadian Confederation; and he spent 40,000 pounds sterling to celebrate his Lord Rectorship of Aberdeen University. A second case is that of R.B. Bennett, Prime Minister of Canada from 1930-1935. The Toronto Star ran a front-page feature on January 21, 1939 entitled 'R.B. Bennett Goes Home' in which Frederick Griffin asked Bennett if his impending move to England meant he was going into exile. "'No, my friend, certainly not to exile", Bennett replied, "...it will be home. Call it what you like, but that's what England is to me. I've felt it always. I felt it the first time I went there, when I was a youth. England to me is home. The countryside is mine, the fields, the shrines, the cities".'[1] Finally, there is William Maxwell Aitken. Within a decade of his arrival in Britain, Aitken was a member of parliament, a baronet, a peer, the owner of Express newspapers and the friend and confidant of that other son of the Canadian manse, Andrew Bonar Law – who became Prime Minister (in contrast to Aitken himself whose highest political post was that of Minister of Aircraft Production in 1940). The causes to which Aitken was attracted – Empire Free Trade in the 1930s and opposition to entry in the Common Market, together with deep antipathy to Lord Mountbatten on the grounds that he gave away India, the jewel of the empire as a whole – were characteristic of this transatlantic world. Bluntly, he loved the British empire more than did the British themselves.

It would be easy to go on, and at length, describing mechanisms of connection or recounting biographical details. Further, the historic pattern has scarcely completely ended. For instance, an old joke about Pierre Trudeau had it that the history of Canada would have been very different had he taken his theory of nationalism from Ernest Gellner rather than from Elie Kedourie whilst he was a student at the London School of Economics. Still, the analytic point to be made remains the same as for the first British Atlantic empire. This transatlantic entity has by and large come to an end. There is at least a Canadian national anthem (or, rather, two of them), the constitution has (at least for every province except Québec) been repatriated, and it would not surprise me were a republican movement to arise in the future to echo the one that is now making inroads in Australia. Conrad Black, the owner of Britain's *The Daily Telegraph*, illuminates matters by sheer contrast. His status as Aitken's presumptive heir seemed assured in 1999 when the British government offered him a peerage. But the Canadian government (whose current Prime Minister Jean Chrétien has reason to dislike the newspaper tycoon) refused to allow him, as a Canadian citizen, to accept this honour. Black renounced Canada, and took British citizenship. National identity trumped transatlantic belonging.

Let me turn to informal transatlantic identities. It may be useful to begin with to say that such identities most certainly have made an impact on the historical record. International relations scholars like to point to the transfer of power between Britain and the United States at the end of the nineteenth century as perhaps the sole example of a peaceful hegemonic transition within the history of the world polity. This transition was certainly eased by geography, but it depended upon shared liberal norms (Doyle, M., 1983) – and perhaps still more on shared Anglo-Saxon culture (Mann, 1993b). Kipling lived in Vermont for a long period, knew Mahan and Teddy Roosevelt, and eventually felt as at home with the key figures in Great Britain's military apparatus, Lords Fisher and Esher. This background transatlantic identity most certainly did a great deal to allow for the creation of a strategy to counter Imperial Germany. A division of military labour meant in particular that Britain could concentrate on designing plans to bottle up the German fleet so as to starve the German population into submission (Offer, 1989).

Is there any more recent equivalent to this situation? The least that can be said about the Atlantic Community was that an attempt was made to create an extensive transatlantic identity (Cf. Schaeper and Schaeper, 1998). All those CIA-funded Congresses for Cultural Freedom sought to cement a shared identity, an enterprise in a sense personified in the vigorous figure of Edward Shils – resident for most of his life half a year in Chicago and half a year at the University of Cambridge. Still, how extensive and deep was this identity? It is worth keeping at the centre of one's mind that identities habitually involve some sort of mix between interest and affect. Is emotional attachment as strong in the Atlantic Community as it was amongst Anglo-Saxons at the turn of the century? Let us consider the most powerful transatlantic link – the 'Special Relationship' between the United States and Great Britain – before characterizing the nature of the Atlantic community as a whole.

The Special Relationship has received enormous attention, not surprisingly since it is with us still. One of the earliest architects was Winston Churchill. The fact that his mother was American lends authenticity to the notion of a transatlantic identity. Still, his behaviour as First Lord of the Admiralty and as Prime Minister had quite as much at its core the pragmatic desire to extend *British* power by means of the American connection. Calculation seems stronger still in Harold Macmillan's celebrated words to Richard Crossman while attached to Eisenhower's headquarters in Algiers in 1942: '[We] are the Greeks in this American empire. You will find the Americans much as the Greeks found the Romans – great big, bustling people, more vigorous than we are and also more idle, with more unspoiled virtues but also more corrupt. We must run [this HQ] as the Greek slaves ran the operations of the Emperor Claudius' (Horne, 1988: 160). This same vein was struck by Keynes, when commenting to his staff before beginning meetings about the British loan: 'they may have all the money, but we've got all the brains'.[2]

If we now revert to continental European cases, the air of calculation rather than of shared identity comes to the fore. As an intellectual, Raymond Aron, despite his fabulous intelligence and carefully nurtured American relationships, was first and foremost French. In more political terms, the 'empire by invitation' that is NATO resulted from the famous calculation, coined by Lord Ismay, that it was necessary 'to keep the Russians out, the Americans in and Germany down' (Lundestad, 1986). A similar point must be made about the nature of transatlantic relations in general, to whose characterization we can now turn.

Nationalist geopolitics in the period from 1870-1945 produced genuine anarchy in the international system. In these conditions, it made sense to grab territory; nationalism became inextricably linked with imperialism, for only extensive territory could secure supplies and markets. The resolution of Europe's security dilemma after 1945 broke this connection. A very particular transatlantic society was created. There are now frequent meetings of the leaders of the Atlantic states, but key transatlantic (and international) institutions are dominated in the last resort by the leading power. This is obviously true of NATO whose commanding officer is, has been, and it is safe to say always will be an American. Europeans have realized that the United States has solved their security dilemma, have occasionally shared anti-communist attitudes, and are well aware that the benefit of being geopolitically supine is their considerable affluence. Nonetheless, the fact that interest in international cooperation is not so to speak automatic can be seen in endless quibbles and in pervasive anti-Americanism. Still, the pretense is that of community, and so it hurts – especially in London – when the United States acts unilaterally, as it does whenever anything of consequence to its own interests is at stake.

The most striking recent portrait of American-European relations, that of Steve Walt's 'The Ties that Fray' (1998/99), suggests that interests have now diverged to such an extent as to destroy any continuing sense of community. It is certainly true that trade between America and Europe is not great (with the United States alone having the option of isolationism), and that economic interests, both in agriculture and in communicative technologies, diverge sharply. All of this will lead, and in the eyes of commentators in addition to Walt, to an economic challenge spearheaded by the new Euro. Further, Europeans calculate the threats in the Middle and Near East in a manner all their own, and clearly resent being subject to American meddling – with the same applying with still greater force in cultural affairs. Despite the cogency of these points, Walt seems to me to be quite wrong. Given that calculation rather than community ruled in the first instance, there is more evidence of continuity than he allows. There is no sign of any real challenge to the United States, much as I might like it, and a good deal to suggest the exact opposite. Who would have predicted, for example, that France would effectively rejoin NATO – a move calculated to balance united Germany by strengthening the American involvement? Does anybody really think it likely that Europe's status as economic giant and military worm will change? Has not the timing of actions in the erstwhile Yugoslavia been dependent, for better and for worse, upon what happens in Washington? Were not European protests about George W. Bush's plans to attack Iraq simply insignificant whines, bereft of any genuine consequence? Is it really likely that the Euro can triumph over the dollar, when the United States remains the provider of geopolitical security?

It is worth trying to highlight the central contention made to this point. Transatlantic political entities are weaker than they once were. On the one hand, formal political entities have disappeared. On the other hand, the large element of calculation in transatlantic relations means that the taken-for-granted quality inherent in the very notion of identity is somewhat lacking.[3] Still, this diminished condition looks, in the absence of any alternative, rather durable. But this is a first approximation; more will be said about the United States.

2. Belongings Beyond One's Nation-State

A proper investigation of images of belonging to social worlds outside one's own state or nation-state would of course be vast. An enormous amount could be said about the images of the other held by people, differentially divided by class, religion and ethnicity, on different sides of the Atlantic. Much here has little to do with belonging. Still less prominent is accuracy of perception. It is difficult for me to describe the loathing that I feel for much BBC drama, so often featuring effete members of the aristocracy, produced for American consumption. This makes a good deal of money, and justifies American views of the backwardness of Britain – but at the expense of any sense of what actually happens in that country. Other images do have much more to do with a sense of belonging, not least amongst intellectuals who dream of mingling in the Café Flore with the heirs of Sartre and de Beauvoir. However, rather than concentrate on such images let me, so to speak, raise the bar higher so as to ask not just about dreams but instead about what might be called networks of interaction – by which is meant those belongings that affect actions rather than dreams.

There is of course nothing novel about the presence of networks of interaction that transcend borders. In medieval Europe, the larger identities of feudalism and of Christianity for centuries transcended states; similar points can be made about most of the world religions, whilst intellectuals quite often have more allegiance to their fellows than to the state in which they live. Still, the standard generalization of historical sociology has been that the rise of the nation-state has increasingly caged social interactions within its borders. This has overwhelmingly been true of the means of violence. Bluntly, Wallenstein was the last of the great military *condottieres*. In the period between 1870 and, say, 1958, capitalists were similarly caged, although I will argue later that their later release is not as great as is often imagined – and that, at least in Europe, it results less from the defeat of the state than from deliberate political intent. Whilst bearing these points in mind, let us concentrate most on peoples. Is it the case that the classical immigrant experience – in which one assimilated, at considerable cost, to the host national culture – has come to an end? Are diasporas now so well connected by cheap travel and the internet that homogeneous national entities can no longer be created? This brings us to key theoretical debates. Bluntly, how much of the ideas of postnationalist and of multiculturalism should we accept?

There most certainly are cases where the extensive search of a diaspora matters for very practical reasons, as most obviously was and is true for the overseas Chinese – many of whom live in genuinely multicultural settings. Is there any transatlantic equivalent? Let us consider Europe and the United States in turn.

At the end of the nineteenth century, the United States was the stuff of which dreams were made, both for peasants in Central and Southern Europe and for the persecuted from regions further to the east. Histories of immigration show that there was much more movement back and forward than we now realize, with perhaps fifty per cent of Italians who came to the United States returning when economic conditions proved too adverse. This is evidence of an extensive network before the era of modern communications, although it is far from sure that this amounted to a genuine transatlantic identity. Irish immigration to the United States in the last thirty years has had a similar character. But the blunt fact is that Europe no longer provides the bulk of immigrants to the United States. American racism of course closed off southern and eastern Europe in 1924. More importantly, most of the nation-states of Europe have made themselves attractive places in which to live, with industrialization now capable of absorbing populations once forced to migrate. Tourism to the United States from across the Atlantic booms, but a transatlantic identity based in Europe does not seem in the cards.

There certainly are cases in North America where an image of transatlantic belonging matters. Capital, the human capital of the young trained in computer technology, and political leadership has come, with varying degrees of benefit, to the Baltics and to the Balkans from the United States. But we need to be very careful before saying that transatlantic belongings are generally strong and on the increase. Three considerations should be borne in mind. First, what is at issue at times is longing rather than belonging: it seems to me to be the case that the Québécois often feel rejected and jilted by the French, who rarely go to live there – often preferring to make jokes about their accent. Secondly, it is very important to note that the images of belonging are imaginary, and that the process of imagining distinctively reflects American culture rather than any primordial identity. The spaghetti with meatballs that marks Italian-American culture is unknown in Italy; more importantly, the support given by Irish-Americans to NORAID was quite often an extreme embarrassment to Irish citizens, amongst them the members of the rock band U2 – who famously and very bravely criticized their 'fellows' in this regard. Third, transatlantic identities are simply not present at all in key circumstances. Recent years have seen the emergence of non-ethnic white Americans, present in striking numbers in the mid-west, who no longer make any pretense at having a transatlantic identity. More controversially, it is worth pointing out the huge difference that exists between African-Americans and Afro-Americans. Except for some very striking exceptions, it is by and large true to say that Afro-Americans have no particular loyalty or link to Africa. There is a vast body of evidence showing that Afro-Americans share mainstream American values, and wish for nothing more than to be full members of their own society – making it all the more cruel, of course, that they cannot gain proper entry into mainstream American society.

It is well worth pausing to consider the United States in a little more detail, not least as this society, the largest and most powerful in the transatlantic world, is the source of recent claims about multiculturalism and postnationality. The central point to be made is that diversity was once much greater in the United States than it is today. Two points should be borne in mind. On the one hand, the United States in 1920 boasted 276 newspapers in German, 118 in Spanish or Portuguese, 111 in Scandinavian languages, 98 in Italian, 76 in Polish, 51 in Czech or Slovak, 46 in French, 42 in Slovenian and 39 in Yiddish – together with the genuinely different culture of the Solid South (Lind, 1995: 75). All of this has of course gone. On the other hand, brilliant research by Mary Waters has demonstrated both that ethnicity is no longer a cage but rather an option – and one, it should be noted, that has astonishingly little actual substance (Waters, 1990). This latter point is not to say for a moment that the constructed identity is not somehow real and important: very much to the contrary, to have an ethnic identity is now almost a constitutional right. But the point about the politics of difference is that so many people are demanding recognition: that so many ask for the same thing is an astonishing demonstration of the continuing powers of American nationalizing homogeneity – for all but Afro-Americans (Hall and Lindholm, 1999). Furthermore, difference is entertained only so far as it is, so to speak, toilet-trained and American: it is fine to express one's Asian background by wearing a sari when graduating from high school – but only on the condition that one does not take caste seriously. As this view is contentious, not to say unpopular, it is worth justifying. Consider that research on Hispanics shows that they are no different from previous immigrants: Cuban-Americans in Florida have out-marriage rates of above 50 per cent within a single generation, together with a set of attitudes in tune with those of the larger society.[4] Perhaps this should not surprise us. It remains the case that immigrants are attracted to the United States because of the opportunities for social mobility that an ever more powerful and nationally integrated capitalist culture offers. If that is to say that the immigrants who come to the United States are self-selected in such a way as to reinforce core American beliefs, there should be no gainsaying of the other side of the picture. Apparently, a stump speech directed against Ann Richards when running to be Governor of Texas had it that 'if English is good enough for Jesus Christ, it is good enough for Texas'. Poll evidence shows very, very high levels of opposition in the United States for any general recognition of a second official language; the votes against such recognition in California are thus entirely representative of strong external pressures placed on immigrants (Wolfe, 1998). All of this can be summarized in the starkest possible terms: no real transatlantic identity will develop from the United States, which will remain a great engine for creating Americans.

3. Conclusion

It may be as well to anticipate an objection to this chapter. Is not the skepticism exhibited deeply unimaginative, blindly ignoring changes to our social reality? Differently put, has not the chapter simply been one of sterile negation? An initial answer to this must of course be Popperian, that conjectures stand in need of refutation. Still, I tend to agree that criticism has greatest force when it is based on some alternative vision. There is, of course, not enough space to spell out my own position fully, but hints can be given – not least so as to make clear agreement as to the need for social science to explain the world. But let me begin by adding fuel to the flames of discontent. My skepticism to this point has in fact been moderate; it is as well to own up to it being far more extensive.

To begin with we should not accept much of what is implied in the term globalization. On the one hand, deep reservations should be held about the supposed emergence of global civil society – about which we know far too little. Most international non-governmental organizations are peopled by and housed in Northern countries; they often give evidence of our sensibilities, of our desire to change others, rather than expressing the feelings of the vast majority of mankind. Further, there is as yet very little evidence that global social movements have had much impact on world politics. On the other hand, a whole set of reasons should make us doubt that the world economy is now globalized (Hall, J., 2000). First, trading patterns go against any naive view of the globe as the key economic unit (Wade, 1996). World trade has only just regained the level of 1913, with most of the increase since 1945 anyway being due most of all to the removal of tariffs within Europe. Further, between 1970 and 1990 the share of the North within world trade increased from 81-84 per cent; importantly, the United States trades only 12 per cent of its GDP – with only 3 per cent of its GDP being involved with the developing world. Second, foreign direct investment patterns show both that external investments – small in any case as a proportion of home capital – go very largely to the North rather than to the South. Third, the most striking research on firms suggests that we should speak of NFIOs rather than TNCs or MNCs, that is, of national firms with international operations rather than transnational or multinational corporations. Profits are still repatriated to the home base, with management reflecting national ownership more and more strongly as one mounts the corporate ladder. Fourth, technological innovation, measured by research and development spending and the taking of patents, continues to reflect the historical differences of nation-states. Fifth, restrictions on labour, to some extent in the United States but much more so in Europe, look set to increase, whilst those of Japan do not look as if they are about to diminish: it is this evidence that makes me doubt the case for post-nationalism. To be set against all this, of course, is the undoubted speed with which money now flows around the world. But here too reservations are in order: stock markets remain very largely national, whilst the floating of currencies reflects the interests of the United States quite as much as any global logic of its own.

Sustained skepticism needs to be shown quite as much to the thesis that the nation-state has been 'hollowed out', putatively assailed both from above and below. States within capitalism have rarely had and have rarely sought total control over their destinies. Historical awareness makes one realize that states are very adaptable, with the loss of power in one arena often being compensated for by an increase elsewhere – as is the case now, for the penetrative power of the state is increasing for all that some monetary powers are being abandoned. Are European states less powerful now that they have been humbled by the attempts made between 1870 and 1945 to become total power containers? Is not less more? Has not security and standard of living been vastly enhanced by a diminution of pretension? Further, exactly how many states are really challenged seriously from below? Were not the great secessionist drives of the last years directed against the last great empire, that of the Soviet Union? Serious analysis makes one realize that the European Union has depended at all times on the motor of the Franco-German alliance – something which goes some way to suggesting that the future of the Union is likely to remain international rather than transnational (Milward, 1992). If the nation-state is still present in Europe, where one can at least argue about new forces, there is little likelihood of it suddenly collapsing in the United States or Japan. The only place where states are collapsing is in sub-Saharan Africa. Awareness of this should make us realize how provincial is much Western commentary when speaking about the state: much of the world needs the powers of the state to increase. It is relevant in this context to note that 'global' – that is, Northern – support can be dangerous. If a minority escalates its claims when confident of external support, it can lead to the counter-mobilization of the majority – and so to civil war, and to the destruction of states in areas where they are desperately needed.

Much of what has been said to this point can be and should be expressed in wholly positive terms. The world has indeed changed. The North is much more integrated. There is general awareness within that world that autarky brings poverty rather than prosperity, in part because participation in high-tech markets increases the knowledge on which late industrial society seems ever more to depend. This is enormously important. It amounts to the replacement of zero-sum nationalist conflict by an increase in positive-sum international society. But we must not exaggerate by claiming that 'global economics and culture...require global politics which will at least be as responsive to popular desires as the most democratic of national states', as elaborated in the editor's introduction to this volume. For one thing, the functionalism of this statement needs to be resisted: my needs have never been met, and I see no sign of any historical process at work suggesting that those of culture and economics will fare better. For another, the international is not the transnational: much order in the world results from deals between heads of governments, whose actions are often not much limited or controlled by their citizens. And this point needs itself to be amplified in a very important way. Behind international order stands the huge powers of the most powerful state the world has yet seen. In retrospect we can see (what in fact could be seen at the time) that the debate about American decline of the late 1980s was utterly misconceived. Only the United States has military, cultural, monetary, economic, and ideological force of primary weight in the contemporary world. One sign of the supremacy of the United States is the simple fact that it has the ability to control or limit the working of any putatively transnational regime, as has recently been wholly obvious in the case of the International Criminal Court. Another sign is that of the ability to run a continual trading imbalance with the rest of the world. The current account of the United States is balanced by borrowing most of the excess capital of the world economy. Such capital is available, it has been argued (Wade and Veneroso, 1998), because of the American insistence on the opening of financial markets – an opening, it should be noted, that helped to cause and certainly to exacerbate the Asian financial crisis of the late 1990s. Still more remarkable is the fact that the United States is responsible for perhaps forty-five per cent of world military spending, thereby spending more than the next seven countries combined. This suggests two final thoughts. First, order can be created through power quite as much as by justice. There is certainly a sense now in which we live within the confines of an imperial republic. Secondly, such inhabitants of the Beltway as Paul Wolfowitz, Dick Cheney and Donald Rumsfeld do not really possess any transatlantic identity (except in the very particular sense that they imagine that beneath the surface of their enemies are little Americans struggling to get out), thereby making traditional realist concepts all-too-relevant. But the fact that much of the motion of modernity is now determined, for better or worse, in Washington means that it behooves Europeans to have a transatlantic awareness (and much of the rest of the world to have international awareness) – even though they lack much sense of transatlantic belonging.

Notes

1   This reference was kindly provided by Sid Noel.
2   I heard this story from James Meade. Though I have learnt a great deal from K. Phillip's *The Cousins's Wars* (1999), the thesis of that book – that there is a united Anglo-America – does not convince this British subject for a simple reason, namely that there have been many occasions when the United States has chosen to act alone. This was true of the shaping of the postwar architecture of the international economy with which Keynes was involved. Equally, Mrs Thatcher was apparently only told about the bombing raid on Libya when American planes were airborne.
3   It may be sensible to emphasize that pure affective identity can and does matter in contemporary Europe. The most obvious example is the desire of many citizens in Central Europe to 'rejoin Europe'.
4   This figure is drawn from the unpublished research of Elizabeth Arias, Department of Sociology, State University of New York at Stony Brook.

Chapter 5

Romancing the State: Sovereignty and the Moral Bases of Self-Determination

Katherine Fierlbeck

1. Introduction

The 'paradox of the state' has been the focal point of much political philosophy in the past decade. According to this account, liberalism has explicitly derided nationalism and other state-building ideologies (favouring instead ideas such as cosmopolitanism and universal human rights) while at the same time implicitly depending upon the self-evident justifiability of sovereign statehood (liberal states being amongst the most vigorous in determining who is and who is not permitted to reside within their borders).[1] As Margaret Canovan (2001: 204) succinctly notes,

> [d]espite their formally universalistic habits of discourse, political philosophers have shared this unconscious tendency to take nations and national boundaries for granted, with the result that crucial questions have remained unasked. Theorists of democracy have rarely worried about the boundaries of the "people" who were to generate representatives to act for them and accept majority decisions as binding, because a nation with limits and unifying bonds was unconsciously taken to be the norm.[2]

Following from this observation, a number of theorists have endeavoured to use the concept of a culturally-oriented 'nationhood' as the moral grounding for national self-determination. In other words, because liberalism tacitly defends the concept of separating 'us' from 'them', the moral desirability of this separation ought to be explicitly recognized in liberal theory. Will Kymlicka (1995: 125), for example, argues that

> liberal states exist, not only to protect standard rights and opportunities of individuals, but also to protect people's cultural membership. Liberals implicitly assume that people are members of societal cultures, that these cultures provide the context for individual choice, and that one of the functions of having separate states is to recognize the fact that people belong to separate cultures.

Neither the existence of this paradox nor the conclusions generated from it have been vigorously challenged. When the philosophical justifications of state sovereignty are discussed at all (which is usually when one country states its intention to invade another, or has already done so), two related but discernable arguments are generally presented. The first argument focuses upon the inherent legitimacy of state sovereignty *per se*: if Western liberal states wish to defend the sovereignty of their nations (historically the result of the flexing of political muscle), so too can non-liberal states. I argue against this claim, holding that what makes the sovereignty of liberal states legitimate is the very liberal nature of the states themselves. That European states *historically* were the result largely of the flexing of political power rather than of reasoned political discourse does not diminish the *contemporary* justification for self-determination that rests upon principles of individual human rights rather than upon political opportunism.

The second argument (generally used in conjunction with the first) does not focus specifically upon historical fact, but rather upon the present constellation of cultural characteristics within and between states. According to this argument, the existence of particular cultural traits shared by a geographically discrete group of individuals is what justifies the claim of this group to self-determination. This right to collective sovereignty is prior to (and independent of) any rights of individuals within the group. Thus, in this account the legitimacy of the state depends upon the protection of cultural traits rather than upon the protection of individuals themselves (the latter being a specifically liberal conception of state legitimacy). I do not believe that this argument is persuasive either, although the case against it is quite complex and has been thoroughly disputed elsewhere.[3] I will, however, present one element of the argument against cultural rights which has perhaps not been sufficiently considered: that a right (or set of rights) dependent upon excessive subjectivity is highly unsatisfactory both philosophically and politically. In sum, then, the argument that liberal states implicitly acknowledge the value of protecting cultural units (and thus implicitly support the right to self-determination for non-liberal groups) is unconvincing. The best (perhaps only) moral grounds for sovereign statehood is the way in which individuals within these states are treated: and liberal states, because of their relatively superior claims in this regard, have a level of moral legitimacy many other putatively sovereign states do not.

The lessons for transnational democracy from the nation-state experience, according to this account, are thus twofold. First, we must never succumb to the romance of the nation-state: as Kedourie states, "'[t]o suppose that nations just are entitled to be self-determined, and that this entitlement is partly constitutive of the concept of nationhood, is simply to embrace the core of nationalism which is a doctrine of political legitimacy'" (quoted in Barry, 2001: 31). The claim to self-determination is a substantial political demand, and must be evaluated rigorously and deliberately on its merits. Second, we can never lose sight of the ultimate importance of the concept of active consent upon which liberal democracy is so firmly grounded. The numinous and revolutionary quality of liberal thought rested largely in the assertion that it was for each individual themselves to judge the legitimacy of their own regimes, and it would be a disastrous mistake to downplay or dismiss this requirement. On the face of it, then, some of the purported impediments to transnational democracy simply do not apply, given that democracy is not to be seen as the moral fulfillment of an integrated cultural community and that it is consent that is crucial from the point of view of democracy. The decline of transatlantic identity ably presented by John Hall (this volume) might not therefore be as damning for democracy's prospects as some might suggest.

As is also stressed by John Markoff and Bruce Morrison (in their chapters in this volume), however, history matters. Both state sovereignty and democracy are products of Western liberal societies (although they have been formed to some degree as well with reference to liberal states' engagement with non-Western societies), and both concepts are tightly linked. It is highly probable that democracy could only ever have evolved within the context of the discrete nation-state;[4] and it is also likely that democracy can only really exist in a practicable manner within the structure of the modern nation-state, notwithstanding the debate over how autonomous contemporary Western nations in fact *are* (or are not). We seem quite prepared to argue for the establishment of democracy (local or transnational) on moral grounds: that is, we are quite prepared to make an ethical case supporting its development and proliferation (notwithstanding the more consequentialist position that democratic states are desirable because they are simply more likely to be stable and nonaggressive). Theorists such as Canovan et al. are also correct that we tend to accept the existence of nation-states as a given even though they are nonetheless subsequently given a significant moral status. Although John Markoff's suggestions that democracy's meaning has always shifted in connection with changed circumstances, and that further adaptation might be a response to the changes we are currently experiencing, is an intriguing one, there seems to be no doubt, as John Hall and Glyn Morgan suggest in their chapters, that we remain at this point in the moral universe of the nation-state and will continue to do so for some time to come. It remains crucial, therefore, to take up the task of disentangling the moral and political claims that are currently made based upon the relationships between liberalism, sovereign statehood, culture, and the distribution of power within and among discrete political units.

The following section of this chapter examines the historical basis for the concept of state sovereignty: what were the original philosophical justifications offered for the nation-state? I attempt to sketch here the theoretical bases of the concept of sovereignty and note the distinction between the historical political developments which led to the formation of discrete state units and the normative accounts that were presented in order to justify the sovereignty of these units. This section argues that because the 'us-them' distinction was simply a practicable strategy for achieving particular goals and was never given any *moral* weight in and of itself, the putative 'paradox of the state' neither is a particularly insightful intellectual idea, nor can be persuasively utilized as a moral basis for contemporary self-determination.

The concluding section looks more closely at the way in which arguments for 'autonomy' and 'dignity' are used in contemporary political rhetoric as philosophical bases for self-determination. The modern state system, to the extent that its development depended upon an ethical justification at all, focused upon the idea of consent as a legitimating account. Precisely why consent was important, however, and how it ought to be made manifest were questions that were addressed in a number of distinct ways, the two most influential being those based upon accounts of autonomy and dignity. The culturally-oriented justification for sovereignty, which has recently become so prevalent, is based emphatically upon the latter, and faces specific problems that diminish its coherence and desirability and, some might argue, its very historical *raison d'être*.

2. The Rights of States and the Rights of Man

Bodin is generally accepted as the first theorist to discuss the concept of 'sovereignty' (to mean the quality of *statehood*, as distinct from *the person of the sovereign*). Facilitated by the break-up of the medieval Church, which forced individuals to consider *which* Church they chose to recognize, late sixteenth-century Europe became fragmented into 'sovereign' units, the attributes of which included the rights to war, peace and political alliances; the right to authorize all appointments to public office; and the right to demand unqualified oaths of submission.[5] The determination of whether any particular sovereign was legitimate, argued Bodin, depended upon whether he recognized the rights of his citizens to liberty and property; these rights, in turn, rested in 'the imprescriptibility of divine and natural law' (Bodin, xxi). In medieval Europe, political leaders were also religious leaders, whose primary moral concern was for the well-being not of their subjects *per se* but of their subjects' souls. It was, in turn, the particular nature of Christianity – the divisive split between Catholicism and Protestantism – which led to the beginnings of the modern state system. Here the principle of *rex est imperator in regno suo* (the king is emperor in his own realm) was transformed for pragmatic reasons to *cuius regio, eius religio* (whose territory, his religion), in which each sovereign respected the religious authority of every other ruler over their respective subjects. It was, in essence, simply a practical principle of political coexistence which was underscored by the internecine battles of the Thirty Years' War. The Treaty of Westphalia, which attempted to resolve this long and bloody period, is thus seen in retrospect as the first major statement of sovereign statehood.[6]

As Christianity fragmented and became less useful in explaining why one ought to obey any particular sovereign, Europe began to see the development of natural rights theories that primarily attempted to provide an answer to the question of why one ought to obey in principle. The answer, of course, rests in the development of consent theory, which in turn depended upon the development of theories of natural right. The precise point regarding the genesis of modern natural rights, however, remains in some dispute: for Richard Tuck, for example, it was Grotius' desire to legitimate Dutch colonial expansion which led him both to defend the authority of the Dutch state and to argue that the sea, unlike land, was not subject to the strictures of private property. According to Tuck, Grotius concluded that 'all rulers owe their authority to the *respublica* which had been constituted by a social contract' (Tuck, 1993: 177): and that this social contract, in turn, rested upon the fundamental natural rights of man. A sovereign state, then, was 'a group who had in some way defined themselves as separate from the rest of human society by particular transfers of rights' (Tuck, 1979: 77). Thus, Tuck sees that the concept of rights, for Grotius, has 'come to usurp the whole of natural law theory, for the law of nature is simply, respect one another's rights' (Tuck, 1979: 67). The distance from the medieval reliance upon God's authority grounding political sovereignty, argues Tuck, can be seen in Grotius' famous passage in *The Rights of War and Peace* where he states that the natural law is binding '"though should we even grant, what without the greatest Wickedness cannot be granted, that there is no God, or that he takes no Care of human Affairs"' (quoted in Tuck, 1979: 76).

Perez Zagorin, in contrast, disputes the account offered by Tuck, and defends the position that the highly original concept of *natural rights,* which confers legitimacy on a state through some mechanism of consent, remains the product of Thomas Hobbes' political thought. Tuck's reading, according to Zagorin, rests primarily upon a mistranslation of Grotius' works in which the concepts of 'law' and 'right' (both confusingly referred to as *ius* in the original Latin) are used incorrectly. Moreover, argues Zagorin, Grotius' passage regarding the force of natural law independent of God's existence was an issue debated by medieval scholastic philosophers, and did not convincingly illustrate 'the secularization of natural law' or 'its emancipation from its theistic roots and ties with theology' (Zagorin, 2000: 16-40).

But whether the genesis of modern natural rights theories began toward the end of the sixteenth century, or three-quarters of a century later, it was clear that the question of political obligation underlying state sovereignty had regardless undergone a radical transformation by the end of the seventeenth century, a product of the English civil war and 'glorious revolution' as much as it was a result of the intellectual endeavours of Hobbes himself. It is of course a recognized irony that the authors of modern natural rights theories were disposed to favour some form of absolutism; nonetheless, by the beginning of the eighteenth century the combination of England's constitutional monarchy and the nation's commercial successes provided a good reason to argue in favour of expanded political liberties. Thus both Adam Smith and Charles de Montesquieu proffered arguments supporting greater political freedom while eschewing popular representation. Liberalism, by the eighteenth century, was seen as incompatible with democracy insofar as liberalism *required* a 'strong' state (counterbalanced by the market and by 'intermediate associations') to protect the very liberties of man which a modern monarchy could provide. Rousseau, likewise, argued that liberalism and democracy were incompatible, although his account reversed the received position and stressed the dangers that excessive individual freedoms or an untrammeled market would pose for a democracy based upon selfless civic engagement.

Historically, then, there is a clear distinction between the political formation of the sovereign state (as a strategy to minimize religious conflict) and the philosophical account developed to justify this new alignment. This historical schism has its reflection in the differing usages of the modern concept of 'sovereignty': while its use in political philosophy generally refers to the legitimate authority of rulers (vis-a-vis the ruled), the literature within the subdiscipline of international relations focuses upon the legitimate relationship between states (the legitimacy of sovereignty largely depending upon whether one is a realist or an idealist[7]). Stephen Krasner, for example, has identified four quite distinct usages of the term (international legal sovereignty, Westphalian sovereignty, domestic sovereignty, and interdependence sovereignty).[8] The contemporary debate over self-determination, however, combines elements of *both*, arguing that the nature of the relationship between individuals within a given community establishes a right to a specific relationship vis-a-vis other political communities. Yet the foundation of each usage is quite distinct, which accounts, in part, for the unsatisfying mishmash present in current political rhetoric.

That liberalism and democracy did in fact become 'liberal democracy' despite the apprehensions of early liberals toward representative democracy (and of Rousseau toward liberalism) may perhaps be linked to the conceptual development of 'individual autonomy' in the nineteenth century: to the extent that state sovereignty was based ultimately upon some manifestation of consent (as early natural rights theorists had argued), liberal theorists began to recognize that the capacity to consent was ultimately meaningless unless it could be exercised effectively and regularly. Given the nature of social contract theory, too, the assumption of *universal* consent also logically required the expansion of universal suffrage. But if the idea of the natural rights of individuals was politically effective in establishing a rationale for effectively circumscribing monarchical powers, others attempted to use natural individual rights as a basis for considering the 'dignity' of these individuals.

'Dignity', as a basis of natural rights, has its roots in the powerful influence of Puritan religious thought. The valuation of what Charles Taylor calls the 'affirmation of ordinary life' (Taylor, 1989: esp. Part III) included an emphasis upon dignity (and specifically the equal dignity of individuals) in place of the classical emphasis upon honour that was, by definition, bestowed only upon a select few.[9] And, while the Diggers and Levellers attempted (unsuccessfully) to argued for a set of political rights for all individuals based upon the natural rights of man,[10] the clearest discussion of how dignity ought to manifest itself politically was perhaps presented at the end of the eighteenth century by the Puritan-raised writer and activist Thomas Paine, who insisted that the inherent dignity of each individual had to be protected by a political framework of universal rights (Paine, 1985 [1791]).[11] Historically, the moral force of rights in a political sense has rested in the simple logic of their universal nature. This principle was recognized quite early by those Puritan factions (such as the Independents) who argued that promoting the toleration of all Christian religious groups was the best strategy for protecting the Puritans' own right of worship. This was a considerably well-founded premise: for despite the fact that 'human rights' were granted historically to white males but not to women or non-whites, the logic of universality over time has indeed corroded the exclusivity of rights and has extended the franchise (as well as other fundamental rights) more widely.

The concept of 'autonomy' is another product of liberal natural rights theory, and has a different intellectual pedigree. 'Autonomy', in contradistinction to 'dignity', focused more emphatically upon the capacity for choice enjoyed by human adults. It was this capacity to make choices, and to be held responsible for them, which, as Rousseau famously noted, differentiated animals from human beings,[12] and it was this discussion of autonomy which precipitated the rise of both democratic and liberal democratic thought. The development of the idea of autonomy, of course, was the culmination of Enlightenment political thought, which, in the Kantian view, placed considerable import upon the idea of 'a radical autonomy of rational agents'. In this view, '[t]he fully significant life is the one which is self-chosen' (Taylor, 1989: 383).

'Sovereignty' writ large, then, has two intertwined yet distinct historical pedigrees: the first, based upon religious factionalism, was a means of preventing virulent and continuous bloodshed. This has its modern manifestation in the 'realist' theory of much contemporary international relations theory. The subdiscipline of international relations, for example, points to Thomas Hobbes as its intellectual founder, for Hobbes was responding to the realities of political and religious conflict in the sixteenth and seventeenth centuries. The second account, based upon a more demanding ethical framework (which contemporary international relations theorists frequently refer to as the 'idealist' approach) paradoxically, *also* sees Hobbes (or Grotius) as its intellectual progenitor; and focuses upon Hobbes' crucial (though limited) use of 'consent', which was based upon the primacy of natural individual rights. But natural right (or natural law) was itself an ambiguous concept even in the seventeenth century, and the accounts of the basis of natural right itself were themselves quite distinct.

Thus the *normative* justification for sovereignty (and also self-determination) is based squarely upon the concept of natural right: contemporary states, in theory, are seen as 'legitimate' not because they simply have the power to maintain their sovereignty, but because they have a right to self-government. And, despite the fancy rhetorical footwork of states and international bodies which must for political purposes recognize states whose genesis is nonetheless unpalatable, no state maintains that its own legitimacy is simply a matter of power rather than of underlying *right*.

State sovereignty is a concept that is, admittedly, far from unambiguous; and the debate about whether human beings' innate dignity is best served through the provision of certain conditions or through the exercise of free will is perhaps the most profound political question of the past two or three centuries. But the *normative* justification for sovereignty is patently not based upon a bifurcation between an account which espouses the desirability of maintaining a clear distinction between cultural groups, and one which promotes the well-being of individuals and the preservation of individual right. *This* dichotomy, that is to say, is not a debate over *moral* principles: to the extent that it exists at all, it is a disjunction between a political reality and the ethical ideas that were articulated in support of such a political organization. It is true that a defense of culture and tradition can easily be found within the European political discourse of this period (that of Burke being the most obvious, but also notably within the reaction to the German Enlightenment), but this is very much a *reaction* to liberal thought rather than a manifestation of it.

Thus Kymlicka and others are quite wrong: there is no clear tradition in liberal thought made evident in the 'paradox of the state' that defends the establishment of a sovereign political unit for the purpose of protecting particular cultural traits or traditions.[13] The 'paradox' is simply another example of the conflict between politics and moral thought, rather than two contesting ethical positions.

3. Autonomy, Dignity, and the Quest for Self-Determination

To sum up the last section, the 'paradox of the state' is incoherent as a moral justification for self-determination simply because, to the extent that statehood was a means of separating cultural or religious communities, such a separation was not justified in the liberal tradition on *moral* grounds. But did the fact that such action was *in fact* taken itself give some normative weight to modern calls for self-determination? In other words, regardless of why such states were established, the fact that they simply *were* set up to separate communities may be enough to justify the establishment of modern communities on similar grounds. The moral component of such a claim simply rests in the acceptance of the modern state system *regardless* of why such states were founded. This claim is substantively different from the argument, outlined above, that the liberal *tradition* itself espouses the desirability of segregated cultural or religious communities.

It is perhaps true that political sovereignty, as it exists today in the international community, is primarily based (as Jackson writes) upon 'the accidents of history' (Jackson, 1999: 425): after the fragmentation of religious authority in medieval Europe the determination of allegiance became largely a matter of the realities of power and what was necessary to preserve peace. But can history alone offer us much in the attempt to give self-determination a strong moral foundation?

There is, for example, a large amount of political rhetoric regarding some issues (such as aboriginal self-determination) which places a great deal of moral force in the historical argument (i.e., the first occupancy argument). Despite the widespread use of the first occupancy argument in political debate, however, it is, as Gans recognizes, 'not clear why self-determination has anything to do with first occupancy' (Gans, 2001: 58-79).[14] Brian Barry has noted that 'real-life nationalists' tend to pitch their claims to sovereignty upon a historical argument ('blood-and-soil' nationalism, in Barry's terms) rather than upon the ongoing cultural composition: 'Indeed, the very simplicity of the structure of blood-and-soil arguments, while rendering them unconvincing to outsiders, at the same time makes them indisputable' (Barry, 1998: 308). And, as Richard Sigurdson observes, '[i]t is these sorts of blood-and-soil arguments, rather than those of the academic nationalists, that are the most powerful ones in places like Québec' (Sigurdson, 1999).

Most contemporary liberal states themselves tend not to base their legitimate claim to statehood upon such accidents of history, but rather upon the felicity of such a system for the individuals within them. The more philosophically sophisticated supporters of self-determination recognize this, and leave the simple but unpersuasive arguments based upon first occupancy in the arena of political rhetoric. They focus instead upon a more current (and intellectually complex) argument: that the appeal of self-determination lies in its evocation of collective dignity, and that 'individual freedom' is an impoverished idea divorced from a sense of the worthiness of one's cultural makeup. The remainder of this chapter will try to evaluate this line of argument.

'[T]he new nationalist concern for self-determination,' writes Margaret Canovan, 'is an offshoot of the liberal commitment to individual autonomy' (Canovan, 2001: 207). The development of the *individual* as the moral foundation for sovereignty was a natural evolution given the gradual acceptance of the claim that individuals had rights of nature which made the condition of *consent* to political authority paramount. In what way does the natural right of individuals impart a moral justification for collective self-determination? Again, there are two distinct accounts offered by modern theorists. The first argues that individuals choose to live under certain governments, thus enhancing their autonomy; and the moral justification lies in this very exercise of choosing. The actual extent of this capacity to choose, of course, varied enormously in the writings of early modern theorists: for Hobbes, sovereignty was absolute (and 'limited sovereignty' was by definition a contradiction); while Locke distinguished between the legislature, or legal sovereign, and the people, or political sovereign (the latter which is 'normally in abeyance' and which 'only takes effect when the government has been dissolved') (Gough, 1950: 114-5).

The second account, in contrast, emphasizes precisely the contingent and involuntary nature of cultural membership. For Charles Taylor, for example, we are simply born into a culture which makes us what we are. And, as all individuals are 'dialogic' creatures heavily influenced by their cultural makeup, to give equal respect to all individuals requires us to give equal respect to all cultures (Taylor, 1991). For Kymlicka, we are manifestly products of our culture, and thus cultural stability ought to be considered a 'primary good' to be protected by group rights. What is similar in both Taylor's and Kymlicka's accounts is the wider acknowledgment that individual well-being 'depends on the successful pursuit of worthwhile goals and relationships': goals and relationships which are thoroughly and profoundly determined by culture.[15] It is this emphasis upon dignity, rather than autonomy, which has had a strong impact upon recent arguments for self-determination: as Greenfield writes, '[t]he popular appeal of nationalism lies in its evocation of collective dignity' (Greenfeld, 1992: 497). How ought we to respond to the call for the preservation of 'collective dignity'?

Underlying the principle of universality itself was the implicit belief in the 'objectivity' of rights, which has its historical basis in the concept of natural law, a moral principle that was naturally comprehensible to all rational individuals. Despite the fact that, for us, the very idea a 'natural law' seems substantially subjective, the modern justification for human rights itself lies in the presumption of some objective quality. Thus 'human rights' are rights because they are applicable not simply to certain people at certain times in certain societies. This, according to Cranston, is one important test in determining whether an alleged right is in fact a *human* right: a right, according to this account, must be 'genuinely universal' if it is to qualify as a human right: that is, it must be both a right of all, and a right against all (Cranston, 1973).

This is one reason, for example, why such resistance exists against the use of 'needs' as a basis for rights: it does not meet the criterion of universality, and thus is seen as too subjective. Claims of need tend to seem ubiquitous and indiscriminate; and the distinction between 'want' and 'need' become blurred.[16] This 'relative indeterminacy of basic needs'[17] is an especial problem in relation to the determination of 'respect' or 'dignity'. That 'all persons need to be respected, in the sense of being treated as persons by others' (Okin, 1981: 235) is a reasonable claim for a number of reasons, the chief amongst them being that a sense of self-worth seems as important to us as an ability to speak freely, or associate with others, or determine our choice of government.

But the focus upon 'respect' or 'dignity' confronts problems that are not as prevalent for other forms of rights. We have a good sense of what it means to be able to speak freely, or to associate with others, or to determine our choice of government. But exactly what it means to have a sense of dignity is manifestly more subjective. I may not be permitted to mount protests when the leader of a foreign country pays a visit to my city, but the issue here is not whether my freedom of speech or freedom of association is being limited (they are), but whether this limitation is justifiable or not. Likewise, if the courts tell me that I am not allowed to follow my religious doctrine, which instructs me to punish my children with a rod, the issue is not whether this is an infringement upon my religious liberty (it is), but whether this infringement is justified.

In contrast, however, whether a person's dignity is infringed upon or not is, except in extreme cases, very much a matter of individual determination. This is why issues of sexual harrassment in the workplace, for example, are so volatile and contentious. Some women may feel harrassed by the presence of Pirelli calendars or by an employer's greeting of 'morning, gorgeous', while others simply may not. This is not to disparage the concerns of those who do feel this way; it is merely to point out that the level of subjectivity in determining whether one's dignity is materially slighted is almost impossible to determine before the fact. This has led to a lowest-common-denominator approach of zero-tolerance for 'offenders', which has in turn led to a significant backlash against what is perceived to be an unbearable level of political correctness.

The same problem exists in the attempt to base self-determination upon the concept of dignity. The government of Québec, for example, has on numerous occasions objected to what it perceived to be instances of 'humiliation' by Ottawa or the rest of Canada; the underlying message being that such humiliation is a justification to push for self-determination. The use of dignity (or the infringement thereof), however, has an added complexity when used as a justification for self-determination, for it is rarely clear whether the dignity in question belongs to that of the individual or to the group. Dignity, it would seem, is a psychological manifestation that is only applicable to human beings, and not to inanimate or abstract bodies. Yet cultural groupings, especially when expressed as 'nations', are very clearly abstract entities: thus, when it is said that Québec is 'humiliated', it must mean that each individual Québécois, by virtue of being a member of that group, feels a diminution of self-worth. But this is probably not what a government official means when, say, Québec is passed over for a substantial federal contract in favour of Ontario or Alberta: the slight is seen to be to the corporate whole. Is each and every Québécois, upon hearing of the federal decision, slumped over in a demoralized stoop? Probably not. But, again, does it make any sense to talk about the 'dignity' of a corporate entity being diminished? What we have here is a simple logical fallacy of the sort that confuses the individual unit with the whole of which the individual is a part (in the same way as to say that 'Canada is a bilingual nation' is not to assume that 'Herbert, being Canadian, is bilingual'). 'Collective dignity' thus has no meaning except as the sum total of individuals' psychological states: it is logically incoherent to speak of the 'dignity of nations' .

To summarize thus far: I have argued here that the idea of the 'paradox of the state' is not a particularly persuasive argument in favour of culturally-oriented self-determination. That this presupposition generates (or supports) a moral right to self-determination is misconceived because, to the extent that state sovereignty did in fact develop around culturally- and religiously-discrete groups, it was a political strategy and not a normative position. And, to argue that cultural or religious groups *ought* to be able to assert nationhood because that *was* how dominant Western states evolved is simply yet another version of the naturalist fallacy. Moreover, to hold that self-determination is important as a means of protecting the collective dignity of a group is an example of the 'fallacy of decomposition', and is unconvincing because the very idea of 'collective dignity' is itself incoherent.

Kymlicka attempts to avoid these problems by arguing that contemporary liberal states still, on principle, shape state policy to deliberately protect and defend their national culture; and that each individual's own sense of dignity rests upon the strength and vibrancy of the culture within which he finds himself. There are two parts to this argument, and consequently two distinct responses. In the first place, there are admittedly some liberal states that are more enthusiastic in espousing national cultural traits (France, for example, is perhaps more enthusiastic than most). But, to borrow an argument I have used elsewhere, 'just because a practice is accepted does not in itself mean that it is logically congruent with stated principles': slavery, overt racism, and the denial of suffrage to women were practiced by 'liberal' states for a very long time, but this did not make such practices liberal. Rather, the logical force of the principle of universalism underlying liberal thought led to the (admittedly gradual) cessation of such practices (Fierlbeck, 1998: 102-3). One of the greatest achievements of liberal thought has been the acceptance of the principle of equal treatment for all individuals, even though the empirical evidence for the equal nature of all individuals has consistently been less than apparent. The reason why the assumption of equality is so important despite its less than manifest character is because, as Hobbes so brilliantly pointed out, it is much easier to secure political cooperation if all participants are given reason to believe that no one of them will be considered to have a privileged position.[18] To the extent that liberal political theory has undergone a dramatic shift in the past generation, it has been to reflect upon the nature of this equality (rather than to question the desirability of the concept of equality *per se*).

Second, in response to Kymlicka's claim that,

> [l]iberals implicitly assume that people are members of societal cultures, that these cultures provide the context for individual choice, and that one of the functions of having separate states is to recognize the fact that people belong to separate cultures (1995: 125),

one can respond that it would seem to most liberals that, if their state did indeed explicitly choose to deny immigration to individuals on the basis of a 'societal culture' such as race (on the grounds that the cultural context it wanted to preserve was a white Anglo-Saxon one), such a practice would be blatantly and insupportably racist. Immigration restrictions in and of themselves are valid in liberal states for the same reason that they are valid in any sovereign state: to protect the 'carrying capacity' or the efficient functioning of the state vis-a-vis the demands of its citizens. No liberal state would permit any public establishment to declare that blacks or orientals were not permitted on the premises by virtue of being black or oriental, but such venues *are* allowed to limit the overall number of people (and, in fact, fire regulations generally require this).

But could we not amend this formulation, and argue that exclusion based upon culture is justified *not* because it is already accepted by liberals, but because individual (as opposed to collective) dignity requires it to be recognized? Charles Taylor, as noted above, has argued that individual dignity is dependent upon a mutually comprehensible 'horizon of significance'; a relationship between society and individual which he draws from the influence of Hegelian thought.[19] This argument is more convincing than that based upon 'the paradox of the state' because, as noted above, state sovereignty was itself defended normatively upon the natural rights of man which, for certain interests, were themselves justifiable with reference to the inherent dignity of man. Yet, again, 'dignity' as a basis of the natural right of individuals (or of groups) is less solidly grounded than that based upon 'autonomy': in the first place, as noted above, 'dignity' is an inherently individualistic notion, and cannot be extrapolated to collectivities. But (as Taylor argues), individuals can feel a diminished sense of dignity when the culture with which they identify is slighted. The moral right to self-determination, on this account, rests in its ability to preserve a culture without which an individual cannot maintain his or her dignity. This is the justification of self-determination, for example, espoused by Margalit and Raz: 'individual dignity and self-respect require that the groups membership of which contributes to one's sense of identity be generally respected and not be made a subject of ridicule, hatred, discrimination, or persecution' (Raz and Margalit, 1994: 113).

But there are two further problems with this account. First, there is a theoretical weakness in accounting for why the political unit – the nation – is any more important than any other social unit in which the individual finds meaning: although a cultural context may provide a 'horizon of significance' for the individuals within it, it does not follow, as David George (1996: 20-1) argues,

> that nations, as ethical communities, are of greater moral value than any other similarly embedding groups, like families, kinship groups or religious communities...whether or not any of these different groups merit that sort of treatment cannot be determined collectively and *a priori*; their actual moral character is an open question which can be settled only by investigating the facts in each individual case.

One might reply, however, that sovereignty is primary because all of these other relationships are contingent upon the existence of a nation. There are two replies to this: one addresses the empirical veracity of the claim, the other the moral value of cultural protection. In the first place, it simply does not seem to be true that cultures cannot thrive without the capacity for self-determination. Very few states are clearly homogeneous; and there is no necessary direct causal connection between not being a member of an ethnic majority, and quality of life (unless, or course, one holds that the 'collective dignity' of the group is maligned without the capacity for self-determination, in which case 'national minority' by definition means a lower quality of life; although the subjective nature of this claim again limits its 'empirical' force). In the second place, however, is the far more unfashionable position (famously held by John Stuart Mill) that some minority cultures would simply be better off as part of a more thriving society. The difficulties of this position have been addressed *ad nauseam,* but the point still remains that there is little reason to believe that *any* cultural autonomy is superior to *any* form of amalgamation simply because, as stated above, sovereignty is primary insofar as all other possibly rewarding relationships are contingent upon the existence of a nation. In other words, nationhood is simply not logically prior to all satisfying relationships, and there is little hard evidence to show that it is requisite for most edifying or gratifying relationships: in fact, it can just as easily *destroy* them.

This ties into the second problem, which is that the right of self-determination based upon the protection of dignity through culture leads to the establishment of bodies that are generally conceived of as involuntarist associations: individuals belong by virtue of some shared features (such as a common language), rather than through a conscious act of will. The assumption is that dignity is created through participation in a shared culture; and this assumption is in and of itself quite troubling. There is, as George noted above, some empirical doubt regarding whether one's cultural community is a necessary (let alone sufficient) source of individual dignity. Despite the popularity of placing the blame for the appalling social conditions of so many reserves in Canada on the abstract concept of 'liberalism', for example (as does Tully, 1995), the political dynamics of reserve politics itself must be acknowledged as the source of at least some of these conditions. Where the distribution of power on reserves is so little governed by requirements of transparency or accountability, abuses of power will occur. To focus upon involuntarist justifications for self-determination (such as a sense of dignity based on a common culture) is to leave unanswered crucial questions such as the determination of what the 'culture' is (language and religion? Just religion? Or just language?) and whether in fact each individual has robust sense of dignity or not. The underlying force of liberal doctrines based upon conceptions of individual liberty is the requirement that the individual must be allowed in some way to be involved in the most important decisions regarding his or her relationship to the state. Concentrating upon the idea of 'dignity' as a moral basis for self-determination, then, too easily gives rise to an involuntarist association, which can be extremely vulnerable to oppressive internal dynamics of power.[20]

4. Conclusion

What, in sum, are the conclusions to be drawn from this discussion? The first is that we must, in general terms, be decidedly wary about the accounts we are given regarding the 'moral' rights to self-determination (to the extent that the basis of this 'moral right' is ever examined at all). The second is that the putative 'paradox of the state' is not as paradoxical as much as it is theoretically confused. And the third is that democrats ought to be suspicious of attempts to base moral claims to self-determination upon involuntarist accounts of 'collective dignity', despite their current fashionability.

Proponents of a moral right to self-determination are abundant in contemporary political thought: Neil MacCormick, Margaret Moore, Avishai Margalit and Joseph Raz, to note but a few, all hold that such a right exists, and that it is based upon some form of national expression. I argue that the case for a 'moral' right to self-determination is quite weak; and, if such a right does exist, it most certainly does not depend upon the intellectual force of any 'paradox of the state'. Moreover, I would add that any arguments for the moral right to self-determination based primarily upon an account of 'dignity' ought to be viewed with a great deal of caution. The historical roots of democracy are replete with references to the dignity of mankind, but, as liberals began to realize by the nineteenth century, abstract conceptions of dignity were rendered useless without some active mechanism of consent to support them.

Certainly diversity of all types is one of the most pressing challenges to modern democracy; and the issue of how formal equality is distorted by subjective perceptions of value is an interesting sociological question. One method of addressing this problem of subjectivity has been the Habermasian conversational model, in which all parties agree to consider those practices or views which are important to each one (see, for example, Lenard and Turgeon in this volume). This model is certainly indicative of good manners, and it would make social and political relations much more palatable should individuals choose to utilize it. But it cannot, without great political cost, be a substitute for formal political equality, negative political rights, or autonomous political decision-making.

Can any satisfactory account of the moral basis of self-determination be found? I would argue that it can, but only to the extent that we accept it in an instrumental sense, rather than as a good in and of itself; and only if the 'instrumentalism' in this sense involves more than the romantic comforts of culture. As David George (citing Elie Kedourie) writes, "'not the least of the triumphs of nationalist doctrine was that its propositions have become accepted as self-evident in the contemporary world'" (George, 1996: 16, 19). This is both unsatisfactory and dangerous. Rather, the *moral* nature of self-determination must rest upon other values and, for the world today, this value seems to be democracy itself (or, stated otherwise, this value is the ability to restrain and regulate the concentration of political power in the political units within which we live). To the extent that democracy is a practice (and a quality) that we as a collective of individuals or of states continue to desire, we must also accept the structure of the nation-state. Stated otherwise, if democracy was once justified by reference to sovereignty ('we shall construct whatever system of political organization we want within the confines of our own borders'), it is now state sovereignty which is justified normatively by reference to its utility in protecting crucial aspects of democratic life.

Such an account, therefore, does not necessarily leave a weakened nation-state fatally exposed to the forces of contemporary international economic change. The crucial point is not that the state, as a political unit, cannot ever articulate its own destiny against the winds of international change; but rather that such a decision must be one freely determined by individual citizens for reasons which they collectively deem to be important (and which they have the capacity to revisit if they so choose). A state, on this account, may certainly decide to make decisions to protect its 'national culture' (e.g., a state's policy actively favouring a national film industry over Hollywood imports), but the *legitimacy* of the decision rests not on the protection of culture *per se*, but rather on the fact that such a choice is clearly supported by the majority of the people.

Nor, however, does this account necessarily preserve the state in the face of the larger threat to sovereignty presented by the prospect of establishing a broader system of political organization in order to offer better institutional protection and promotion of democratic values. The most obvious concern, and one dealt with at length in this book, is the effect of the forces of globalization upon the autonomy of the state (and, by extension, upon the decision-making capacity of the citizens within it). Yet it is important to remember that states in general have never been totally autonomous (unless they were so isolated or impoverished that they did not excite the interest of their neighbours). And while examples can easily be presented where globalization diminished the democratic capacity of states (most pointedly because of the mobility of capital, in which real democratic choices do still exist but only by imposing high economic costs), other examples can be found where democratic opportunities are enhanced through the same processes of globalization (such as the coordination of environmental controls). The European Union probably exhibits both of these traits; and a balance sheet regarding the influence of each would require some detailed consideration (and could easily shift over time). A continual hope is that new international organizations can be developed to restrain the worst excesses of the most immoral while enhancing the freedoms of the most civil; but this development, while certainly possible, will always face the dilemma that the centralization of power needed to reign in the rascals could be used by them to undermine the most relaxed and trusting regimes.

However, if political developments surpass the limited imagination of this stolid author, then so be it: the key implication of the preceding analysis is that any system shown to protect a wide array of individual freedoms (including, pointedly, the freedom of association), and which can be held clearly accountable through a transparent system of governance, and which does so more efficiently than a system of state sovereignty, certainly should not be feared. Western civilization has existed at various points independently of sovereign statehood; there is no reason to reify statehood into something that has value beyond its utility.

Thus we come full circle: post-medieval Europe saw the development of the sovereign state as a means of protecting a set of values that would be endangered otherwise; we do likewise today. It is merely the values to be protected which have changed. There is nothing inviolable about state sovereignty except, perhaps, insofar as such inviolability is accepted as a politically advantageous *quid pro quo*. But to talk of the *right* to self-determination of cultural groups based upon the premise that we already recognize the rights of culturally distinct sovereign states is little more than weak reasoning based upon a naturalist fallacy. Meanwhile, the pressure placed upon these states in today's world, and the cultivation of transnational connections and prospects as outlined elsewhere in this volume, has perhaps begun to challenge this naturalist foundation. Finally, the language of rights also poses a problem for debates over self-determination insofar as the critique of rights language, as Beiner recognizes, 'presents an important challenge to nationalism, with its foundational appeal to a universal *right* to self-determination' (Beiner, 1998: 163). Let us do battle, if we must, over the felicity of democracy, at local, national, and perhaps even transnational levels, and leave the justification for state sovereignty upon more consequentialist grounds. This will surely leave us enough to debate.

Notes

1	See, for example, Tamir, 1993; MacCormick, 1996, 34-52; Kymlicka, 1995; Black, 1991.
2	See also Canovan, 1996, 69-84.

3 See, especially, Barry, 2001.

4 Although, Dunn has noted, '[t]he idea of the modern state was invented precisely to repudiate the possible coherence of democratic claims to rule or even take genuinely political action, whether these claims were advanced under secular or religious inspiration' (1992: 248).

5 See Bodin, n.d., xxv.

6 As Jackson points out, the peace treaties of Westphalia did not include much evidence for the claim that Westphalia was 'the crucial turning point in the emergence of sovereignty'; nor was there any mention of the word 'sovereignty' itself. Nonetheless, he notes, '[b]y the time of the Peace of Utrecht (1713-1717) the rulers of Europe understood each other as 'essentially ... self-determining actors, none of which was entitled to dictate others'. Some, he adds, only see the 'full historical manifestation' of state sovereignty in the Concert of Europe in the 1820s. Jackson, 1999: esp. 438-440.

7 For an excellent discussion of the concept of sovereignty considered within the field of international relations see the special issue of *Political Studies* (v. 47, 1999), edited by Robert Jackson.

8 See Krasner, 1999: chapter 1.

9 See Taylor, 1991.

10 For clear, brief account of the politics and principles of the Puritan factions mid-seventeenth century England, see Woodhouse's excellent 'Introduction' to his edited volume on the Clarke Manuscripts, entitled *Puritanism and Liberty* (1938).

11 This account was influential for feminist theorists such as Mary Wollstonecraft, and also for early black activism in the United States.

12 'Nature speaks to all animals, and beasts obey her voice. Man feels the same impulse, but he at the same time perceives that he is free to resist or to acquiesce; and it is in the consciousness of this liberty, that the spirituality of his soul chiefly appears...' (Rousseau, 1967: 187). This position is increasingly debated see, for example, Masson and McCarty, 1995.

13 It is perhaps more accurate to suggest that there is no clear tradition in Anglo-American liberal thought defending this position. It is possible that one might find a more compatible basis for this claim if one mined the more recent history of European liberalism outside of this tradition. This, however, has not been the focus of those who see the 'paradox of the state' as an argument supporting their claim to cultural rights.

14 See also Waldron, 1988, 284-90: 'it seems to me that the bare idea of occupancy – of taking possession of a resource – cannot seriously be regarded as carrying much justificatory weight on its own'.

15 See Kymlicka, 1995, and Raz and Margalit, 1994.

16 'This indeterminacy does not mean that the notion of "basic need" is entirely without value but it does mean that any set of rights founded upon basic needs will be infected with a similar indeterminacy' (Jones, P., 1994: 153).

17 For a discussion of this, see Griffin, 1986.

18 'If Nature therefore have made men equall, that equalitie is to be acknowledged: or if Nature have made men unequall; yet because men that think themselves equall, will not enter into conditions of Peace, but upon Equall termes, such equalitie must be admitted.' (Hobbes, 1968 [1651], 211).

19 It is perhaps worthwhile to note, for the sake of historical accuracy, that, to the extent that Hegel discusses the concept of culture at all, he seems strongly in favour of a heterogenous and multicultural society rather than one in which individuals are drawn together by dominant homogeneous traditions. As he writes in The German

Constitution, '[i]n our day, the tie between members of a state in respect of manners, education, language may be rather loose or even non-existent. Identity in these matters, once the foundation of a people's union, is now reckoned amongst the accidents whose character does not hinder a mass from constituting a public authority. Rome of Athens, like any small modern state, could not have subsisted if the numerous languages current in the Russian Empire had been spoken within their borders, or if amongst their citizens manners had been as different as they are in Russia or, for that matter, as manners and education are now in every big city in a large country. Difference in language and dialect (the latter exacerbates separation even more than complete unintelligibility does), and difference in manners and education in the separate estates which make men known to one another is hardly anything but outward appearance – such heterogeneous and at the same time most powerful was able to overcome and hold together, just as in modern states the same result is produced factors the preponderating weight of the Roman Empire's power (once it had become great) by the spirit and art of political institutions. Thus dissimilarity in culture and manners is a necessary condition of the stability of modern states' (quoted in Knox and Pelczynski, 1967: 158).

20 In Canada, for example, aboriginal policy is conducted almost exclusively at the elite level. While native leaders have pushed the issue of self-government for years, the first ever national survey of Canadian natives living on reserves showed that self-government was supported by only half of the population. See *The Globe and Mail* (2001: A1).

Part II

Actors, Institutions, and the Potential for Transnational Democracy

Chapter 6

Searching for
Democratic Potential in
Emerging Global Governance

Chadwick F. Alger

1. Transnational Social Movements

The *Yearbook of International Organizations* reports that the number of transnational associations, i.e. private, voluntary, nonprofit groups with members from three or more states, a decision-making structure with voting members from at least three countries, and cross-national and/or international aims, escalated rapidly in the twentieth century to some 5800. These organizations are widely referred to as non-governmental organizations (NGOs), although the more accurate term is international non-governmental organizations (INGOs). Of particular relevance to those concerned with potential for democracy in global governance are those INGOs actively seeking social change, labelled as Transnational Social Movements (TSMOs)[1] by sociologists. By coding the INGOs appearing in the *Yearbook of International Organizations,* Jackie Smith found that the number of TSMOs grew from 183 in 1973, to 348 in 1983 and to 631 in 1993 (Smith, Jackie, 1997: 47). After coding the policy issues on which these organizations are focused she divided them into transnational social movement industries (TSMI). In Table 6.1 she lists the seven most prominent TSMIs, with human rights, environment and women's rights leading the list.

A volume edited by Smith, Chatfield and Pagnucco (1997) provides nine case studies of the involvement of these TSMOs in a wide array of global issues. Analysis of these case studies illuminates five dimensions (Table 6.2) of a global political process in which most effective TSMOs must be involved (Alger, 1997). Obviously they (1) *create/mobilize global networks*, as a *sine qua non* for becoming global actors. It is equally obvious that they must (2) *participate in International Governmental Organization (IGO) conferences*. It might not be as obvious that in most issues their success depends upon their capacity to (3) *facilitate interstate cooperation*. At the same time, it is not always fully

Table 6.1   Transnational Social Movement Industries

	1973 N=183	1983 N=348	1993 N=631
Human Rights	23%	23%	27%
Environment	6	7	14
Women's Rights	9	7	10
Peace	8	6	9
World Order/Multi-Issue	7	9	8
Development	4	4	5
Self-Determination/Ethnic	10	11	5

Source: Yearbook of International Organizations, 1973, 1983, 1993 (Smith, Jackie, 1997: 47)

appreciated that success in these three endeavours often requires (4) *activities within states.* Furthermore, it is sometimes forgotten that success over the long term necessarily requires TSMOs to (5) *enhance public participation.* Whether the development – or any other issue – eventually sustained solutions for global problems must be implemented in the human settlements of the world. And this requires broad public understanding and participation.

Table 6.2   Activities of Transnational Social Movements (TSMOs)

I.   Create/Mobilize Global Networks
1. Create transnational organizations
2. Gather information on local conditions through contacts around world
3. Alert global network of supporters to conditions requiring attention
4. Create emergency response network around world
5. Mobilize pressure from outside states

II.   Participate in Intergovernmental Organizaton (IGO) Conferences
6. Mobilize TSMOs around issues in IGOs
7. Build TSMO coalitions
8. Raise new issues
9. Support IGO development
10. Address IGO meetings
11. Submit documents to IGO meetings
12. Improve TSMO skills in conference diplomacy
13. Increase TSMO expertise on issues

III.   Facilitate Interstate Cooperation
14. Prepare background papers and reports
15. Educate delegates
16. Educate representatives of states to narrow technical gap
17. Serve as third party source of information
18. Expand policy options

19. Facilitate agreement
20. Bring delegates together in third-party fora
IV. Engage in Activities Within States
22. Linking to local partners
23. Linking TSMOs with complementary skills
24. Working in national arenas to harmonize state policies
25. Humanitarian Aid
26. Development
27. Protective Accompaniment of persons in danger
V. Enhance Public Participation
27. Remind government delegates that they are being watched
28. Enhance public understanding
29. Increase transparency of international negotiations and institutions
30. Link to local partners
31. Provoke public protest

Source: (Alger, 1997: 262)

At the same time, this portrayal of activities helps to illuminate the diversity of arenas in which TSMOs must be active: (1) within their own networks, (2) in IGO conferences, (3) in the cooperative interstate activities that provide supportive background for these conferences, (4) within states, and (5) within the various settings in which the larger public can be educated and mobilized – both within and across states. These nine cases reveal that TSMOs are growing in their awareness that success in global politics requires successful multiple-arena strategies.

2. NGOs in the UN System

The kinds of activities of NGOs in the UN system that we will be presenting fall within the definition of TSMO, but are customarily called NGOs in the UN context. It will make our exposition less complex if we use this term in the UN context. The UN Charter provides only for NGO consultation with the Economic and Social Council (ECOSOC), but NGO involvement has expanded widely at UN System headquarters in New York and throughout the UN System (Alger, 1995: 26-31). We will examine a diversity of kinds of access that representatives of NGOs have to representatives of states, and members of secretariats, at UN Headquarters, followed by a look at the spread of NGO involvement throughout the UN system. A primary purpose of this effort is to illuminate the diversity of kinds of NGO activities that take place in the parliamentary settings provided by interstate organizations (Alger, 2003, 2002a).

2.1 Involvement in UN Decision-Making Bodies Obviously, NGOs are observers at public meetings of UN decision-making bodies. In addition, some of these bodies have developed a diversity of styles for involving NGOs in their political processes that range from public meetings to more private meetings that are always part of parliamentary style decision-making (Table 6.3). Opportunities for NGOs to address public sessions has spread beyond ECOSOC to include committees of the General Assembly. They have also appeared in what have been labeled as 'formal panels' and 'informal panels' of General Assembly committees.

Table 6.3   Modes of NGO Involvement with UN Decision-Making Bodies

Public meetings
1. NGOS address public sessions
2. Formal panel and dialogue sessions
3. Informal NGO panel discussion

Private meetings
1. Observers
2. Private sessions linked to public decision-making
3. *Ad hoc* meetings
4. 'Non-internal deliberations'
5. NGO group meetings with officers or members of a UN decision-making body

All parliamentary bodies require private meetings, including a diversity of committees, that prepare for the public decision-making phase. It is very significant that NGOs have acquired access to a broad range of these meetings. When NGOs made presentations to the General Assembly Working Group on Financing of Development in 1999 it was called a 'Private Session Linked to Public Decision-Making'. When the Secretary General of Amnesty International briefed a private meeting of the Security Council in 1997 it was called an '*ad hoc* meeting'. The UN Administrative Committee on Coordination's Sub-Committee on Nutrition welcomes relevant and competent NGOs to sit as equals in its 'Non-Internal Deliberations.' NGOs also have private meetings with an officer of a specific body or with members of a delegation. One example is a 'Consultative Group' of the NGO Working Group on the Security Council, composed of members of several NGOs, that has met informally with Presidents of the UN Security Council.

2.2 NGO Relations with UN Secretariats In recent years, Secretaries General have paid increasing attention to NGOs. Secretary-General Boutros Boutros-Ghali, addressing NGO representatives at the UN in September 1994, made this very clear when he said: 'I want you to consider this your home. Until recently, these words might have caused astonishment. The United Nations was considered to be a forum for sovereign states alone. Within the space of a few short years, this attitude has changed. Non-governmental organizations are now considered full participants in international life' (Rice and Ritchie, 1995: 256-7).

Members of secretariats are, of course, deeply involved in parliamentary diplomacy. They are present at all public meetings, often sitting on either side of the Chair. In this context NGOs can establish contact with those who organize public meetings and those who are expected to carry out the decisions. This can build contact, and collaboration, with relevant offices in UN secretariats. In Table 6.4 we briefly enumerate the diversity of kinds of secretariat relations that have emerged, and list one UN office or agency as an example of each.

Table 6.4   Modes of NGO Relations with Secretariats

1. Secretary General (Focal point: Special Political Advisor)
2. Regularly scheduled meetings with NGOs (Office of Coordination of Humanitarian Affairs)
3. NGO representation on committees (World Bank)
4. NGO Annual Consultation with Secretariat (International Fund for Agricultural Development)
5. Secretariat symposia for NGOs (World Trade Organization)
6. Secretariat posting of policy papers on web for NGO comment (World Bank)
7. Secretariat creation of national steering committees (World Bank)
8. NGO training (Communications Coordination Committee for the UN)
9. UN Financial support of NGOs (UNDP)
10. NGO Financial support of UN (Human rights monitoring in Rwanda)
11. NGO creation (UNESCO)
12. Joint research (World Meterological Organization (WMO))
13. Joint implementing and Monitoring of a program (United Nations Volunteers)
14. NGO as stand-in for UN (World Refugee Year)

Source: Items 9 to 14 taken from Rice and Ritchie, 1995: 262.

In 1995, the Secretary General designated his Special Political Advisor as the focal point in his executive office for matters pertaining to NGOs. This officer was made chair of an interdepartmental working group on relations with NGOs. She was requested to make proposals for innovative mechanisms to the Secretary General, as well as to develop a strategy to enhance relations with NGOs (*Go-Between*, 54, October/November 1995: 5).

The diversity of modes for NGO contact with members of the Secretariat are impressive. They include regularly scheduled meetings with NGOs, representation of NGOs on committees, Annual Consultation meetings with NGOs, symposia for NGOs, and NGO participation on national steering committees. Policy papers are posted on the web for NGO comment. Support for NGOs is provided through training, financial support and NGO creation. NGOs support secretariats financially and serve as their stand-ins. Secretariats and NGOs collaborate through joint research and joint implementation and monitoring of programs. NGO cooperation with secretariats ranges across a diversity of agencies, including the World Bank, UNDP, WMO, UNESCO, WTO, and UN Volunteers (World Bank Group, 1999; World Trade Organization, 1998). It also involves an array of issues, including agriculture, refugees, human rights, and communications.

In conclusion, our effort to provide typologies of emerging NGO roles in UN decision-making bodies and secretariats offers an astounding contrast with the reluctance of member-states to make significant changes in formal rules established in for NGO access to the UN in 1950. It would seem that the nature of societies that are established at headquarters of multilateral organizations tends to create conditions that inevitably lead to an array of opportunities for public and private NGO participation in member state decision-making bodies and a diversity of relations with secretariats. These opportunities are seized both by representatives of NGOs and members of decision-making bodies and secretariats. Particularly fascinating is the fact that on some occasions secretariats support and even finance NGOs, and on other occasions the support flows in the opposite direction. Thus our inventory leads to challenging research questions about the present significance of this dimension of emerging global governance (Alger, 1999b).

2.3 NGO Liaison Offices in the UN System Because the UN system of some thirty organizations is dynamically responding to a growing array of global issues (Alger, 1998), it is not surprising that NGO participation has spread throughout the system. This is vividly reflected in Table 6.5, listing the location of 93 NGO Liaisons.

Table 6.5   NGO Liaison Offices in the UN System

1. 9 Service Offices: New York (4), Geneva (3), Vienna (2)
2. 54 liaison offices in substantive offices of the UN Secretariat (New York, Rome, Geneva, Vienna and Nairobi)
3. 6 UNEP regional offices (Washington, Bangkok, Athens, Bahrain, Kingston, Mexico City)
4. 5 offices in UN Regional Economic and Social Commissions (Geneva, Bangkok, Santiago, Baghdad, Addis Ababa)
5. 19 Specialized Agency liaison offices. (New York, Geneva, Vienna, Rome, Montreal, London, Washington, Paris, Berne)

Source: Developed from UN, Office of the Under Secretary General, 1990.

Offices located at headquarters of UN agencies in eighteen cities. Table 6.6 provides a quick view of the breadth of issues covered by these liaison offices. The 24 issues that are the focus of the liaison offices range from aging and apartheid to social development and welfare policies.

Table 6.6   Issues Addressed by UN Liaison Offices

1. Ageing (Vienna)
2. Apartheid (New York [NY])
3. Children (NY)
4. Cooperatives (Vienna)
5. Crime (Vienna)
6. Decolonization (NY)
7. Desertification (NY)
8. Development (NY [5], Vienna)
9. Disability (Vienna)
10. Disaster Relief (Geneva, NY)
11. Disarmament (NY)
12. Emergency situations (NY)
13. Environment (Nairobi, NY, Geneva, Athens, Bahrain, Bangkok, Kingston)
14. Family (Vienna)
15. Food/Hunger (Rome [2])
16. Human rights (Geneva, NY)
17. Human settlements (Nairobi, NY)
18. Law of the sea (NY)
19. Migrant workers (Vienna)
20. Narcotic drugs (Vienna)
21. Palestinian rights (NY)
22. Peace studies (NY)
23. Population (NY [2], Geneva [2])
24. Refugees (Geneva, Vienna, NY [2])
25. Social development (Vienna)
26. Welfare policies (Vienna)

Note: bracketed numbers indicate number of offices in that city.

Source: Compiled from UN, Office of the Under Secretary General, 1990.

3. NGO Participation in UN Conferences at Sites Outside UN Agency Headquarters

Over the years conferences involving UN members have spread far beyond headquarters, including special UN conferences on global issues and treaty negotiation conferences. At the same time, internet extensions of headquarters societies have emerged. These developments have offered opportunity for participation of a growing number of NGOs, and they have offered important opportunities for NGOs to develop their own meetings parallel to those of UN member-states.

3.1 The Impact of Special UN Conferences on Styles of NGO Participation The practice of holding UN conferences focused on specific global issues at various sites around the world builds on a tradition that reaches back as far as the 1932 World Disarmament Conference (Spiro, 1995: 49). These conferences have had a significant impact on the development of NGO involvement in the UN system in at least four respects. First. the practice of having NGO conferences that run parallel to these governmental conferences has spurred the development of NGO collaboration in the development of policies on specific issues and in presenting them to assemblies composed of government representatives. Second, NGOs have become increasingly involved in the preparatory phases of UN conferences, thereby offering NGOs experience in wider involvement in pre-public phases of parliamentary diplomacy. Third, because sites of these conferences have been scattered around the world, they have been accessible to a growing number of NGOs, particularly those in the 'Third World'. Fourth, conditions at these *ad hoc* meeting sites have required the development of *ad hoc* procedures for NGO participation that have led to demands for wider NGO access at permanent headquarters.

3.2 NGO Involvement in Treaty Negotiation and Implementation   Another significant venue for NGO participation in interstate decision-making that is closely linked to the UN system is conferences called for the drafting of treaties. The significant contribution of NGOs in the development of the landmine treaty was recognized by awarding of the Nobel Peace Prize to the leader of the International Campaign to Ban Landmines. This successful campaign linked one thousand NGOs in 60 countries, largely through e-mail.

During negotiations on the International Criminal Court Treaty, 'NGOs participated informally, but effectively, alongside governments in a high-level negotiating process. They spoke, circulated documents, met frequently with delegations and had a major impact on the outcome' (Paul: 3). In preparation for the International Criminal Court conference, the NGO Coalition for an International Criminal Court brought together a broad-based network of hundreds of NGOs and international law experts to develop strategies and foster awareness. Again, the key to their network was e-mail and the World Wide Web.

It is also well known that NGOs have been very active in efforts to secure implementation of treaties. Prominent examples are those concerned with human rights and environment. The UN Convention to Combat Desertification (CCD) places unusually strong emphasis on the role of NGOs in implementation. There are 22 references to the role of NGOs in the text.

3.3 NGO Conferences   We have already indicated that mobilization of NGOs for participation in UN world conferences has spurred expanded activity of NGOs at UN system headquarters. At the same time, NGO gatherings in the context of these interstate conferences has spurred four other NGO conference formats.

First, a number of NGO conferences have convened as follow-ups to UN world conferences with an issue focus. For example, the NGO Forum on Social Development provides NGOs a platform for discussing their role in the implementation of the recommendations of the World Summit for Social Development (Copenhagen, 1995). They met immediately preceding the 37th Session of the UN Commission for Social Development, on February 9, 1999. This has now become a tradition prior to the meetings of this commission, organized by the International Council on Social Welfare (ICSW) and the Friedrich Ebert Foundation (FEWS). A similar forum was held on February 6 and 7, 1999, in The Hague, as a follow-up to the International Conference on Population and Development, held in Cairo in 1994.

Second, building on NGO conferences linked with UN conferences focused on a single global issues, broad agenda-free standing NGO conferences, often referred to as 'people's assemblies', have emerged. They include The Hague Peace Conference (May 1999), the Pilot People's Assembly (San Francisco, June 1998), Milenio Gathering (December 27-January 1 2000), University of Peace in Costa Rica and Earth Citizen's Assembly (2000/2001). An NGO world conference held at Kyung Hee University in Seoul (October 1999) focused on the role of NGOs in the twenty-first century. It was advertised as the first-ever conference of NGOs to address issues across the whole spectrum of human development.

Third, on December 16, 1998, the General Assembly adopted a resolution (A/53L.73) designating the fifty-fifth session of the General Assembly as a Millennium Assembly. As the proposal for a Millennium Assembly emerged, Secretary General Kofi Annan joined the call for a companion Peoples Millennium Assembly (PMA) in his Reform report. This proposed assembly met on 22-26 May, 2000, under the name Peoples Millennium Forum. Participating in the Forum were 1,350 representatives of over 1,000 NGOs from more than 100 countries. The Forum declared its intent to build on UN world conferences and civil society conferences of the 1990s toward the end of drawing 'the attention of governments to the urgency of implementing the commitments they have made and to channel our collective energies by reclaiming globalization for and by the people'.

Fourth, for several decades there have been proposals for a second General Assembly that have included differing proposals for the nature of its members, including members of state legislatures, representatives of non-governmental organizations and directly elected members. More recent proposals include the International Network for a Second Assembly (1982), Childers and Urquhart's proposal for a UN Parliamentary Assembly (1994) and a proposal for an annual Forum of Civil Society, Report of the Commission on Global Governance (1995). Many working for the Peoples Millennium Forum saw it as a building block toward a permanent second assembly, but certainly not all.

In conclusion, here there is only space for briefly noting our seven most significant findings with respect to NGO participation in the UN. *First*, practices evolving out of the 'consultation with non-governmental organizations' provision of Article 71 have 'infected' the entire UN system and spread beyond issues on the ECOSOC agenda, thereby affecting virtually all issues on UN system agendas. *Second*, NGO privileges for participation in public meetings have often been extended to include private preparations for public meetings. *Third*, the contributions of NGOs to UN political processes include mobilizing NGOs, facilitating interstate agreement, preparing background papers and reports, and reminding government delegates that they are being watched. *Fourth*, the modes of NGO involvement with members of secretariats are also broad and diverse, including regularly scheduled meetings and symposia, joint implementation and monitoring of programs, and posting of secretariat policy papers on the web for NGO comment. *Fifth*, involvement of NGOs in UN conferences on specific issues has led to dramatic changes in the style of NGO participation and in the number and types of NGOs involved in regular meetings at various UN headquarters. *Sixth*, NGOs have played significant roles in conferences called to draft treaties on issues such as an International Criminal Court and banning of land mines, and in follow-ups to these conferences. *Seventh*, all of these developments in the involvement of 'civil society' in the UN system have contributed to proposals for a Second UN Assembly that would eventually be directly elected.

Despite this remarkable evolving expansion of NGO involvement in the UN system, there are, of course, significant restraints. Important to scholars is Secretary General Annan's assertion, in a report on NGO participation, that the UN lacks adequate knowledge 'about this complex and expanding universe' (UN Secretary General, 1998). Also highly significant is his emphasis on lack of financial resources for strengthening relations with NGOs. Noteworthy too is the fact that James Paul, an active NGO representative, does not feel comfortable with the right to participate being 'extended through practice' and suggests the need for these practices to be codified. It is apparent that new forms of global governance are emerging that are very widespread and very complicated (Alger, 1997: 268-70), but we still have very limited knowledge on which to base a sound assessment of their present significance and future potential.

4. Local Authorities

Local communities have always been connected with distant places in a diversity of ways, as a result of immigration, emigration, travel, trade, investment, media, the arts, religion, academic connections and many other dimensions of human life. Recent local responses to escalating local-global links suggest that the roles of cities and local regions in world politics are undergoing fundamental change. These responses include (1) movements for local 'foreign policies' on critical issues such as human rights, environment, and nuclear weapons; (2) energetic local efforts to foster foreign investment and trade; (3) the creation of international offices in city governments; (4) the emergence of regional and global organizations of cities; and (5) efforts by these organizations to participate in decision-making in UN agencies (Alger, 1999a, 2002b). It is useful to briefly review the emergence of a diversity of efforts by local people to exercise influence over their world relations (Table 6.7).

Table 6.7   Evolving Procedures for Projecting Local Concerns on Global Agendas

I.   Local Activities
1. Individual Exchange Programs
2. Sister City relationships
3. Mundialization of cities
4. City policies for generating exports and foreign investment
5. Local efforts that replace or supplement foreign activities of states
6. Mobilizing local people in order to change the 'foreign policy' of their state
7. Mobilizing local people in order to impact the domestic policies of foreign states

8. Local efforts to change the international activities of business

II. Regional and Global Activities
9. International organizations of municipalities
10. Cross-state border associations of local and regional authorities
11. Transregional functional associations
12. World Assembly of Cities and Local Authorities
13. Municipalities in the UN System
14. Transnational Discourse Communities
15. Regional and World declarations and charters for local self-government
16. Direct participation of cities and local regions in regional governance

In many communities **(1) Exchange programs** have arisen, particularly after World War II, in which people attempted to 'internationalize' their community, and to stimulate distant connections in order to facilitate international understanding and peaceful relations. In many cities these exchange activities evolved into **(2) Sister city** relationships, in which two cities developed cooperative programs for exchanges between city officials, the general public, and individuals in specific professions and occupations in the two cities. **(3) Mundialization** programs in which a 'global identity of cities' is encouraged through exchange and educational activities. At the same time, the international involvement of many city governments has been primarily focused on the development of **(4) City policies to generate exports and foreign investment**.

In some areas, sister city relationships have also evolved into **(5) Local efforts that replace or supplement foreign activities of states**. Prominent here are efforts by 'First World' cities to facilitate the economic development of their sister cities in the 'Third World' in what is referred to as decentralized development cooperation, as exemplified by Towns and Development and Municipal International Cooperation (MIC) programs in Europe. Local campaigns have declared local communities nuclear free zones, and have demonstrated against local military production, and local military bases housing foreign troops. At the same time, there has been local mobilization in support of local immigrants determined to be 'illegals' by the state and local efforts to protect these immigrants from deportation by these authorities, i.e. **(6) Mobilizing local people in order to change the 'foreign policy' of their state** through local action.

Another challenge to traditions of the state system has been efforts to **(7) Mobilize local people in order to impact the domestic policies of foreign states**. A very obvious example is campaigns against Apartheid in South Africa that took place in many countries.

Closely related are **(8) Local efforts to change the international activities of business** in which government is not significantly involved. An example here would be the In-Fact Campaign against the marketing of infant formula in the Third World, primarily waged against the Nestle Corporation and a few other companies.

Governments of cities throughout the world have joined together to create **(9) International organizations of municipalities**, they are both global and regional, with some having general purposes and some more limited concerns. Table 6.8 provides a quick overview of those that are global.

Table 6.8 Global Organizations of Local Authorities

1. **General purpose:**
   a) International Union of Local Authorities (IULA) – www.iula.org
   b) Federation Mondial des Cities Unies (FMCU) – www.fincu-uto.org
2. **Larger cities:**
   a) Summit Conference of Major Cities of the World (SUMMIT)
   b) METROPOLIS – www.metropolis.org
   c) World Assn. of the Major Metropolises, Metropolis (WAMM) – www.int/ina-ngo/ngo
3. **Environmental focus:** ICLEI – www.iclei.org
4. **Peace focus:** World Council of Mayors for Peace Through Inter-city Solidarity – www.pcf.city.hiroshima.jp/mayors

Global Membership, General Purpose. The oldest in this category is the International Union of Local Authorities (IULA) founded in 1913 in Ghent, with its headquarters now in the Hague. Its aims are to promote local autonomy, contribute toward improvement of local administration, study questions concerning life and activities of local authorities and welfare of citizens, promote the idea of participation of the population in civic affairs, and establish and develop international municipal relations.

Global Membership, Larger Cities. More recently two organizations focusing on the problems of the world's largest cities have emerged. The Summit Conference of Major Cities of the World (SUMMIT) first met in Tokyo in 1985 with the objective of addressing urban problems contributing to the formation of societies suitable for comfortable and safe living. METROPOLIS, with 65 member cities and headquarters in Paris, held its sixth conference in Barcelona in 1999.

Global Membership, Environmental Focus. Founded in 1990, the International Council for Local Environmental Initiatives (ICLEI) is dedicated to the prevention and solution of local, regional and global environmental problems through local action. It was established through the partnership of the UN Environment Program (UNEP), the International Union of Local Authorities (IULA) and the Center for Innovative Diplomacy (CID).

Global Membership, Peace Focus. Another initiative with a global policy focus is the World Council of Mayors for Peace Through Inter-city Solidarity, involving 405 cities from 98 countries in all continents, as of July 1995. This activity was initiated by the cities of Hiroshima and Nagasaki and held its Fourth World Conference, August, 1997, in Hiroshima and Nagasaki.

Regional Membership. There are also many regional organizations of municipalities, such as Arab Towns Organizations (ATO), CITYNET (Asia and

Pacific), Eurocities, *Red de Associationes de municipios de America Latina, Union des Villes Africaines* (UVA), and Union of the Baltic Cities.

The creation of the World Academy for Local Government and Democracy (WALD) in Istanbul, Turkey, in 1992, illuminates collaboration that occurs between worldwide, regional and local organizations. It is a joint project of IULA, IULA-EMME (IULA Eastern Mediterranean Middle East), the Union of Municipalities of the Marmara Region and the Istanbul Metropolitan Municipality.

(10) Cross-state border associations of local and regional authorities. The creation of states has often arbitrarily divided people on different sides of new borders. At the same time, these regions tend to be located in a peripheral position, distant from centres of decision-making by states. At times, border areas are the most dissatisfied and disruptive areas within the boundaries of a state. In a study of 'Co-operation Between Local Authorities in Frontier Regions', Professor Orianne of Louvain has described their predicament in poetic fashion:

> Time and mankind patiently strive to put together again what treaties and systems of law once tore asunder to meet the requirements of a particular type of political organization. (Orianne, 1973: 1)

Border regions in Europe have been particularly active in efforts to collaborate across state borders. In 1980 a Convention on Transfrontier Co-operation was approved by the Council of Europe, followed by an additional Protocol in 1995. A number of cross-border organizations have been established pursuant to this convention. Two examples are the Working Communities of the Alps and the Working Community of the Pyrenees. Some 40 European cross-border and frontier regions have come together to form the Association of European Frontier Regions.

(11) Transregional functional associations. Associations have also been developed among regions in different states who share a common problem as a result of their common kind of geographic environment or economic activity. Aygen Aykac (1994) reports that there are over thirty of these transborder structures linking local and regional authorities in Western Europe.

(12) Federation of International Organizations of Municipalities. On the eve of the HABITAT II Conference of the United Nations on Human Settlements, held in Istanbul in June 1996, international local government organizations called together the first-ever World Assembly of Cities and Local Authorities. The World Assembly emphasized the importance of ongoing coordination of the movement of cities and local authorities worldwide and the need for local government input to the United Nations. The World Association of Cities and Local Authorities Coordination (WACLAC), formed in Paris in September 1996, is the resulting world alliance of international associations of cities and local authorities committed to responsible and effective local self-government for sustainable development. Its mission is to represent the local government sector in the international arena, particularly in the United Nations system.

(13) Municipalities in the UN system. Surprising as it might seem for an organization of states, there is now increasing involvement of local governments in the UN system. Cities are even on the agenda of Secretary General Kofi Annan, who has said that local governments should be given more authority to deal with problems that come with explosive growth as the world enters the 'urban millennium'. Only six months earlier a UN Advisory Committee of Local Authorities was established in Venice, in January 2000, at a meeting called by the Head of UNCHS (Habitat), and attended by mayors from all over the world and presidents of international associations of local authorities.

Although we have not made a complete inventory, Table 6.9 offers evidence of the diversity of kinds of involvements of local authorities in the UN System. Not surprising is the fact that organizations such as UNEP, UNDP, UNICEF, the World Bank and UNCHS have projects assisting the economic development of cities. Less expected are WACLAC demands for participation of cities and local authorities in the proceedings of the UNCHS (Habitat), and on its Commission on Human Settlements. Responsive to these initiatives has been the creation of a UN Advisory Committee on Local Authorities.

Table 6.9   Local Authorities in the UN System

UN Commission on Human Settlements – www.unchs.org
Urban Managements Program (UMP)
Sustainable Cities Program (SCP)
Municipal Development Program (MDP)
Global Campaign on Urban Governance
Urban Sanitation and Solid Waste Management
World Assembly of Cities and Local Authorities (WACLA), Istanbul, 1996, before
    Second UN Conference on Human Settlements (Habitat II)
World Urban Form (Before UN Conf. on Environment and Development
    (UNCED) 1994)
UNDP   Colloquium of Mayors, 1995 (New York, before Copenhagen Social
    Summit)
World Bank, Municipal Development Program – www.worldbank.org
UN Development Program (UNDP) Urban Mangement Program – www.undp.org
UNICEF Mayors Defenders of Children Initiative, periodical meetings of mayors –
    www.unicef.org
UN Advisory Committee on Local Authorities

Source: www.unsystem.org

(14) Transnational discourse communities. At the same time that local officials are participating in the activities of international organizations of cities and in their efforts to influence agendas of the UN system, there is obviously a feedback impact on local government. One study asserts that local government is being reshaped in the global discourse known as New Public Management (NPM), a 'hegemonic discourse' since the 1980s. It evolved from 'international administrative experts working for the UN, [was] taken up by the Carter administration and then processed and refined by the OECD' (Salskov-Iversen, et al., 2000: 183). 'Not only are distant localities being linked together by very real and rapidly increasing flows of capital, flexible production processes, and people in motion; they are also becoming connected through networks of expertise' (Salskov-Iversen, 2000: 185).

(15) Regional and world declarations and conventions on local self-government. In 1985 the Council of Europe drafted the European Charter of Local Self-Government which has now been ratified by over thirty members of the Council. The preamble concludes that local self-government 'entails the existence of local authorities endowed with democratically constituted decision-making bodies and possessing a wide degree of autonomy with regard to their responsibilities, the ways and means by which those responsibilities are exercised and the resources required for their fulfillment'.

The European Charter has served as a model for a movement to develop a World Charter for Local Self-Government. Before the second UN Conference on Human Settlements (Habitat II), WACLAC called on the international community to develop a world charter of local self-government and presented this proposal to the Habitat II Conference. Following up on this initiative, a memorandum of understanding was signed in New York in July 1997 between the UN Centre for Human Settlements (UNCHS) (Habitat) and WACLAC which committed both parties to a world charter of local self-government.

(16) Direct participation of cities and local regions in regional governance. In fulfillment of its support of democracy, the Council of Europe (COE) created The Congress of Local and Regional Authorities of Europe (CLRAE) in 1994. As a consultative body its responsibilities include helping new member states to make progress in establishing effective local and regional self-government. CLRAE has two chambers, the Chamber of Local Authorities and the Chamber of Regions, comprised of 291 members and 291 substitute members that represent more than 200,000 European local and regional authorities. The members of CLRAE, composed of only elected local and regional authorities, are representative of the various types of local and regional authority in each member state. Projects developed by CLRAE in fulfillment of its goals include efforts to establish and strengthen local democracy that include training local officials and transfrontier cooperation. Included in its projects are three conventions. The European Outline Convention on Transfrontier Co-operation recognizes the right of local and regional authorities to cooperate across frontiers in providing public services and environmental protection. Rights of foreigners are protected by the European Convention on the Participation of Foreigners in Public Life at the Local Level. There is also a Charter for Participation of Young People in Municipal and Regional Affairs.

In many respects the creation of the Congress of Local and Regional Authorities of Europe (CLRAE) is the most surprising development in our inventory. Although advisory, it does establish the CLRAE as a third component, along with the Parliamentary Assembly and the Committee of Ministers, in the Council of Europe. Significant in CLRAE is the fact that this body is composed of already locally elected local authorities. At this point it would seem that participation of cities and local regions in interstate regional organizations is primarily a European phenomenon. But this conclusion cannot be reached without a systematic inventory of other regional organizations.

Table 6.10 Vienna, Austria. An Example of the Network of Involvements of One City

1. Committee of the Regions (CoR) (222 representatives of regional and local authorities in the European Union (EU))
2. Assembly of the Regions of Europe in European Union (ARE)
3. Union of Capitals of the European Union
4. Council of Local Authorities and Regions of Europe (CLRAE) (European division of IULA)
5. Conference of Mayors of South Eastern European Capitals
6. Eurocities (European cities with 250,000 or more population)
7. Council of Local and Regional Authorities of Europe (CLRAE), Council of Europe
8. Working Group, Danube Region
9. Airport Regions Conference (ARC)
10. Summit Conference of Major Cities of the World (SUMMIT)

Source: www.magwien.gv.at

As we conclude this brief overview, it is informative to obtain a snapshot of the involvements of only one city. Table 6.10 presents the network of involvements of one city, Vienna Austria, as reported on their web site. They range across very local regions, to Europe and to the entire world.

This survey has revealed growing awareness by some involved in local governance that maintaining and extending local democracy requires efforts that range from local to global contexts. This is reflected in the array of strategies being employed by cities and local regions to strengthen local democracy and enhance the participation of cities and local regions in world affairs. *First*, there are local efforts to enhance the capacity of local people to become more self-conscious about their world involvements and to participate in local response to the needs of distant people. *Second*, there is an array of activities that facilitate worldwide exchange of knowledge and experience among cities and local regions, including workshops, study visits, training seminars, courses, published reports and manuals. *Third*, sharing and training takes place through institutions especially established for this purpose by international organizations of cities and local regions. *Fourth*, these international organizations have also developed projects that are directly engaged in local government capacity-building. *Fifth*, out of these collaborative efforts 'transnational discourse communities' on local governmental practice have emerged. *Sixth*, regional conventions creating local government standards have been put into practice and a world convention is now being developed. *Seventh*, cities and local regions are directly participating in regional governance in the Council of Europe. *Eighth*, organizations of cities and local regions are actively involved in projecting their interests into relevant units of the UN system.

Overall, our brief overview of evolving procedures for projecting local concerns into emerging regional and global governance has revealed growing recognition by local governments and local civil society that their daily life, and fate, is extensively affected by local-global links; and growing recognition that they must become directly involved in shaping the character of these linkages. Of course, it must be frankly recognized that available information does not permit us to assess the impact of these efforts. Nevertheless, these innovative locally-based efforts do challenge us to ponder their present significance, investigate further their impact, and evaluate their potential contribution for emerging global governance. Indeed, it is puzzling, in a time in which so much consideration is being given to the emerging role of civil society in global governance that this literature has given scant attention to the emerging involvements of local actors (Alger, 1999a).

5. Conclusion

What are the implications of this growth in the array of actors in world politics? Why are those involved in local government and civil society now extending their activities into global governance? As we said in establishing our introductory context, it is because the boundaries of all significant public policy issues now reach across the entire globe. Nevertheless, each of these public policy issues has a diversity of local dimensions. Thus, efforts at global governance confront the need for simultaneously coping with issues on a global scale and in the context of governance for a diversity of more local boundaries (see Shaw, this volume). This is, indeed, a difficult challenge. Although individual actors have not explained their behaviour in these terms, the totality of their efforts implies this hypothesis: *in a world of escalating interdependence, local democracy is not feasible without global democracy, and global democracy is not feasible without local democracy.* Upon drawing this implication we are immediately reminded of Dahl and Tufte's 1973 treatise on *Size and Democracy*. After observing that democracy is most compatible with small political units they note the challenge to democracy presented by problems that transcend political boundaries:

> The central theoretical problem is no longer to find suitable rules, like the majority principle, to apply within a sovereign unit, but to find suitable rules to apply among a variety of units, none of which is sovereign. ... At the same time that transnational units will increase the capacity of the system to handle critical problems ... transnational units will also increase the ineffectuality and powerlessness of the individual citizen.... Theory, then needs to do what democratic theory has never done well: to offer useful guidance about the appropriate relations among units (Dahl and Tufte, 1973: 135, 140).

Certainly those engaged in the activities that we have been describing are engaged in 'experiments' that are responsive to the needs identified by Dahl and Tufte. But these practitioners have no theory to guide them. They have invented new procedures supportive of local democracy by responding to challenges confronted in everyday practice.

Finally, what principles for democratic global governance are suggested by our brief exploration into innovations in three arenas? Here are only a few:

First, all territorial units, no matter how small, have world relations. It is necessary that all residing in these territories become aware of the 'world relations of daily life' and become cognizant of their impact on those involved, both locally and in distant places.

Second, decisions on the external relations of all territorial units must be made democratically.

Third, people in each territorial sub-unit in a larger territorial entity must participate in the formulation of policies for external relations by the larger unit.

Fourth, all of the primary types of territorial units, both governmental and non-governmental, require their own representative global assembly, e.g. the UN General Assembly (states), World Peoples' Assembly, and World Cities Assembly.

Fifth, procedures must be developed for relations between these assemblies. They could eventually become separate assemblies in a single organization.

Sixth, global democratic standards for participation in all units, and for relations among them, must be established in global assemblies, based upon contributions from all territorial entities.

No doubt the reaction of most to these principles is that they are too complicated to implement. On the other hand, thousands of thoughtful and reasonable people, responsive to the challenges presented by globalization in their daily lives, are already creatively engaged in practicing some of these principles. We believe that significant insights on democratic potential in emerging global governance can be attained by closer monitoring of the diversity of modes for participation in global governance that are now being invented in a vast array of 'laboratories' in global society.

This approach is suggested by an insight offered by Eugen Ehrlich a decade before the UN was founded:

> Whence comes the rule of law, and who breathes life and efficacy into it? At the present as well as at any other time, the center of gravity of legal development lies not in legislation, nor in juristic science, nor in judicial decision, but in society itself (1936: 12).

Finally, it is quite obvious that a critical democratic deficiency in current practice is that many of the participants in the activities that we have described have very limited formal responsibilities to most of the people who live their daily lives in networks of world relations. This is because most of the citizens represented in global governance do not even know about the world relations of people who are representing them (Alger 1999a). This is a challenge that merits the devoted attention of researchers and teachers, including those whose focus ranges from local to global affairs.

Note

1   The 'O' emphasizes the organizational character of transnational social movements.

Chapter 7

Human Development, Security, and the Prospects for African Governance in the Twenty-First Century: Lessons from/for Uganda and the Great Lakes Region

Timothy M. Shaw

...the spread of the term 'global civil society' reflects an underlying social reality. What we can observe in the 1990s is the emergence of a supranational sphere of social and political participation in which citizen groups, social movements, and individuals engage in dialogue with each other and with various governmental actors – international, national and local – as well as the business world...global civil society both feeds on and reacts to globalization.
– Anheier et al. (2001: 4, 7)

Effective governance is often the 'missing link' between national anti-poverty efforts and poverty reduction. For many countries, it is in improving governance that external assistance is needed – but not with a new set of poverty-related conditionalities imposed on top of existing economic conditionalities.
– UNDP (2000a: 8)

...neither Africa's post-colonial history nor the actual practice engaged in by successful 'developmental states' rule out the possibility of African 'developmental states' capable of playing a more dynamic role than hitherto.
– Mkandawire (2000: 289)

After two decades of structural adjustment, as well as years of open conflict in many parts of the continent, the definition and sustainability of human development/security in Africa are increasingly a function of novel forms of 'governance' encompassing the local, national, regional, and also global levels. 'African governance' in the new century involves a dynamic mix of state, civil society, and private sector actors responding to a set of new policy issues with multi-level appeal, such as biodiversity, debt, environment, gender, genocide, HIV/AIDS, and landmines. Uganda constitutes a particularly interesting case in this regard because – having experienced post-conflict reconstruction, a no-party polity, and an economic revival leading to the Heavily Indebted Poor Country (HIPC) agreement on a poverty reduction strategy, multilateral but orchestrated by an NGO coalition, the Uganda Debt Network (www.udn.or.ug) – it stands at the point of conjunction between 'success' and 'failure' in the African context, and has on both counts revealed the potential for local-to-global interactivity. Similarly, the Great Lakes Region (GLR) illustrates the variety of effects of a regime's regional context, from market opportunities and ecological pressures to population movements and security challenges. Overall, 'Africa' today illustrates a variety of formal and informal transnationalisms, the democratic character of which at least bear discussion.

Definitions of and relations among states, economies and civil societies are everywhere in flux as a consequence of globalizations, regionalisms, migrations, neo-liberalism and other transformations. Yet, as indicated below, contemporary texts on government, international relations and/or political science rarely appreciate the extent of change. Likewise, the post-bipolar 'world community' now consists of some 200 mainly poor, small, and weak countries, but most orthodox studies of 'foreign policy' fail to recognize their tenuousness or vulnerability (Khadiagala and Lyons, 2001), unlike the state of analysis in the less ominous/global 'world' of the 1960s and possibly that after 11th September 2001. Some scholars, such as Anheier et al. in the opening passage, are just beginning to pay attention to the complex interactions that arguably constitute a global civil society. Meanwhile, certainly only a minority of critical analysts focus on the other side of globalizations (Gills 2000; Klein 2000; Mittelman, 2000): the regional and global networks of informal/illegal trade in people and products, mafias/militias, drugs and guns, and the like (Cox, 1999). Yet the formal governmental regimes of over half the members of the UN and the World Bank exert at best a tenuous control over their territories, economies and civil societies.

This chapter suggests, then, that we need to rethink the assumptions and analyses of comparative politics to accommodate a range of irrefutable current phenomena such as contracting-out, 'corruption', flexibilization/feminization, fundamentalisms, money-laundering, narco-diplomacy, regionalisms, smuggling, the privatization of security, and supply chains. These are no longer aberrations but rather central features of the political culture/economy of the majority of the world's states, increasingly typical of regions like Africa, Central America, Central Asia, and Eastern Europe. Yet just as there are 'failed' states in Asia there are also a few 'developmental' states in Africa, as attested to by Mkandawire (2001) above. Furthermore, the existence of distinctive 'capitalisms' confirm that there are important differences amongst its major regional variants, not just in the 'trilateral' world – marked out by the liberal Anglo-American, corporatist continental European, and statist Japanese cases (Cox, 1999) – but also in the 'overseas' Chinese, Latino, Islamic and 'African' experiences. Thus, the current political culture/economy of 'Africa' has to be situated in a range of interrelated contexts, involving 'continuous patterns of relations, decisions and/or policies among the heterogeneous trio of state, market and civil society actors over a diverse range of issues and levels' (Quadir, MacLean and Shaw, T., 2001: 4; also Shaw, T., 1999). As the above UNDP quotation suggests with regard to the treatment of poverty, it is 'effective governance', increasingly broadly defined, that has become the 'missing link', which creates an 'urgent need for governments and intergovernmental organizations to examine and define the rules of engagement with civil society in the coming years' (Culpepper, 2001/2: 9-10).

1. Global

First, just as states are highly heterogeneous – from Switzerland and Singapore to Somalia and Sierra Leone – so likewise are non-state actors. In addition to the state on one 'corner' of the 'governance triangle' (see page 115 for diagram), the other corners include global corporations and local micro-enterprises on the one, and informal and illegal enterprises as well as formal and legal on the other. This framework provides the complexity required to recognize that 'global capitalisms' are in fact heterogeneous rather than homogeneous: relationships around the governance triangle vary between Anglo-American 'liberal', European 'corporatist', Scandinavian welfarist and statist Asian varieties, notably Chinese (mainland and 'overseas') versus Japanese, with Africa having its own distinctive form of for-profit structures, increasingly under the influence of South African capital and brands.

Similarly, NGOs vary from familiar global INGOs to very local grassroots/community-based organizations (Anheier et al., 2001; Desai, 2002; Van Rooy, 2002; Alger, this volume). In particular, NGOs can be distinguished in terms of whether they are primarily engaged in policy advocacy as think tanks or service delivery as subcontractors, although most do both in varying proportions. In fact, major INGOs have become increasingly engaged with international agencies in the UN and IFI nexuses in terms of both advocacy and subcontracting (Nelson, 1995 and 2002b). Meanwhile, organizational variety is enhanced by the fact that such legal arrangements are matched by illegal transnational networks amongst mafias, militias, private armies etc (Cox, 1999; Mittelman, 2000).

'Global civil society' is thus very heterogeneous (Anheier et al., 2001), with global social movements coming to play increasingly salient yet quite incompatible roles. On the one hand, many contemporary INGOs have been the sources of new global issues, such as ecology, genetic engineering, gender, global warming, international criminal justice, landmines, ozone depletion (van Rooy, 2001) and now 'conflict diamonds' (Smillie, Gberie and Hazelton, 2000). These have led to major global coalitions such as the International Campaign to Ban Landmines (ICBL) which resulted in the 'Ottawa Process' (Hubert, 2000; Tomlin et al., 1998), now replicated in the 'Kimberley Process'. But they have also advanced 'anti-globalization' sentiments, as reflected in the 'battle of Seattle' against the Multilateral Agreement on Investment (MAI) (Anheier et al., 2001: 60-1) and subsequent alternative summits and counter-demonstrations at major global and regional summits (Klein, 2000; Van Rooy, 2001; www.attac.org; www.nologo.org). In turn, major global corporations increasingly seek to insulate themselves from popular pressures/boycotts through a variety of strategies, from association with the UN Global Compact to corporate codes of conduct/responsibility (Pearson and Seyfang, 2001), ethical as well as fair trade initiatives, and strategic alliances with certain international organizations or NGOs. Thus, many of the multinational corporations which are featured in Naomi Klein's *No Logo* (2000) as targets of anti-corporate campaigns – for instance, McDonald's, Nestlé, Nike, and Shell – are most active in the UN Global Compact (www.unglobalcompact.org; Parpart and Shaw, 2002)!

One novel aspect of South-North trade in the new global political economy is 'supply chains' which link local producers to global markets in novel ways in a variety of sectors, including 'new' horticulture. Typically, these link producers of fresh flowers, fruits and vegetables to major supermarket chains and use information technology for communication and airfreight/containers for transportation (Fold, Gibbon, and Ponte, 2003). These are in turn open to pressure from advocacy groups over ecology, gender, labour and other concerns, leading to Ethical Trade Initiatives as well as Fair Trade, and conditionalities over gender, housing, and labour practices. One result, as is apparent in thumb-print sketches of sources of specialized coffee beans in Aroma, Coffee Republic, Costa, Second Cup, and Starbucks, is the emergence of 'value chain' governance (Gereffi and Kaplinsky, 2001; cf. Pearson and Seyfang, 2001).

There is a growing revisionist debate about whether the three corners of the governance triangle are really better conceived of as separate rather than as different points along a continuum. Certainly, there is continuous communication and interaction along the three sides of the triangle; yet, crucially, there is also some autonomy at particular times and in particular instances over particular issues. In short, notwithstanding the continual possibility of cooptation, many actors at all levels in the governance nexus do maintain a degree of independence, as increasingly demanded by their stakeholders (UNU, 2002).

2. Continental

Second, inter- as well as non-state relations in Africa are changing at the turn of the century (Khadiagala and Lyons, 2001) as a result of both the extra-continental impact of globalization/neo-liberalism and the emergence of new threats/leaders intra-continentally, now advanced in terms of an 'African Renaissance' – encompassing the movement from African Union and African Economic Community to New Partnership for Africa's Development (NEPAD) (www.dfa.gov.za/events/nepad) – and resonance within the G8 community (www.g8.gc.ca) reinforced by bilateral Blair and Chrétien (see below) 'initiatives' for the continent. These may inform as well as legitimate regional peace-keeping responses to resilient regional conflicts. And they might even facilitate, perhaps unintentionally, non-state definitions of 'new' regionalisms such as ecology, ethnicity, brands, religions, and sports (Parpart and Shaw, 2002).

Coinciding with such promising developments are moves away from orthodox structural adjustment programmes (SAPs) and conditionalities towards poverty-reduction programmes. SAPs were widely criticized as being onerous and ineffective. Given the pressures on the IFIs, as well as the sequence of the Asian, Russian and Argentinian 'crises', they moved towards special programmes for Heavily Indebted Poor Countries (HIPC I and II). To qualify, African regimes had to meet SAP terms and design acceptable poverty reduction strategies in association with civil society. In the case of Uganda, one of the few currently successful HIPC cases, in the late 1990s the Uganda Debt Network (UDN), composed of myriad national, regional and global NGOs, 'acted as an intermediary between state and private sector on the one hand and civil society on the other, at both the design and the implementation stages, moving from policy advocate to policy agent or subcontractor, and achieving along the way the status of an authoritative epistemic community' (Callaghy, 2001). As UNCTAD (2000: 148) indicated in a 'box' (#7) on the Uganda case, its Poverty Eradication Action Plan (PEAP) was founded on four pillars: 1) creating a framework for economic growth and transformation; 2) ensuring good governance and security; 3) directly increasing the ability of the poor to raise their income; and 4) directly increasing the quality of life of the poor.

Thus Uganda is something of a model – potentially a 'democratic developmental state' similar to Botswana and Mauritius (Mkandawire, 2001)? – in terms of designing a Policy Framework Paper (PFP) and then maintaining the momentum through Poverty Reduction Strategy Papers (PRSPs) in collaboration with a wide network of ministries, NGOs, international organizations and NGOs, both local and global. According to UNCTAD (2000: 143):

> The PRSP is intended to be a country-owned document prepared through a participatory process which elicits the involvement of civil society, other national stakeholders and elected institutions. 'Ownership' in this context refers to the Government's taking the lead in the preparation of PRSP, including the animation of the participatory process (which is expected to increase public accountability) and the drafting of the action plan.

Such a poverty reduction network constitutes an example of partnership for rural development as advocated by IFAD in its *Rural Poverty Report 2001: the challenge of ending rural poverty*: a mix of state-NGO-private sector governance facilitated by decentralization.

Similarly, given their recent espousal of 'human security', countries like Canada commit more resources to the continent than 'national interest' alone would justify, in part because of notions of 'human security' and in part in response to concerned diaspora communities. As Chris Brown (2001a: 194) suggested, at the turn of the century:

As a continent where human security is manifestly at risk, Africa came to figure more prominently in Canada's foreign policy during 2000 than a narrow examination of national interests might suggest.

3. National

Third, patterns of 'governance' in Africa are in flux at all levels – local to continental – and in all sectors – from state and corporate to NGOs (i.e., the three corners of the governance 'triangle'). Contemporary notions of governance have a variety of conceptual, ideological, institutional, political and theoretical sources and correlates (Jenkins, 2000; Quadir et al., 2001). Governance on this continent as on others varies over time and between regions (Reinikka and Collier, 2001; Shaw and Nyang'oro, 2000; UNU, 2002). And it reveals similarities and dissimilarities with other continents. As elsewhere, notions of comparative politics/development have evolved profoundly over the last decade as the mix of 'globalizations' and 'liberalizations' has had a cumulative impact. The focus on the state has been superseded by recognition of the diverse and changeable patterns of governance reflected in concepts like public-private partnerships, networks, and coalitions (see, for example, www.copenhagencentre.org, www.unglobalcompact.org) (Fowler, 2002; Mbabazi, MacLean, and Shaw, 2002). If the state has not been rendered irrelevant, its continued role presents an interpretive challenge to scholars as well as to myriad political and economic actors. For further discussion of the status of the state, see the Morgan, Hall, Fierlbeck, Morrison, and Markoff chapters (this volume).

So, for instance, the debate continues over whether 'globalization' offers opportunities for some African states, civil societies and companies at all levels, with the more optimistic 'liberals' insisting that it does, despite all the negative evidence and press over the last two decades (Bond, 2002; Makhan, 2002; Nsouli and Le Gall, 2001; Reinikka and Collier, 2001). The key, however, may lie in noting that the changes associated with globalization are altering the terrain, and even calling some of our main conceptual categories into question. Certainly, SAPs generated much scepticism, even defeatism, on the continent (Arrighi, 2002), but their *de facto* successor, offering a distinctive form of globalization – negotiated debt relief through HIPC (Anena, 2001; Gariyo, 2002) – is both rooted in and leading towards a novel form of governance. As Callaghy (2001: 138, 142) suggests:

> ... all HIPC debt relief is now to be tied directly to poverty reduction. This is to be ensured by the creation of Poverty Reduction Strategy Papers (PRSPs) put together by debtor countries *in consultation with civil society groups.... If seriously implemented*, this new process could be an important change in international governance on debt, aid and development more generally and may have major implications for the unfolding of democratization processes in Africa and elsewhere.

The UDN continued to grow and increase its capabilities. By 2000, it had more than 60 members as well as strong ties to the Uganda Joint Christian Council and to business, student, and labour organizations. It was becoming very active in coordinating civil society participation in the PRSP process, which it was doing with the help of Northern NGOs. Lastly, it had improved its own organizational capabilities and was running its own independent website.

'HIPC governance' by definition involves the state negotiating Poverty Reduction Strategy Programmes with a range of non-state actors at local to global levels, a process facilitated in the Ugandan case by the Uganda Debt Network (UDN), itself a heterogeneous coalition of (I)NGOs, think tanks, and religious groups, among others. In the process of negotiating, and thereby facilitating, HIPC governance, the UDN has itself been somewhat transformed not only in status, but also in practice – in terms not just of advocacy but of delivery as well – thus raising the question of cooptation (Nelson, 1995 and 2002b). If the national state is, therefore, far from out of the picture, it is also the case that redevelopment has not been evenly distributed across Uganda (Anthony, 2002): the north (61 per cent support for multiparty politics) remains more impoverished and alienated than the south (39 per cent support for multiparty politics in the West) as reflected in opinion polls as well as support for opposition parties and guerrilla movements (Sunday Monitor, 3 February, 2002). Conversely, Museveni gets most support for his handling of the political debate from the West (52 per cent) and least from the North (30 per cent). There is, therefore, no single form of relationship between the state and civil society.

Nor is the democratic impact of these various relationship types altogether clear. In particular, there may be a danger in privileging civil society to the detriment of formal, multiparty politics, especially under a unique, not uncontroversial, no-party constitution: can civil society, especially when legitimated or reinforced by global donors/media, 'squeeze out' other democratic processes like elections? The distinctively 'Ugandan' debate about Movement versus multiparty formal politics is not separable, therefore, from the parallel discourse about occasional formal elections versus continuous civil society activity/advocacy. As John Makumbe (1998: 305) suggests:

> For most of Africa … civil society would include trade unions; professional associations; church and para-church organizations; resident, student, business and other special interest associations; the media; and various types of NGOs.

Whilst he recognizes the weakness of contemporary civil society in much of the continent, including its tenuous democratic features, Makumbe (1998: 317) concludes that with extracontinental support it can continue to develop.

The resurgence of civic protest in virtually all sub-Saharan African countries since the late-1980s has resulted, inter alia, in the transformation of the continent's governance and political systems, with civic groups in most of these countries demanding that their governments be democratic, transparent and accountable to the people. Although much has already been achieved, much also remains to be done if Africa is to have an effective and vibrant civil society.

Similarly, extra-continental actors are also increasingly concerned about the continent, in part because of a variety of non-state connections, from diasporas/refugees to biodiversity, conflicts, drugs and guns, and sustainability; hence the debates in Canada at the turn of the millennium about countries like Angola, Congo, Sierra Leone, and Sudan emphasizing civil societies, communities, companies, media, as well as the government (Brown, 2001a; Van Rooy, 2001).

Overall, therefore, Kevin Dunn (2001: 46, 49) has some justification in chiding orthodox analysts for their increasingly outdated and inappropriate analytic approaches which, he feels, reveal a lack of nuanced understanding of the new and distinctive patterns of dynamic, mixed-actor governance on the continent; ie 'developmental governance':

> Just a few of the labels attached to the African state over the past decade or so include 'failed', 'lame', 'fictive', 'weak', 'collapsing', 'quasi', 'invented' and 'imposed', 'shadow', 'overdeveloped' and 'centralised', 'swollen', 'soft', 'extractive' and 'parasitic', premodern', and 'post-state'.... What needs to be recognized is that the African state is not failing as much as is our understanding of the state.

4. Local

Fourth, and finally, decentralization and urbanization have greatly enhanced the importance of the local level of governance – city and community – to human development/security concerns (see Alger, this volume). Attention to this level reveals patterns of partnership similar to those at the other levels, in the sense of increasing roles for non-state actors in terms of service, delivery, and the like. As we will see in the case of Mbarara municipality and county, such innovations as subcontracting to local companies for education or to local NGOs for AIDS hospices have become commonplace. Over the last decade there has been approximately 10 per cent growth in Western Uganda, albeit from a very weak base established by the Amin/Obote II regimes. This has advanced both human development and human security (Mbabazi and Shaw, 2000; Mbabazi, MacLean and Shaw, 2002). The former is defined by the UNDP (1994: 13) as expanding human capabilities and choices whilst minimizing vulnerabilities and the latter (UNDP, 1994: 24) as *'freedom from fear and freedom from want': human security is not a concern with weapons – it is a concern with human life and dignity'* (UNDP, 1994: 22).

5. Conclusions

Building upon a *variety of interrelated disciplines and debates* – from political science/economy and international relations to African, development and security studies – to which I return at the end, this chapter draws insights from the juxtaposition of generic concepts like 'civil society', 'governance', and even the 'democratic developmental state', with cases drawn from Africa. While it concentrates on the Great Lakes Region (GLR), it reflects analyses and debates from Sub-Saharan Africa as a whole (Villalon and Huxtable, 1998). The attempt is also made to bring in notions of human development/security, given their salience in the contemporary continent (Hampson, Hillmer and Molot, 2001; UNDP, 1994 and 1998), while reflecting on peace-building and reconstruction in today's Uganda with particular attention to the roles of NGOs and think tanks.

5.1 Civil Society and the State in Contemporary Africa: Beyond Liberalization

At the start of the twenty-first century, NGOs are engaged in service delivery and/or policy advocacy from the local to global levels (Clark, J., 2002; Desai, 2002; Nelson, 2002b), leading to partnerships of multiple types (Fowler, 2002) which affect the state whether it seeks such links or not: *NGOs create alliances and networks to place pressure on the state* (Desai, 2002: 497).

One side of the governance triangle – that between the state and civil society – is focused on democratization or 'political liberalization'. By contrast, the other side - that between the state and the private sector – is preoccupied with 'economic liberalization' or privatization. There is cause to wonder about the compatibility of these two forms of 'liberalization'. Furthermore, both affect the bottom, horizontal axis of the triangle, that between the two non-state elements – i.e. civil society and private companies – which is no longer an exclusively antagonistic one; rather, a series of partnerships has come to characterize some of these horizontal relations. In short, there appears to be something of a stand-off (contradiction?) between global competitiveness and a democratic deficit, raising questions as to which is primary for local and global interests/institutions.

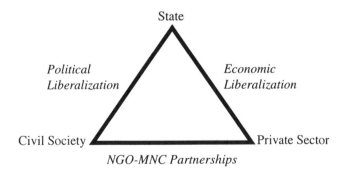

Figure 7.1 The Governance Triangle

In such a fluid context, the role of 'think tanks' as well as NGOs (covering the spectrum in Uganda from Private Sector Foundation and Economic Policy

Research Centre [see more below] to Centre for Basic Research (CBR) and UDN versus 'old', established research institutions like MISR at Makerere), are in flux, as indicated in the broad-based (winning?) coalition supporting the PRSP process (UNCTAD, 2000).

5.2 Civil Society and the Economy in Contemporary Africa: Beyond Privatization 'African capitalism' in contemporary Uganda is quite distinctive. It includes not only traditional and contemporary 'colonial' commodities and supply chains but also informal (and illegal?) as well as formal regional exchanges. It thus now includes fruit, horticultural, and vegetable exports as well as coffee and tea; and at a regional level it includes electricity, Coca Cola, Mukwano soap products, UHT milk, and so on. In addition to serving as an entrepot for Central African resources, meanwhile, it also serves as an informal conduit for outgoing coltan, diamonds, and gold and incoming guns and other basic needs. The mix of legal and illegal economic interaction is problematic and controversial, to the point of drawing the UN into the debates. On the whole, however, the Ugandan economy has benefited from its external linkages, as in the case of the clear gains deriving from the Congolese conflict/expeditionary force. In addition, the termination of apartheid has enabled South African capital, franchises, links, and technologies to enter Uganda, thereby establishing competition with local (African and Asian), British/European and Asian capital sources: examples include Century Bottlers' Coca Cola franchise, MTN cell-phones, MNet cable and satellite TV, Nandos, Spur and Steer fast-food franchises, Shoprite supermarket and Metro Cash-and-Carry wholesaling, South African Airways, and South African Breweries.

Such alternatives lead towards new opportunities and new regionalisms: beyond the established interstate East African Community (EAC), now augmented by the East African Legislature, and onto new security provisions, as well as the specification of the Great Lakes Region (GLR), to flexible non-state forms of regionalism defined by ecologies, ethnicities, infrastructures, technologies, viruses, and the like (Shaw, T., 2003).

5.3 Governance in Contemporary Uganda: Beyond Peace-Building to Human Development/Security? For Uganda, the future looks too ghastly to contemplate. The elections have not only confirmed the traditional divide between the south and the north but, more critically, opened another internal divide within the NRM. These are very sensitive issues which will require delicate handling if Uganda is to avoid a return to the lawlessness of the 1970s and 1980s. The wild card in this whole question remains the generals returning form the DRC (Ajulu, 2001).

Human development/security at the turn of the millennium in a small 'fourth world' state like Uganda at the periphery is a function of the balance between the local/national and the global/regional (Shaw, T., 1999). And at all levels, 'governance' is dynamic rather than static: the balance among state, economy, and civil society varies between levels and over time. Uganda has made a remarkable comeback in the last fifteen years in terms of basic human development/security, at least for most of its regions (Baker, 2001; UNDP, 1998). But the sustainability of such an 'African renaissance' is problematic unless a judicious balance is maintained among patterns of governance at all levels. In particular, the notion of 'national development' or 'developmental state' is problematic when the gap between, say, Kitgum and Kabale, is rather wide (Baker, 2001; UNDP, 2000b), as indicated in the continued tensions and violence (Ehrhart and Ayoo, 2000; UNDP, 2000b).

Local governance offers a variety of advantages over centralized government, but accountability/transparency need to be continually demanded/monitored and democratic decentralization perhaps encouraged. Governance at the local level, meanwhile, may require a continually changing mix of state as well as non-state resources and relationships (Kasfir, 1998 and 2000), as our own work on Mbarara suggests (Mbabazi and Shaw, 2000; Mbabazi, MacLean and Shaw, 2002).

5.4 Lessons From/For Governance in Africa at the Start of the Twenty-First Century The official, optimistic scenario emerging from Uganda in the early-twenty-first century in terms of African or HIPC governance is that of a continuous negotiation among corporations, NGOs/networks, state and partnerships involving new capital/franchises/technologies and commodity/supply chains, and so on (Holmgren, Kasekende et al., 2000). By contrast, the critical, pessimistic preview suggests arbitrary decision-making, exponential corruption, state violence, and regional aggressiveness, as reflected in growing concerns regarding accountability and transparency (Lewis and Wallace, 2000). Nevertheless, given Uganda's comeback in the 1990s, are there lessons to be learned for local to global decision-makers about such embryonic 'democratic developmental states' (Mkanadwire, 2001)?

Here, I look briefly into possible insights for established disciplines such as political science, international relations, and political economy as well as for interdisciplinary fields such as African/Development/Security Studies. In terms of orthodox canons, case studies like contemporary Uganda suggest the imperative of going beyond the state and formal economy to examine myriad links between these and the non-state/formal realm, the yield being access to real triangular forms of mixed-actor governance (UNU, 2002). And in terms of more recent interdisciplinary perspectives, there is a need to reflect on new issues/relations around developing countries and communities, so questions of traditional and 'new' security cannot be separated in the GLR. Indeed, Uganda in the twenty-first century, as in the nineteenth and twentieth, suggests the imperative of situating 'external' challenges and opportunities in the context of state-society relations – what we now know as 'globalization' (Dunn and Shaw, 2001). The place of new, poor, small, weak states in a globalizing, even turbulent, world is crucial for analysts and citizens alike. Callaghy (2001: 144) concludes his own suggestive study of 'HIPC governance' in Uganda with a rejection of the tendency to disregard Africa on the political and analytical front:

Africa has been central to the evolution of the international regime on public debt, although not its primary driving force. New actors and processes have been unleashed in response to Africa's plight that might significantly alter the way the larger development regime functions. In the long run, the most significant changes may well not be HIPC itself, but rather the new processes and transboundary formations that it helped to unleash.

Chapter 8

European and North American Integration: Some Implications for Transnational Democracy

John N. McDougall

According to the 'retreat of the state' school of thought, globalization is undermining familiar forms of democratic accountability by reducing the scope and effectiveness of national governments. On the assumption that the majority of citizens in most currently democratic societies continue to wish their governments to solve a variety of outstanding social and economic problems, anything that reduces or impedes the capacity of those governments to do so must be regarded as inherently undemocratic. Because one of the main sources of this 'democratic deficit' is the fact that economic and social interactions are no longer coextensive with the boundaries of national political authority, some democratic theorists are beginning to argue that democracy, too, must 'go global', that is, must operate at a supranational or transnational level (see Archibugi and Alger, this volume). Similarly, to the extent that states have begun to pool their authority in intergovernmental organizations, it is argued that democratic activists must organize on a transnational basis to ensure that global cooperative arrangements are at least as democratically responsive and accountable as national institutions (discussion of which can be found in Alger, Markoff, Morrison, and Morgan, this volume).

As part of this challenge, the widening movement toward transnational democracy is exploring ways of building public accountability into international processes of economic integration, at both regional and global levels. Accordingly, the present discussion is aimed to focus on the problems of democratic accountability specific to two prominent instances of regional integration, the European Union (EU) and the North American Free Trade Agreement (NAFTA). A central empirical point established in the chapter is that the 'institutional deficiency' of the NAFTA makes the issue of democratic accountability even more problematic for its North American members than the emerging institutional and political order of the European Union does for its members. Theoretically, the chapter provides empirically grounded instruction on the potential for democratic accountability within the global process of integration by extrapolating to that level some of the contrasts between the political adjustments to economic integration taking place in the two continental settings.

The conclusion is that the institutional model of political integration associated with economic integration within the European Union is more democratic – in fact and in potential – than the policy harmonization model of political integration associated with economic integration under the NAFTA. However, this good news for Europeans cannot be elevated into good news for transnational democracy more broadly because, as argued here, the emerging North American version of the relationship between economic and political integration is much more likely than the European one to become the model for the governance of global integration. This is because the European process – which is essentially the re-creation of the state at the regional level – at least tends toward significant institutionalization and pressures for the democratization of those institutions. Therefore, the European Union's global counterpart is, if not a world superstate, at least a set of institutions combining intergovernmental and transnational elements that have some potential for democratic accountability. Meanwhile, the political counterpart to economic integration in North America is essentially the contraction of the states (especially Mexico and Canada) within the region. As such it translates globally into something fairly close to what the 'retreat of the state' school of thought believes is happening already: the 'withering away of the state' – and with it, the democratic accountability of national governments – under conditions of the private ownership of capital and the primacy of the United States of America within global capitalism.

It is difficult to imagine how recognizable forms of democratic accountability can be built into universal supranational institutions resembling those created within the European Union. It is even more difficult for this observer to see how democratic accountability can survive in a world of nation-states that have been severely hollowed out by global processes resembling those currently at work under the NAFTA. As a consequence, promoters of transnational democracy might be wise to take a lessen from the NAFTA and direct their energies toward 're-democratizing' the nation-state, that is, *restoring* democratic accountability to the state as we know it, in both its domestic policies and its participation in interstate organizations and processes. As limited as the prospects for this development might seem, they appear to this observer to be significantly brighter than those for the alternative, which is to take lessons instead from the European Union and attempt to devise ways to ensure the democratic accountability of mammoth and remote structures of world government, which we are unlikely to see in any event.

The discussion proceeds in three stages. The next section tries to clarify the relationship between economic and political integration, making the case that neither economic nor political integration need necessarily involve the degree of institutionalization that marks the European Union's experience with both. The following section then reviews the evolution of the European Union in a little more detail, highlighting the historical, practical and game-theoretical reasons for the higher degree of institutionalization of the integration process there, compared with North America. The third section follows with an overview of the institutions and decision-making processes established under the NAFTA and an assessment of their potential to promote political integration in the form of policy harmonization among its members. A final section concludes the discussion with some of the implications it holds for the preservation of democratic accountability, and the prospects for transnational democracy, under conditions of global economic integration.

1. Economic and Political Integration

A key point about the relationship between economic and political integration is that the reduction or elimination of barriers to the movement of economic factors is largely independent of any particular international institutional arrangements. Specifically, moves toward international economic liberalization do not require the creation of common decision-making structures, certainly not ones with the scale and scope of those found in the European Union. Theoretically, economic integration could be fully accomplished through mutual but independently enacted adjustments to national policies that do not involve significant transfers of authority from national to international levels of authority.

In fact, the prospects for 'deep integration' within trade associations depend far more critically on the national policies adopted (or abandoned) by each of their members than on the creation of common institutions among them.[1] That is to say, deep integration, which is generally deemed to be an intensification of *economic integration,* is essentially about reducing *political* differences between countries – that is, differences between national policies, regulations, and standards that restrict the ease and efficiency with which goods, capital and people move between national jurisdictions. The substitution of common, 'supranational' policies for existing national policies is certainly one way of removing these differences, but it is not the only way.

Despite this, the identification of political integration with institutionalization is generally taken for granted. For most of the history of the international economy since World War II, economic integration was taken to be synonymous with trade liberalization, seen essentially as the reduction or removal of national tariffs on the importation of goods (i.e., shallow, at the border integration). The single major exception to this was found in the commitment of members of the European Community (now the EU) to the goal of deeper integration, a goal they pursued – for some special reasons to be reviewed in the next section – through the creation of a customs union, a common market, and eventually a full economic union. Member governments promoted the objective of removing trade- and investment-distorting differences in national policies by replacing or overriding them with European-wide policies enacted through newly established supranational institutions. In other words, in the Western European experience, the political integration that accompanied deep economic integration has been identified with the creation of common policies by means of state-like central institutions.

The conventional understanding of the relationship between economic and political integration has been heavily influenced by this tendency to associate deep integration strongly (if not exclusively) with the institutional form that it has taken in Western Europe. However, this obscurity is compounded by a related failure to give explicit recognition to the extensive domestic impact of all forms of deeper, behind the border integration, however arrived at. The pervasiveness of such impact is undeniable, even where a commitment to supranational institutions plays no part in moves toward market liberalization. For instance, the pressure for extensive changes in domestic policies effectively derailed the latter stages of the Uruguay Round of negotiations under the General Agreement on Tariffs and Trade (GATT), as the 'trade' agenda increasingly involved such matters as services and intellectual property rights that collided with the determination of most national governments to preserve deep-seated differences in their national business environments.[2]

Apart from the historical association of political integration with institution-formation in Western Europe, confusion over the relationship between economic and political integration is not helped by the failure of most theories of international integration to identify very clearly what the *outcome* of the integration process is posited to be, either economically or politically. (That is, these theories fail to specify with any precision what the 'dependent variable' in the relationship between economic and political variables is hypothesized to be.) Typically, both political and economic integration are modelled essentially as processes, but without identifying the determinable end (or outcome) of such processes.

Most economists would probably agree that 'factor-price equalization' provides one good measure of economic integration: markets have become fully integrated when the returns to land, labour and capital (respectively) have become uniform.[3] Unfortunately, there is no widely accepted measure of the end-point of political integration comparable to the economic concept of factor-price equalization. A measure of political integration that parallels factor-price equalization to some extent might be termed 'subject-value equalization' (or possibly 'citizen-value equalization'). While perhaps lacking in elegance and familiarity, the notion of subject value equalization is at least capable of reasonably objective measurement: political integration has taken place when the nationals of all member states are treated in the same manner by all governments. Significant progress toward political integration can thus be defined as the absence of discrimination on the basis of nationality in the implementation of government policies, as well as the elimination of differences in national policies. In other words, political integration has been fully realized when *government policies no longer favour members of their own society above members of other societies* or when *government policies on all trade- and investment-related matters are the same.*

In some respects, of course, the notion of subject-value equalization is only a more explicit political extension of the notion of 'national treatment' that has become a central feature of trade associations, including the GATT (now the World Trade Organization, or WTO). The key to the principle of national treatment is that, while each country is permitted to maintain 'its own' laws and policies, those policies must be applied in the same manner to all economic actors – domestic or foreign-based – operating within its jurisdiction. As the cliché goes, national treatment 'levels the playing field' for all competitors within each country.

However, recent trade negotiations are more concerned than in the past with creating 'the same playing field' across all countries, a development that extends policy integration beyond the principle of national treatment and further into the realm of subject value equalization. National governments are increasingly coming together to reduce the differences in their policy and regulatory regimes, to the point where all economic actors everywhere will be subject to the same – or at least less different – laws. Their objective is to reduce significantly the 'system friction' in the global economy that is created by diverse national economic, social, environmental, and cultural policies.[4]

In sum, in the current dynamics of market liberalization, system friction is intended to succumb to the harmonization and standardization of all trade- and investment-related national policies. The ultimate end of such a process is equal standing before the law of all subjects in all countries, a condition here defined as political integration. As such, the world as a whole is unlikely to witness the achievement of significant political integration for a long time, if ever. But its realization at a regional level, probably in Western Europe and at least plausibly in North America, may not be far off. The fact that the two regions have embarked on their journeys toward that destination at different times and by different routes does not mean that they will not end up in the same place at roughly the same time.

2. The 'Deficient Institutionality' of North American Political Integration[5]

Despite the prospect just noted that the processes of political integration in Europe and North America may be headed toward the same destination, it is important not to understate the profound differences that exist in the respective means they have adopted to get there. There are, first of all, countless differences in the circumstances under which the process of economic liberalization got under way in Western Europe fifty years ago compared with those under which, more recently, it was undertaken in North America. However, it may be useful to review what the most significant differences are and, more importantly, to establish how they may have placed an enduring stamp on the two processes.

The most obvious contrast between the two cases of integration is the fact that, from the start, the Europeans were self-consciously seeking political unity as well as economic integration, a fact that arose out of the historical and geopolitical conditions that prevailed in Europe in the immediate aftermath of World War II. Another significant difference is the fact that – even among the founding members – the European process was marked by a larger number of more equal national actors. It will be helpful to review a few of the details concerning each of these differences.

2.1 Historical and Geopolitical Factors   It is generally agreed that the European Union represents the high-water mark of both economic and political integration over the past fifty years. The problem lies in accepting this correlation of economic integration with political integration as evidence of causation (not least because it is not even clear which direction the arrow of causality should be pointing). Sorting out the economic chicken from the political egg of European integration would be very like (to shamelessly pursue a related metaphor) unscrambling an omelet.

However, it seems difficult to dispute the interpretation that the unusually high degree of 'supranationalism' in the European system – defined as the creation of authoritative central institutions to decide and administer common policies for all members – is largely attributable to the political, rather than the strictly economic, objectives of the founding states. In fact, the primary motives for the integration of Western Europe can be summarized as peace, power, and prosperity: peace between erstwhile major combatants, France and Germany; power both to defend against aggression from the (then) Soviet Union and to counter the pre-eminence of the United States; and prosperity to meet the postwar demands of a devastated population.

Frederick Abbott (1995: 1) has provided a succinct summary of the key point here:

> The modern concept of an integrated Europe developed in the aftermath of World War II. The economies of the continental European countries had been devastated. Economic integration was viewed as a means to accelerate the rebuilding process by permitting European enterprises to take advantage of economies of scale. The modern integration process also embodied the political goal of creating inter-state political linkages which would reduce the possibility of another conflict such as the two which had plagued Europe in the first half of the twentieth century.

Thus, most observers take as given that European integration differs significantly from North American integration, partly because of the former's explicit commitment to supranationalism, but also because of the consciously political origins of that commitment. Less frequently recognized, however, is the primary consequence (or corollary) of that fundamental difference, namely that in Western Europe – unlike North America – the process of trade liberalization has been associated with the (re-)creation, rather than the contraction, of state power.

The sovereign power of European states – most notably France and (West) Germany – to take up arms against one another could not be reliably contained simply by diminishing the power and scope of the member governments to manage and otherwise intervene in their own domestic societies. To ensure peace between them, those sovereign powers needed to be overridden by the gradual creation of a 'super sovereign', one with the capacity to run all of the members' common affairs, and eventually their societies. The fact that this ultimate objective has been (as yet) only partially and imperfectly realized does not diminish the effect that the historical origins of the integration process in Europe has had on the balance between state and markets that has prevailed there throughout. The process of integration in Western Europe is about pooling state authority, not eroding it.

In the meantime, the governments of the countries of North America have set out more modestly to achieve only one of the three European goals for integration – prosperity – and the institutional component of their steps in that direction has been correspondingly more limited. It is likely to remain that way. Nobody expects Canada and/or Mexico to go to war against the United States of America and, oddly enough, this means that the *formal* sovereignty of all three members of the NAFTA is untouched by their commitment to economic integration. The 'peace' and 'power' objectives were either a foregone conclusion or beside the point in the North American context, given the inevitable deference of Canada and Mexico to the overweening power of the United States (Smith, P., 1993: chapter 14).[6] One can at least speculate, therefore, that the three-item rationale for integration motivating political elites in Western Europe is responsible for their long-standing commitment to the achievement of 'supergovernment' there, whereas the single-item agenda – or, rather, the absence of the peace and power agendas – of elites in North America is responsible for their lack of a comparable commitment to institution-building.

However, the fact that the North American commitment to economic integration, for all of the foregoing reasons, has not been accompanied by the creation of a supergovernment does not at all imply that it will not involve significant degrees of political integration. As this discussion will demonstrate in greater detail below, the NAFTA has set in motion a number of joint decision-making processes with considerable potential to bring about common economic policies and standardized treatment of investors across the three parties to the agreement. In doing so – as discussed in the third section, below – the NAFTA represents for the United States the achievement in its own neighborhood of an agenda it originally set for the entire international economy in the aftermath of World War II – the convergence of national economic policies and greater accessibility of foreign markets to American-based firms.

2.2 Game-Theoretical Factors The prospects for supranational decision-making in North America seem meager enough, given the discussion presented in the previous subsection. Moreover, as I argue in the present subsection, the likelihood of its emergence is reduced further by the difficulty of designing the rules according to which such institutions might operate, particularly given the small number of unequal partners involved in the integration of North America. Once again, special circumstances can be seen to have favoured the 'political integration as supra-nationalization' model for Europe, but only for Europe.

The number of actors in an organization and the degree of equality (or symmetry) among them are important characteristics of international organizations because they affect the manner in which each member weighs the costs and benefits of membership. For each party to the formation of any organization, the net benefit from joining it is the sum of the gains that forming the group is expected to promote minus the anticipated costs of belonging to it, such as the transaction costs involved in creating and running it, as well as the disadvantages that may flow from any unwanted decisions it may make. Thus, even where the creation of central authorities with particular supranational powers may seem to promise benefits, the perceived costs of designing, operating, and – not least – acting in conformity with such authorities may be reckoned too high, and the expected extra gains from trade or the elimination of negative externalities seem too modest by comparison.

Finally, even if a purely transactions-cost analysis proves positive, particular problems of institutional design may still render the creation and ongoing operation of joint decision-making institutions difficult, or even impossible. The literature on international organizations does not pay much attention to the problems of institutional design in general, or to decision rules in particular. This overall lack is equally true, to date, of studies of the NAFTA. Peter Smith, however, has drawn several conclusions about the prospects for joint decisionmaking in the NAFTA (and possible enlargements of it) using a combination of broadly theoretical perspectives and comparisons with the European Union (Smith, P., 1993: 14). Writing just before the NAFTA went into effect, he foresaw, first, that the three-party agreement would implicitly or explicitly entail unanimity among the members; second, that, for this reason, the decision-making machinery within it would be cumbersome and slow; and, third, that it would be subject to institutional paralysis (Smith, P., 1993: 376-7).[7]

Smith recognized further that the considerable disparity in size among NAFTA members would reinforce their determination to hold on to the unanimity principle. By the same logic, he cited the absence of a 'hegemon' in Western Europe as an important factor in promoting a spirit of give and take in negotiations within the (then) European Community. As he contended, it is 'this condition of relative parity - or, better said, lack of acute disparity - that has enabled the Community to establish its system of decision-making by qualified majority'(Smith, P., 1993: 379).

As Peter Smith (1993: 381) pointed out, there is no such prospect for North America, or even for the Western Hemisphere. The power of the United States relative to all its neighbors is so overwhelming that

> it is difficult to conjure up any form of qualified majority rule for decision-making within the Americas. The United States would naturally resist any scheme that would allow it to be outvoted, and Latin Americans (and Canadians) are likely to resist any scheme that would assure US domination.

3. Institutionalization and Harmonization Under the NAFTA

Both history and theory, therefore, suggest strongly that national governments on this side of the Atlantic are not very likely to take a path of political integration similar to that of the European Union. While both the European and North American experience represent a blend of the 'political integration as supranationalization' and the 'political integration as policy harmonization' models, the former clearly dominates in Europe and the latter prevails in North America. However, the NAFTA does create joint decision-making institutions – in fact, quite a number of them. However, the capacity of these institutions to super-sede national governments appears minor, while NAFTA provisions relating to policy harmonization – involving such matters as national treatment, rights of establishment, government procurement and international arbitration – are substantial.

A general review of the institutions created by the NAFTA will serve to document its relative balance in favor of the integration-as-harmonization model.

3.1 Institutional Provisions in the NAFTA At first, the North American Free Trade Commission (created directly under Article 2001) appeared to be the most prominent institution associated with the NAFTA. The Commission on Labor Cooperation and the Commission on Environmental Cooperation (created, respectively, by two Supplementary Agreements) were also conspicuous because they were intensely debated during ratification by the US Senate. Since the early years of the NAFTA regime, however, the Environmental Commission is the only one of the three to maintain a reasonably high profile, as measured by the degree of academic attention and interest group activity it has attracted. Also of interest to Americans, but less so to Canadians because they are not a party to them, are the Border Environmental Cooperation Commission and the North American Development Bank, both of which are primarily concerned with joint US-Mexican environmental projects.[8]

These NAFTA commissions are not invested with supranational authority comparable to the chief agencies of the European Union. The Free Trade Commission (FTC) is composed of cabinet level representatives and was assigned the role of overseeing the implementation of the Agreement, as well as supervising its dispute resolution processes. These roles are implemented on the basis of consensus (i.e., unanimous agreement) among the Parties (Abbott, 1995: 28). In any case, apart from routine administration by its Secretariat – which operates strictly under mandates delegated by consensus among the Parties – the FTC seems practically dormant.

Arguably, one activity of the FTC that does merit attention is the oversight and general direction it gives the Secretariat's management and coordination of the NAFTA's widening constellation of committees and working groups.[9] As of 1997, according to Sidney Weintraub, there were 24 committees and working groups under NAFTA and 'in each case their duties correspond to a particular clause in the agreement' (Weintraub, 1997: 71). More specifically, the NAFTA creates (among others) committees on Trade in Goods, Agricultural Trade, Standards-Related Measures, Small Business, and Financial Services. There are also working groups bearing titles such as Rules of Origin; Agricultural Subsidies; Meat and Poultry Inspection; Dairy, Fruit, Vegetable and Egg Inspection; Trade and Competition; Procurement; Services and Investment; Import Surges; and

Subsidies/Countervailing Duties and Anti-Dumping. Finally, the agreement contains articles creating the Land Transportation Standards and Telecommunications Standards Subcommittees.

According to de Vanssay and Mahant, despite the presence of the FTC and the operations of some of its delegated agencies, the NAFTA's institutional structure is 'decentralized and apparently uncoordinated' compared with the quasi-federal institutional structure of the European Union. Over all, they conclude that, 'NAFTA's institutional structure is far behind that of the European Union in terms of supranationality, if not in complexity' (de Vanssay and Mahant, 1996: 138). In fact, the functional specificity of the responsibilities delegated by the NAFTA is, in itself, a measure of this lack of supranationality; the assignment of narrow, essentially technical tasks is generally acknowledged to be a hallmark of international organizations designed to promote cooperation without impinging on the sovereign powers of member governments.

Despite the lack of supranational powers attached to these various agencies, however, their potential contribution to the harmonization of national policies – and, therefore, their contribution to North American political integration by that definition – should not be dismissed out of hand. Indeed, a recent article has described the NAFTA 'as an ongoing framework under which deeper and even broader economic and policy integration will occur' (Rugman, Kirton and Soloway, 1997: 200). According to this study, the NAFTA's elaborate set of 'new intergovernmental bodies' – meaning its commissions, committees and working groups – are a key element in a wider dynamic of community formation, that is, 'the emergence of a sense of North American community, beginning with an acceptance of a significant and irreversible interdependence and common future among those in the three countries – at the governmental, corporate, NGO, and individual levels' (Rugman, Kirton and Soloway, 1997: 204).[10]

In fact, when the mandate for each committee or working group is tied back to its corresponding clause in the agreement, one can see that the standardization of national approaches is often an important part of that mandate. The NAFTA provisions with respect to 'Standards-Related Measures' (Chapter 9, Article 913) are a case in point. According to Chapter 9, each party pledges nondiscriminatory treatment in the application of any such measures it adopts.[11] However, Article 913 also establishes a Committee on Standards Related Measures charged, among other things, to facilitate the process by which the parties make these measures compatible. In doing so, it is also meant to 'consider non-governmental developments in standards-related measures'.

Similarly, part of the terms of reference for the Working Group on Trade and Competition Policy is 'to make recommendations on relevant issues concerning the relationship between competition laws and policies and trade in the free trade area' (Chapter 15, Article 1504). Among the tasks consigned to this working group are a review of 'differences in mergers and vertical-restraint regimes', as well as possible participation with the private sector in a roundtable on trade and competition.

Further work on the actual operations of these agencies will be necessary before anyone can legitimately assess their impact on Canada-US trade and investment relations. Yet even this bare sampling of the institutional provisions contained in the agreement indicates their potential to promote, at the very least, mutual recognition of the parties' standards and practices and possibly harmonization of those standards and practices. Moreover, there are similarly strong indications, both in the language of relevant provisions of the Agreement and in academic studies of the performance of NAFTA's committees and working groups, that business corporations are highly active players in the process of policy harmonization.[12]

Indeed, the 'political integration as policy harmonization' model dovetails perfectly with the role of multinational corporations in the process of policy standardization. International firms have an interest in the preserving the sovereign power of states to maintain property rights and to enforce international contracts. At the same time, such firms have no wish to see those sovereign powers invested in a global superstate, and therefore they have no strong desire to see existing nation-states disappear. However, they do hope to ensure that maintaining a multiplicity of sovereign states does not continue to represent a patchwork of trade- and investment-related policies at the national level that both complicates their global management of assets, production and marketing and inflates their transaction costs. Thus, to join actively in the negotiations among governments to reduce differences in national policies – whether through universal trade organizations such as the WTO or through regional organizations such as the NAFTA – is the preferred remedy for the costs and complexities that system friction causes for multinational enterprises.

This conclusion is consistent with the past fifty-five years of United States leadership of the international economy. Sylvia Ostry has ably and convincingly demonstrated that a primary objective of American economic foreign policy makers since the end of World War II (apart from the reduction of foreign tariffs) has been to make the domestic economic policy environment in other countries more open to competition from American multinational corporations – what we today refer to broadly as 'rights of establishment' (Ostry, 1997: 233). Indeed, one of the principal reasons for the America's failure to achieve international acceptance of a prospective International Trade Organization (ITO) after World War II was the inability of the United States government to get its principal post-war economic partners to agree to measures designed to reduce the differences in national economic systems and to improve the contestabilty of foreign markets by American-based producers of goods and services.

Even more telling, the American administration's ITO initiative was ultimately aborted by the US Congress, and the weaker GATT was all that the United States and its international negotiating partners could bring into being. Ostry contends that behind this congressional opposition, apart from some academic and ideological perfectionism, was the protectionism – or, perhaps more fairly, the counter-protectionism – of powerful American business lobbies. At the heart of this American business opposition, she argues, 'was a rejection of the idea that there can be many variants of market systems, with different institutional arrangements including different mixes of government and business roles. And where such differences existed, they were, in the view of American business, probably unfairly protectionist' (Ostry, 1997: 65).

In the present context, it is worth remembering that back then the United States' preferred means of advancing this agenda was emphatically *not* to bring nations together under a world government, but merely to make national economic policies everywhere conform more closely to those of the United States – a posture it has retained more recently with the last round of the GATT negotiations and the creation of the WTO. From this perspective, the NAFTA represents the realization of the United States' postwar global economic agenda in its 'own' regional trade association.

4. Implications for Democratic Accountability

The above analysis appears to have at least two general applications to the issues of democratic accountability and transnational democracy under conditions of globalization. One of these is simply to examine the implications of the NAFTA for democracy in its three member countries. The other is to examine the implications for democracy of deepening economic integration worldwide, using the experience of the EU and the NAFTA as contrasting templates. With respect to the first of these applications, this discussion will do no more than to focus on a few observations concerning the impact of the NAFTA (so far) on Canadian democracy and accountability. With respect to the second, this discussion will conclude with a brief defence of the view that a projection of the NAFTA model, rather than the EU one, is the most appropriate and fruitful way to appreciate the implications global economic integration for democracy and transnational democratic movements.

4.1 The NAFTA and Canadian Democracy   One of the most important conclusions supported by the foregoing analysis is that government authorities in the three NAFTA countries have not been very forthcoming with their publics when it comes to the politics of trade liberalization. The 'official line' on trade agreements tends to reject or simply ignore two of their critics' most persistent and forceful complaints: first, that they are more about investment and the rights of corporations than they are about trade and, second, that as such they have the potential to bring about significant changes in national politics and government policies.

Despite these (and other) shortcomings in the debate over market liberalization, few Canadians are likely to join demonstrations against future free trade agreements, let alone hurl tear-gas canisters back at thin black lines of municipal swat teams. In fact, to the contrary, opinion polls tell us that a significant majority of Canadians support being part of the NAFTA in principle, and a plurality of them believe that the overall effects of the NAFTA have been favourable.[13] However, similar polls suggest strongly that a majority of Canadians (to date) have done exactly what their elites, as argued above, have consistently wanted them to do, namely to associate free trade agreements simply and exclusively with the reduction of trade barriers. When large numbers of Canadians associate free trade agreements closely with things they do not regard positively, such as the possible erosion of Canadian social policies or increased foreign ownership of Canadian business, the proportion of them who endorse such agreements is noticeably weaker, or at least more qualified.[14]

In fact, it appears that the global trade liberalization agenda encounters greater and greater skepticism – if not outright opposition – the more that international trade agreements and associations are perceived to impinge on domestic social, labour, and environmental policies, and the more that intergovernmental decisions in these fields are perceived to favour the interests of corporations at the expense of populations at home or abroad, especially in the Third World. Matthew Mendelsohn and Robert Wolfe make essentially this point in a carefully researched and argued survey of Canadian attitudes toward free trade over time. These authors observe that '[d]omestic framework policies are now at the heart of the trade agenda' and note, further, that recent opposition to the WTO and the ongoing free trade agenda is largely focused on the domestic impact of market liberalization:

> [t]he WTO has come to be seen by some activists as globalization incarnate because trade is the vector that brings policies in different countries into conflict, and when the WTO mediates such conflict, it can be portrayed as favouring multinational enterprises. The WTO may become even more of a lightning rod for concerns about globalization because it seems to displace parliament from its role with regard to formerly domestic decisions about the environment, human rights and many other policy domains – telecoms, competition, health, education, magazines, asbestos, beef hormones, and others (Mendelsohn and Wolfe, 2000: 14).

It seems highly probable that, as the NAFTA's working groups and other institutions begin to affect national policies in many of these same fields and in similar ways, a growing number of Canadians will begin to associate free trade with two things they very well may not like: first, their own disenfranchisement and, second, a decline in the capacity of their governments – as Mendelsohn and Wolfe put it – to help Canadians help one another (2000: 15).

For the present, however, the majority of Canadians seem content in their belief that Canada's autonomy in the domestic policy domains highlighted by Mendelsohn and Wolfe is secure, mostly because they accept the argument that associations such as the GATT/WTO and the NAFTA are exclusively about reductions in trade barriers. In this, they appear to believe that political integration is outside the scope of such agreements, precisely because the latter do not entail formal transfers of power to European-style governing institutions.

4.2 Global Economic Integration and Transnational Democracy   The comparisons between the EU and the NAFTA presented in the foregoing discussion support the conclusion that the NAFTA is the more valuable model for understanding the manner in which deep global integration will affect the prospects for the accountability of national governments across the world. There are two principal reasons for this. One reason is that the United States, as noted above, has no interest in witnessing (much less leading) the creation of world institutions modeled on the supranationalism embedded in the central institutions of the EU. Instead, the United States has a strong interest in promoting global political integration in the form of policy harmonization, which has been the guiding strategy of its economic foreign policy since the end of World War II and which it has already achieved to a degree in many provisions of the NAFTA. The other reason is that the prospects for building democratic accountability into global supranational institutions modeled on the EU seem extremely remote.

For both reasons, moreover, there is a case for making the 're-democratization' of national governments (or simply their democratization, where democracy does not currently exist) the central focus of the transnational democratic movement. As Ian Clark has argued persuasively, globalization is not *promoting* state transformation, it *is* state transformation. Moreover, one aspect of this transformation process is that states are becoming less democratic and accountable to voting majorities and the demands of domestic groups. In Clark's view, the persistence of what he calls 'the Great Divide' – essentially, the fundamental separation within the International Relations paradigm between the 'internal' domain of national politics and the 'external' domain of international politics – continues to obscure the impact of globalization on democracy. Analysis under the influence of the Great Divide, he writes,

> maintains that the democratic shortcomings of the contemporary state have arisen because of the growth of globalized forces that disempower it from outside. As a result, its democratic procedures barely conceal the nakedness within. If the situation is to be retrieved, the scope of democratic accountability must be extended beyond the state so that it matches the global reach of the influences that wash up on its shores. Such an analysis fails to take due account of the reciprocal manner in which democratic deficits on the inside have been the necessary accomplices of globalization (Clark, I., 1999: 165-166).

This is not the place to explore, even in principle, the most promising agenda for the politics of 're-nationalizing' democracy. However, this discussion's brief look at the Canadian case suggests that such an agenda would probably have a lot to do with restoring the balance between the requirements of the 'embedded liberal state' and the demands of the international economic order that prevailed in the West during the Cold War. Whatever specific objectives it might entail, the prospects of genuine democracy emerging (or re-emerging) from the pursuit of such an agenda seem far less remote and fanciful than hopes for democratizing global institutions. In any event, unless one (somewhat bizarrely) envisages a world parliament analogous to the European Parliament – presumably along the lines of a directly elected United Nations General Assembly – any genuine democratization of intergovernmental organizations (as the term itself implies) can only be achieved by holding governments that assemble under the auspices of these organizations accountable to their respective publics.

Finally, it is worth noting that the re-democratization of national politics argued for here need not take place to the exclusion of transnational social movements and advocacy networks, as discussed in Markoff and Morrison and outlined in detail in Alger (all this volume). Indeed, it might not succeed in the absence of connections with such developments, given that one of the positive aspects of globalization is surely the manner in which national protest movements can and do inspire, inform and support one another through advanced communications technologies and the reduced cost of travel. The points made here do not add up to an argument for limiting the geographic scope of democratic movements, but only to focus them and their campaigns on the task of keeping national governments democratically accountable. This includes holding them to account for both what they do at the level of international organizations and what they do to their national societies in the course of implementing international agreements at the national level. Here the primary reference is to Susan Strange's complaint that what is lacking in global governance to date is an opposition. By this she expressly does not mean a 'loyal opposition' in the formal sense of some parliamentary systems, but more generally 'some combination of forces to check the arbitrary or self-serving use of power and to see that it is used at least in part for the common good' (Strange, 1996: 198). She goes on to compare this formula for democratic accountability to Daniel Deudney's notion of 'negarchy', or the power to negate, limit or constrain authority.

The final point of this discussion, then, is that Deudney's negarchy is still best realized at the level of national politics. As John Hall and Katherine Fierlbeck also recognize in this volume, national sovereignty still matters – not least to transnational corporations who know that they cannot conduct international exchanges without a binding legal authority at each end of them and, further, that a global leviathan to regulate world markets would become their worst nightmare. National governments exercise that national sovereignty, whether acting alone in domestic affairs or in concert with others in international fora, and therefore remain the primary agents in world politics. Negarchy could thus take the form mass protests at the venues where the intergovernmental mechanisms of economic integration are set in motion, as recent demonstrations against the WTO and the like have shown. However, it is possible that it could more productively take the form of national protests against respective national governments on their return home from such meetings.

As Ian Clark would have it, if globalization 'does' anything, it does it through actions performed by existing national and subnational governments. The point of transnational democracy should be to have national oppositions mutually inform and support one another in efforts not only to bring the state 'back in', but also back home. In sum, opposition to globalization should consist primarily of transnational cooperation among national oppositions, each devoted to convincing its own national government that it will not survive if its actions fail to promote the common good of its citizens. If national democratic movements are unable to succeed at this objective, it is hard to imagine how transnational ones can be expected to succeed in making global government accountable to anyone.

Notes

1 Some readers may find it useful to pause over some of the terminology involved here. The politics of international economic integration is essentially about reducing the ways in which – and the extent to which – government policies impede the international movement of the factors of production. Government policies can block or encumber such flows *at the border* by prohibiting the entry of some or all such factors into national markets, or they may inhibit such flows *behind the border* by discriminating against foreign producers or investors in the application of national policies and regulations.

    The distinction between impediments 'at' and 'behind' national borders roughly corresponds to a further distinction between *shallow* (more purely economic) and *deep* (more expressly political) integration. Governments engage in shallow integration when they agree to lift restrictions at their borders through commonly accepted changes to national trade policy, most typically by removing tariffs or quotas against one another's goods. Additionally (or alternatively) governments engage in deep integration when they afford each other's citizens 'national' (that is, non-discriminatory) treatment in behind-the-border measures, such as the application of standards or performance requirements. Beyond this, governments may deepen integration even further by agreeing to reduce or eliminate differences in national policies, economic or any other, that impinge on the ability of each country's producers to sell in the other's markets. See Keohane and Hoffmann, 1990: 299, fn38.

2 See Ostry, 1997: 100-10.

3 Richard N. Cooper identifies factor-price equalization, defined as 'uniform wages (except for differences in skills, etc.), common interest rates on comparable financial assets, and equal profits on comparable investments,' as one of three useful definitions of economic integration (along with an end to discriminatory national policies and the achievement of optimum economic cooperation). See Cooper, 1968: 10.

4 See, for example, Lipsey, Schwanen and Wonnacott, 1994: 7-8. The phrase is attributed to Sylvia Ostry's *Governments and Corporations in a Shrinking World* (1990).

5 The quoted phrase is taken from Appendini and Bislev (1999).

6 Viewed from a slightly different angle, however, the power dimension may not have been totally absent in relation to the NAFTA. Some international trade observers have argued that one of the American motives in seeking North American free trade was to hedge against the consolidation of the world economy into European and Asian blocs; the NAFTA was a shot across the bow of the members of the other regional blocs, warning them to pursue more seriously the agenda for deeper economic integration through the GATT/WTO. A few such observers label this the 'domino effect'.

7 Peter Smith (1993: 376-7) sets out the logic that led to this conclusion as follows: 'The range of decision rules bears a direct relationship to the number of parties involved. Almost by definition, bilateral arrangements entail the principle of unanimity: both parties possess a veto. Trilateral agreements present the theoretical possibility of majority rule, but without any system of qualification. The risk of losing out in a two-to-one vote leads parties to prefer unanimity (or to refrain from joining in the first place).'

8   See Abbott, 1995: 28-30.

9   See McKinney (2000: 26-7): 'In addition to their annual meetings, the Free Trade Commission has established other mechanisms for fostering communication and for overseeing the work program of the various NAFTA committees and working groups. At their meeting on 29 April 1998, the Free Trade Commission members directed their deputy ministers to meet regularly twice a year, "to provide high-level, ongoing oversight of the NAFTA work program".... Furthermore, NAFTA coordinators (chosen from within each of the respective ministries) ... confer monthly by telephone to discuss the progress of the various committees and working groups and to help keep their work organized'.

10 In the conclusions to their analysis (215), the authors succinctly characterize the FTA/NAFTA as 'a quasi-political regime to complement the integrated economic and business systems of Canada and the United States'.

11 The section reads, in part, as follows: 'Each Party shall, in respect of its standards-related measures, accord to goods and service providers of another Party: (a) national treatment in accordance with Article 301 (Market Access) or Article 1202 (Cross-Border Trade in Services); and (b) treatment no less favorable than that it accords to like goods, or in like circumstances to service providers, of any other country'.

12 The author has not been able to find many academic treatments of business participation in NAFTA decision-making. Rugman, Kirton and Soloway develop a brief case study of business-government relations under the auspices of the NAFTA in the chemicals sector (1997: 212-15). Indirect evidence that such activity is both present and significant is available in Blank and Haar, *Making NAFTA Work: U.S. Firms and the New North American Business Environment* (1999). This study presents an excellent account of the close interconnections between North American business rationalization and deepening continental integration. The authors conclude (84) that 'pressures on U.S. firms to integrate across North America will continue and even intensify', and they therefore 'speak with confidence of a dynamic, rapidly evolving and deepening North American economy'. Finally, Susan K. Sell has shown how U.S. firms actively lobbied for favorable treatment of intellectual property rights under the WTO (modeled on provisions they had already achieved under the NAFTA) in Sell (2000: chapter 5).

13 See Media Release Center, 2001. The release points out that 'this is down from its highest level of support (70 per cent) in October 1999 but well ahead of and Ipsos-Reid poll of February 1999 that showed only 46 percent in favour of the initiative'. The release also reports that 40 percent of Canadians believe that the country has benefitted since being part of the agreement, as opposed to 32 percent who believe it has been hurt and 23 percent who believe it has had no impact.

14 Despite overall support for the NAFTA, eighty-four percent of Canadians surveyed by the Canadian Centre for Research and Information on Canada said that they would place restrictions on American investment in Canada to prevent investors from taking control of Canadian companies. (This was up ten percentage points from 1964, when the same question was put). As CRIC points out, these respondents seem to be ignorant of the fact that any such (new) restrictions would contravene the FTA and the NAFTA, a fact which tends to confirm the point made here that most Canadians who support so-called free trade agreements are generally not aware that they are about much more than simply trade relations. See CRIC Papers (2001: 15).

Part III

Fashioning and Evaluating Transnational Democracy

Chapter 9

Assessing Democracy at National and International Levels

David Beetham

For a number of years prior to 2002 I was working for the International Institute for Democracy and Electoral Assistance (IDEA), Stockholm, directing a programme of democracy assessment in countries from different regions of the world. This work involved developing a framework and methodology for assessing or 'auditing' democracy in any country, developed or developing, and piloting its use with in-country partners in eight selected countries (Bangladesh, El Salvador, Italy, Kenya, Malawi, New Zealand, Peru and South Korea). The programme has so far produced a number of different types of publication: full-length country assessments published in-country; a comparative volume of assessment summaries, comparative tables and conclusions about the achievements and challenges of the democratization process (Beetham et al., 2002b); and a handbook on democracy assessment for anyone to use for their own country (Beetham et al., 2002a). The last of these publications has inspired or contributed to many projects of democracy assessment across the world.

The purpose of the present chapter is to explore three questions arising from this programme that are relevant to the theme of the nation-state and transnational democracy. They are:

Q1. What assumptions about the global reach of democracy are implicit in a project of individual country assessments, and how can they be justified?

Q2. What issues about the transnational aspects of democracy are raised in the assessment of individual countries?

Q3. How far can the criteria used for assessing democracy at the level of the nation-state be used for the assessment of international institutions?

1. Q1. What assumptions about the global reach of democracy are implicit in a project of individual country assessments, and how can they be justified?

A brief explanation is in order to begin with about the purpose and methodology of our project. There are many different purposes that a democracy assessment might serve. The primary purpose of our assessments has been to conduct a systematic analysis of the strengths and weaknesses in the different aspects of a country's democratic life, as a contribution to public debate and possible reform in that country. Only secondarily have we been concerned to draw comparative conclusions from the separate country studies for wider analysis. The first of these purposes has required that the assessments be conducted by citizens of the country involved, who take the responsibility for the judgements made, and that the preliminary findings be exposed to a domestic panel of reviewers with different expertise and viewpoints. The second purpose has required that the assessments be conducted according to a common framework of enquiry, with common search questions guiding the investigations in each case. Although this framework had its origins in a project of auditing democracy in the UK, it was subsequently revised and considerably expanded in discussions with participants from the countries being assessed, together with other contributors from both North and South. We have ourselves used this expanded framework in our latest audit of the state of democracy in the UK (Beetham et al., 2002c).

A copy of the assessment framework, with the full list of search questions, is appended to this chapter. The framework starts with an assessment of citizens' rights, including social and economic rights; continues with the institutions of representative and accountable government; analyzes the character of civil society; and concludes with the international dimensions of a country's democracy. All the questions for investigation are phrased in the comparative mode (how much? how far? etc.), on the assumption that democracy is not an all-or-nothing affair but is a matter of degree. They are also all so arranged that the stronger the answer, the more democratic the aspect of a country's political life can be deemed to be. However, we reject the view that the different aspects can be summed together to produce a quantitative score or 'league table' of democracy. Most countries will be better in some respects than others, and it is the task of an assessment to identify these through a differentiated approach such as our framework makes possible. At first sight the list of questions looks formidable, but they can be answered at different levels of detail; and our experience shows that an assessment team comprising different types of expertise can achieve a thorough assessment in a relatively short space of time, provided the work is clearly focused.

Any programme of democracy assessment, especially one with ambitions to a global reach as ours has, makes a number of assumptions which it would be useful to spell out explicitly, even if there is not the space to defend them in full.

The *first* is that democracy is to be defined primarily by a set of principles or regulative ideals, and only secondarily by the institutional arrangements and procedures through which these principles are realized to a greater or lesser degree. Starting with institutions begs the question of what it is that makes them democratic in the first place. It also encourages disillusionment with 'democracy' when these institutions turn out to operate in a non-democratic way, or are used for anti-democratic purposes. To start with principles enables us to show what contribution particular institutions make to their realization; and it establishes the criteria against which we can assess how democratically these institutions are working in practice. It also allows us to investigate arrangements which may not usually be thought of as part of democracy, but which may prove to be democratically significant in certain societies (or at the international level – see below).

The accompanying table (Table 9.1) sets out how we get from our core democratic principles (popular control and political equality) via a set of 'mediating values' (participation, authorization, representation, accountability, transparency, responsiveness, and solidarity) to the different institutional arrangements of a typical representative democracy. As should be evident, some institutions serve to realize more than one value (as the electoral process does the values of participation, authorization, representation, and accountability simultaneously), while some values require a variety of institutional arrangements for their realization (e.g., the accountability of office holders).

The *second* is that these principles have a global reach in two quite distinct (though complementary) senses. At the *philosophical* level of the discursive justification of normative principles, any justification of them requires us to make universalistic claims which do not stop at the shores of the West or the North. Although this is a contested doctrine, it seems to me self-evident that democracy can only be defended against paternalism in all its varieties (which is the only serious alternative) by reference to some universal features of human nature. In brief, it is human equality that makes democracy *desirable*, human capacities that make it *possible*, and all-too human limitations that make it *necessary*. No defence against our own home-grown forms of paternalism, let alone exotic ones, is possible without reference to these considerations; it cannot be done simply in terms of 'the way we do things here'.

At the *empirical* level, it is a matter of common observation that there are numerous people in all societies across the globe who subscribe to democratic principles, and who want them for, or are struggling to realize them in, their own societies. Whereas, on the other hand, the paternalist alternatives (some elite 'knows best') have only a limited range, either territorially or in terms of the populations to whom they are claimed to apply. This does not mean that democratic principles have yet won universal acclaim. But their reach is certainly global, and the contestation over them occurs as much *within* all societies as *between* them.

The *third* assumption is that the same framework of assessment questions is applicable to both developed and developing democracies, since what counts as 'democratic' is the same in both. To say this is not to assume that all political systems which are not dictatorships are necessarily 'transiting' towards some teleological goal called 'democracy' (see Carothers, 2002). All that is required is that enough people in a given country should find some value in taking stock of where they stand from a democratic point of view, and in what respects. Nor is this to commit the fallacy of 'voluntarism', which has been levelled against the 'crafting democracies' approach (Di Palma, 1990). What a project of democracy assessment recognizes is that, whatever the limiting conditions or circumstances, democratization in any degree never occurs without conscious collective struggle.

Table 9.1   Democratic Principles and Mediating Values

Basic principles:
- *popular control* over public decision making and decision
- *equality* of respect and voice between citizens in the exercise of that control

Mediating values	Requirements	Institutional means of realization
participation	rights to participate capacities/resources to participate agencies for participation participatory culture	civil and political rights system economic and social rights elections, parties, NGOs education for citizenship
authorization	validation of constitution choice of office holders/programmes control of elected over non-elected executive personnel	referenda free and fair elections systems of subordination to elected officials
representation	legislature representative of main currents of popular opinion all public institutions representative of social composition of electorate	electoral and party system anti-discrimination laws affirmative action policies
accountability	clear lines of accountability, legal, financial, political, to ensure effective and honest performance civil service and judicial integrity	rule of law, separation of powers independent auditing process legally enforceable standards strong parliamentary scrutiny powers
transparency	government open to legislative and public scrutiny	freedom of information legislation independent media

responsiveness	accessibility of government to electors and different sections of public opinion in policy formation, implementation and service delivery	systematic and open procedures of public consultation effective legal redress local government close to people
solidarity	tolerance of diversity at home support for democratic governments. and popular democratic struggles abroad	civic & human rights education international human rights law UN and other agencies international NGOs

Defining what you are striving for, and identifying what the key obstacles may be, constitutes a necessary, if modest, part of this process.

To say that the same framework of assessment questions can be used for both developed and developing democracies does not mean that they will necessarily apply the same standards of what counts as a good level of democratic practice. The choice of appropriate comparators is a matter best left to domestic assessors. They may wish to concentrate on a historical benchmark, from which they may chart significant progress or regress. Or they may wish to assess themselves against comparator countries in the same region. Or against targets set by their own government. Or against standards of best practice internationally. Or some combination of all four. This is a matter of political and not just academic judgement.

One important conclusion, however, that has emerged from our pilot studies, is that the sites of greatest democratic deficit in recently democratizing countries are precisely the sites where long-established democracies have also experienced the most intractable problems. This is perhaps hardly surprising if one acknowledges that inegalitarian and counter-democratic tendencies are intrinsic to capitalist economies and the structure of the modern state everywhere. It is these tendencies that make the agendas of democratization similar in different places, and that also serve to justify a common framework of investigation for a democracy assessment.

As I shall argue below (see Q3), we cannot simply take it for granted that democratic criteria are the appropriate ones for the assessment of international institutions, or that, if so, they should replicate those applicable to individual countries. However, the universalistic assumptions explored in answer to this first question provide at least a necessary jumping-off point for consideration of the international level. To know that democratic principles, if they have any validity and applicability, must do so universally, at least puts them into serious contention for the assessment of global institutions.

2. Q2. What issues about the transnational aspects of democracy are raised in the assessment of individual countries?

It is frequently said nowadays that democracy has been 'hollowed out' at the national level, since increasingly decisions that are important for the welfare of a nation's people are taken beyond its borders, whether by other governments, international institutions, multinational companies or a variety of other non-state actors. What is the use of the democratic principle of popular control if the government to be controlled has little power itself over the issues that matter for its citizens' well-being? We do not have to engage in debate as to whether this concern has been exaggerated (or, conversely, whether there ever was a golden age when nation states had full control of their own affairs) to acknowledge that a democracy assessment which omitted the external dimension of a country's governance would be inadequate. Indeed, the perspective of separate country studies shows up the variability of external influences at work, and their differential impact on different states, in contrast to generalized claims about the effects of 'globalization'.

A number of questions in our assessment framework (see appendix) can be used to explore the impact of external agencies which may affect a country's democratic performance. Q1.3 about the degree of consensus on state boundaries can reveal any cross-border influences on national security. Q2.1 about the reach of the rule of law can be used to explore the significance of international mafia, drugs cartels, mercenaries, arms distributors, and so on (compare Q8.4). Section 4 on economic and social rights can identify the decisions of external agencies which constrain a government's economic and welfare policy. Q4.6 on the regulation of corporations can be used to explore the extent of regulatory evasion, tax avoidance, etc., by multinational companies. The general question at 7.1 about government control over the policy arena can be used to identify external as well as internal obstacles to effective self-governance. Q10.1 asks explicitly about foreign media ownership. And so on.

However there is also a whole section of the framework (section 14) which is explicitly devoted to the international aspects of a country's democracy, and the problems raised by the questions in this section are worth discussing briefly, as they touch on many of the themes of this volume. Taken as a whole the section tries to strike a balance between externally imposed limitations on a country's decision making (Q14.1), and those which are voluntarily assumed through international treaties, or which can be reasonably expected of a country that claims to be democratic (Q14.3 to 14.5). Admittedly this distinction is not watertight, and Q14.2 occupies a somewhat uneasy boundary between the two, depending on how we interpret the term 'partnership', and which side of an unequal partnership relation a country is deemed to fall. Most countries in the South which have been at the receiving end of IMF structural adjustment policies regard these policies as an external imposition, and as evidence of 'subordination to an external agency' (Q14.1), even though they may technically be members of the organization concerned. This is because they see no genuine partnership in the organization, but rather the dominance within it of the creditor countries and their banks, which follow an orthodox 'Washington consensus' (Stiglitz, 2002).

Even institutions whose membership is reasonably fair and equal, however, such as the European Union or the Council of Europe, can be perceived as agencies of subordination from the standpoint of individual countries. Admittedly this is more likely to happen where a particular decision runs counter to public opinion or government policy or both. At the same time a perception of subordination is given weight where there is a lack of transparency or accountability in the operation of the organization concerned, or a lack of serious public debate about a country's responsibilities towards it. So the character of the internal organization of an international body will make a difference as to whether its decisions are seen as externally imposed or voluntarily assumed from the standpoint of any individual country.

Should our view about the democratic significance of some externally determined decision be affected if the decision in question leads to an enhancement of democratic rights in a country? A number of decisions about UK law or administrative practice made by the European Court of Human Rights at Strasbourg, which the government has contested, have improved particular civil and political rights in the country. The same can be said about decisions made by the EU on employment and consumer rights which have run counter to government policy. A useful distinction can be made here between the democracy-enhancing *content* or *substance* of a policy, rule or decision, and the *procedures* by which it is arrived at. What makes organizations like the IMF, World Bank, WTO, etc., seem so biased to many in the South is that both the procedures of decision making and their consequences are experienced as disempowering.

This distinction between democratic procedure and substance is particularly relevant to Q14.5 about a country's support for human rights and democracy abroad, especially if we read it in conjunction with Q14.3 about its respect for international law. When the UK government gave support to the elected President of Sierra Leone who had been deposed, and did so through the mercenaries and weapons provided by a private company, Sandline, it was in clear violation of a UN resolution. How should we view this? Or when former imperial powers impose conditions on aid and trade with former colonies, which may trigger sanctions in cases of flagrant government violation of democratic norms, does this count as 'support for democracy'? Almost invariably such actions entail siding with one set of internal political forces over another, and can readily be interpreted as interference in a country's internal affairs and as 'neo-colonialism' (see the sharp division within the Commonwealth and between the EU and SADCC over the imposition of sanctions on President Mugabe in the run up to the Presidential elections of 2002).

The potential conflict between democratic procedure and substance, or between means and ends, is at its starkest when military force is involved, and the invasion of state sovereignty. The US-led invasion of Afghanistan, originally justified in terms of self-defence against the al-Qaida network, was rapidly extended to include the removal of the Taliban regime and the imposition of a democratic system of government. Yet the war's bombing raids predictably brought widespread violations of the human rights to life, health, and shelter for Afghan civilians, and left a highly unstable regime behind once the war was declared officially over. Judgements about the legal and moral justifiability of such actions are bound to prove controversial. The wording of our Q14.5, however, attempts to provide some guidance in the phrase '*support* for human rights and democracy abroad', and by inviting assessment of the *consistency* of a government's record over time.

To be sure, it is partly the absence to date of any recognizably impartial body with enforcement powers to adjudicate serious violations of democratic and human rights norms, that leads states to take unilateral initiatives. Yet we should not imagine that the existence of such a body would resolve all controversy about what, say, counts as 'democratic' in a given country, nor avoid decisions which privilege one set of internal political forces over another. The European Court of Human Rights (ECHR) is rightly regarded as a model for the impartial international adjudication of civil and political rights questions, involving the key right of individual complaint and an enforcement mechanism for its judgements. Its position, however, gives it a substantial and sometimes controversial right of determination over the internal organization of its member states, which would be even more contested if such a body were to be established at the wider international level.

Consider, for example, a recent decision by the Court (July 2001) about political parties in Turkey. Turkey's own constitutional court had previously taken a decision to order the disbandment of the Welfare Party and the sequestration of its funds, on the grounds that its Chairman and some of its leading MPs were on record as having advocated the introduction of sharia law for the country's Muslim majority, though no such proposal was mentioned in the party's programme or manifesto. The party had the most popular support in the country and was a member of the coalition government of the time. The MPs in question (who had also been dismissed from parliament) appealed to the ECHR on grounds of violation of their fundamental freedoms of expression and association. The case divided the court. A majority of four judges argued that 'there can be no democracy where the people of a state, even by a majority decision, waive their legislative and judicial powers in favour of an entity which is not responsible to the people it governs.' A minority of three argued *per contra* that democracy was meaningless without the free expression of electoral opinion, and that this was 'inconceivable without the participation of a plurality of political parties representing different shades of opinion' (Council of Europe, 2001).

The case went in favour of disbanding the Welfare Party, though it could easily have gone the other way. In effect, the ECHR was ruling that the introduction of sharia law was incompatible with democracy, and that a country's electorate required protection from the unfortunate consequences of its own decisions, if necessary with the support of an international judicial body. Whatever we may think about the content of this judgement, it shows that deciding what counts as democratic in given circumstances may be deeply controversial, and that the introduction of an international dimension makes it even more so.

Given that the questions of our section 14 are especially likely to involve contestable judgements, therefore, it is important that those engaged in an assessment should at least acknowledge the main potential disagreements of evaluation, even if they come down clearly on one side of the argument. It may not be possible or desirable to achieve a political balance within an assessment team, since a variety of disciplinary expertise is a more pressing requirement. However, it is important that a draft country assessment should be openly debated in a conference comprising a full range of political viewpoints, including some regional and international contributors, as we have done in our pilot studies in the IDEA project. In this way, a country assessment can serve to open up debate about the meaning of democracy itself, as well as about the specific evaluation of a country's record.

3. Q3. How far can the criteria used for assessing democracy at the level of the nation-state be used for the assessment of international institutions?

The previous section has already touched on some of the issues raised by this question, since it has proved impossible to answer questions about the external profile of a country's democracy without some assessment of the international agencies to which it is exposed or in which it is itself involved. These issues now need addressing more systematically. I shall do so by again posing a series of questions.

First, which institutions are appropriate subjects for assessment? My answer is: all those engaged in governance at a supranational level. That is to say, those institutions that are involved in regulation, law-making and/or adjudication which applies to a number of states. This definition includes regional bodies such as the EU, Council of Europe and their equivalents elsewhere, international organizations such as the IMF, WTO etc., and the UN and its various sub-bodies. Almost all of these bodies are sector-specific, and in that respect they do not resemble governments, not even yet the EU. What they all share with governments, however, is that they exercise a regulatory authority which limits the freedom of those subject to it, and which also has distributional implications (taking 'distributional' in its broadest sense).

Naturally, these bodies are not the only actors in international space; there are also states, MNCs and other non-state actors which affect people across borders. Yet even the most significant of these should be described as exercising power at the international level, not authority. From an international perspective, democracy requires that they be appropriately regulated in the public interest, though not necessarily that they be run democratically themselves. We may well sympathize with the international lawyer, Michael Byers, when he writes: 'One regularly hears talk of a "democratic deficit" with regard to supra-national institutions.... Perhaps it is time to start speaking of a similar deficit with regard to the US. The importance of decisions made in Washington today eclipses that of decisions made in the UN – and not just for Americans. Citizens of other countries find themselves victims of a twenty-first century form of "taxation without representation", subject to the governance of a foreign power but deprived of any voice' (Byers, 2002: 15). However, this should properly be a matter for international regulation rather than for us all to have a vote in US elections. How that might be done is thankfully not a subject for this chapter. What is important here is to make the distinction between power and authority, a distinction that is made rather brutally by another North American expert, Ivo Daalder, when he says, 'Europe emphasizes norms, treaties, institutions, because they don't have an alternative; the US emphasizes power' (quoted in Engel, 2002).

Democratic principles have authority as their focus, though certainly they concern themselves with the distribution of power *within* authority, and with the *scope* of that authority over other powers that significantly affect people's well-being. As far as the latter goes (the scope of authority), then some version of our questions 4.6 about the regulation of economic organizations, 7.1 about the capacity of authority to control those issues that significantly affect people, and 14.1 about its subordination to other agents, could well be replicated at the international level. However, an important difference is that the subjects of authority of international institutions are typically states, not non-state actors, and the latter can only be regulated indirectly through the legal enforcement mechanism of states. This question about the scope of regulatory authority raises a whole set of different issues for the particular sectoral institutions in the international arena which will have to be left on one side here, except to signal that this dimension is important for any democratic assessment.

Second, are democratic criteria the appropriate ones against which international institutions should be assessed? A number of possible objections can be distinguished here. One is that what is required of an institution exercising authority is that it should be plausibly legitimate, and there are other principles of legitimacy than democratic ones more appropriate to the international arena. One is some version of Hobbesian contract theory, supplemented by Lockean consent (Hobbes, 1960 ed., chapter 18; Locke, 1952 ed., chapter 8). According to this version, international institutions are rendered legitimate by the agreement of the states which originally authorized their establishment. Late-comers express their consent to the rules of the institution and its distribution of power by becoming members. To this, the standard replies are, in order: to the Hobbesian part, that the principle of original equality of participants can only be preserved by an effective equal right of all to make revisions to the original agreement; to the Lockean part, that the choice of joining is no more than a 'Hobson's choice' for latecomers. Neither contract nor consent versions of legitimation can be realized in practice without democratic procedures.

Another legitimating principle that has been canvassed is a technocratic version of paternalism. Experts in the relevant sectoral discipline are entitled to decisional authority within international institutions, so the argument goes, by virtue of their special training and knowledge. The model is that of the judiciary or central bankers within nation-states (Majone, 1997; Morgan, this volume, makes such a case). However, the analogy does not hold. Judges and central bankers alike take decisions on the basis of rules that are determined by elected legislators; they do not determine the rules themselves. Admittedly, the distinction between law-making and its interpretation is often blurred in practice, but the distinction is vital to maintain in principle. As was argued in the first section, the irreducibly evaluative judgements involved in rule determination cannot be legitimated today in an international forum without reference to popular authorization and accountability. That such decisions may as a matter of fact be taken by technocrats does not of itself guarantee their legitimacy (for a fuller discussion of these points see Beetham and Lord, 1998: chapter 1).

A different set of objectors simply assert the impracticality of democratic principles at the international level. Impracticality may be of two kinds, institutional and political. The claim of *institutional* impracticality is a version of 'ought implies can': democratic principles are irrelevant unless it can be shown how they might plausibly be operationalized. Answering this objection is a subject for other chapters in this volume. The claim of *political* impracticality involves the assertion that the most powerful actors, whether states, MNCs or other actors, will simply not submit to democratic arrangements, and these must therefore be heavily qualified to accommodate the 'realities' of power. To be sure, most arrangements of governance in practice involve some degree of compromise between democratic principles and non-democratic or pre-democratic social and political forces. But the point of a democracy assessment is precisely to expose how far this is so, as a contribution to the process of greater democratization. This process will simply not happen if people abandon their democratic principles at the outset.

Third, if democratic criteria are the only appropriate ones for the legitimation and therefore the assessment of international institutions, what exactly would count as 'democratic', or its converse – evidence of a 'democratic deficit'? So far I have made a number of distinctions which need to be borne in mind when answering this question. There is the distinction between the procedures of decision-making and the democracy-relevant consequences for the states and peoples affected by the decisions. There is the distinction between the distribution of decisional power within an authority and the scope of that authority over other relevant powers. Let me now concentrate on the issue of decisional procedures and the distribution of power involved in them, which for many is the subject of democracy *par excellence*.

One advantage of the framework we have used for the democratic assessment of nation-states is that it is not tied solely to the institutions typical of this level of governance, but starts from principles and values that have wider applicability. But how are values such as participation, representation, accountability, etc. to be assessed at the international level? Should we look for their realization by direct or indirect means? Are the proper subjects of democracy at this level peoples or the states that are taken to represent their peoples? If the latter, then participation is by states; the authorization of international institutions is effected by governments; fair representation might require that state members have votes according to the size of their respective populations (as in the EU); accountability of officials is to state representatives, and through these to their national parliaments; and so on. And then the democratic character of the international tier is only as sound as the internal democracy of the states which comprise it. If however it is peoples who are the proper subject of democracy at this level, as forms part of Chadwick Alger's vision in this volume, then how are they to be constituted? Formally and territorially, through elections to a global assembly? Or informally and by a variety of cross-national groupings or associations? Or by some other mechanism yet to be devised?

No doubt we could conceive of combining the direct and the indirect modes, as in the EU. But attempts to assess the 'democratic deficit' in the EU are fraught with disagreement as to what should be the appropriate balance between the two, between the intergovernmental and the supranational components of democracy. Moreover, the experience of the EU also shows what are the respective difficulties with each mode. The indirect or intergovernmental mode suffers from the fact that there is very inadequate accountability of state representatives to their national parliaments, and through them to their respective publics, though this varies from country to country. The direct or supranational mode suffers from the lack of what might be called the preconditions of democracy: there is no common identity as a people (except possibly as Euro-users), no common political language, no common political media, and a consequent low turnout and low legitimacy for electoral politics at the European level (see Archibugi, this volume, for an opposing view). The problems of both modes could be expected to be enormously magnified at the global level.

In the light of these difficulties, it may be that the agenda for a democracy assessment at the international level should be a relatively modest one. That is, to take some of the main international institutions we actually have, rather than might have, and explore what are the assumptions about membership, representation, accountability, and so on that are embedded in their existing practice. These could then be assessed so as to identify what are the most glaring deficiencies from a democratic point of view. Such an assessment should also, to revert to the distinctions made earlier, seek to identify the most glaring inadequacies in the *scope* of the respective institutional authority and in the democracy-relevant *consequences* of its decision making. Such a project would not require us to come up with proposals for a fully workable set of democratic arrangements at the international level, though it might suggest pointers towards them. And it might also, as any democratic assessment should, identify instances of democratic achievement as well as deficit, that is examples of good democratic practice, which could be generalized more widely.

In making such an assessment two final considerations should be borne in mind. The first is that establishing effective administrative, regulatory, and law-making institutions at a new spatial level of governance has in the past usually taken place *prior to* their democratization, as is argued by Morrison and Markoff (this volume). This is the experience of the European Union, and also currently of the development of regional government within England. There is a political logic to this sequencing. Effective administrative and regulatory systems have to be put in place, and people have to experience them working and to recognize themselves as common subjects of their authority, before democracy can become meaningful. Only once effective authority is being exercised will the perception of a 'democratic deficit' be possible, and demands for democratization emerge. In other words, legitimation by function and performance is prior to legitimacy through democratic control (Beetham and Lord, 1998: chapter 1).

Democratization is thus an evolving process, and any assessment of international institutions should recognize this. But if the process depends on the demand for it, then an assessment should also be able to identify relevant agents who are able and determined to press such demands. Democratization is as much about political agency as about institutions. At the international level we can discern a motley coalition emerging of non-Western governments, INGOs, aid agencies, protest movements, former international bureaucrats, and even some businesses responding to consumer pressure all pushing an agenda of institutional democratization. Admittedly their concerns are not all the same: some are concerned more with the transparency of decision making, others with stricter accountability, others again with fairer systems of representation. Yet the direction of the demands is clear, even if there is no agreement on the precise institutional forms in which these core democratic values should be realized.

4. Conclusion

I realize, in reviewing my text, that it may read like three quite separate chapters. However, the conclusion I would draw is of the essential interconnectedness of the three questions posed at the outset, and of the issues they raise. So the democratic principles and values applicable to a national-level assessment are also relevant for the assessment of international institutions, since they are based on universalist considerations. At the same time, the assessment of a country's external profile will depend upon the character of the international bodies of which it is a member, as well as on its relations with other agents in the regional and global arena. Finally, the extent to which international institutions themselves can be judged to be democratic is in part dependent on the democratic character of the states to which they are formally accountable, as well as on the effects they may have on these in turn. If all this seems like an unmanageable assessment agenda, its main purpose may be to provide a map of the terrain, so that the assessment of any one feature can be undertaken with some understanding of how it is to be positioned in relation to the rest.

Appendix 9.1: List of Assessment Questions

1.   Citizenship, Law and Rights

1.0   Nationhood and citizenship
Is there public agreement on a common citizenship without discrimination?

1.1   How inclusive is the political nation and state citizenship of all who live within the territory?
1.2   How far are cultural differences acknowledged, and how well are minorities protected?
1.3   How much consensus is there on state boundaries and constitutional arrangements?
1.4   How far do constitutional and political arrangements enable major societal divisions to be moderated or reconciled?
1.5   How impartial and inclusive are the procedures for amending the constitution?

2.0   The rule of law and access to justice
Are state and society consistently subject to the law?

2.1   How far is the rule of law operative throughout the territory?
2.2   To what extent are all public officials subject to the rule of law and to transparent rules in the performance of their functions?
2.3   How independent are the courts and the judiciary from the executive, and how free are they from all kinds of interference?
2.4   How equal and secure is the access of citizens to justice, to due process and to redress in the event of maladministration?
2.5   How far do the criminal justice and penal systems observe due rules of impartial and equitable treatment in their operations?
2.6   How much confidence do people have in the legal system to deliver fair and effective justice?

3.0   Civil and political rights
Are civil and political rights equally guaranteed for all?

3.1   How free are all people from physical violation of their person, and from fear of it?
3.2   How effective and equal is the protection of the freedoms of movement, expression, association and assembly?
3.3   How secure is the freedom for all to practise their own religion, language and culture?
3.4   How free from harassment and intimidation are individuals and groups working to improve human rights?

4.0   Economic and social rights
Are economic and social rights equally guaranteed for all?

4.1   How far is access to work or social security available to all, without discrimination?

4.2   How effectively are the basic necessities of life guaranteed, including adequate food, shelter and clean water?

4.3   To what extent is the health of the population protected, in all spheres and stages of life?

4.4   How extensive and inclusive is the right to education, including education in the rights and responsibilities of citizenship?

4.5   How free are trade unions and other work-related associations to organize and represent their members' interests?

4.6   How rigorous and transparent are the rules on corporate governance, and how effectively are corporations regulated in the public interest?

2.   Representative and Accountable Government

5.0   Free and fair elections
Do elections give the people control over governments and their policies?

5.1   How far is appointment to governmental and legislative office determined by popular competitive election, and how frequently do elections lead to change in the governing parties or personnel?

5.2   How inclusive and accessible for all citizens are the registration and voting procedures, how independent are they of government and party control, and how free from intimidation and abuse?

5.3   How fair are the procedures for the registration of candidates and parties, and how far is there fair access for them to the media and other means of communication with voters?

5.4   How effective a range of choice does the electoral and party system allow the voters, how equally do their votes count, and how closely does the composition of the legislature and the selection of the executive reflect the choices they make?

5.5   How far does the legislature reflect the social composition of the electorate?

5.6   What proportion of the electorate votes, and how far are the election results accepted by all political forces in the country and outside?

6.0   Democratic role of political parties
Does the party system assist the working of democracy?

6.1   How freely are parties able to form and recruit members, engage with the public and campaign for office?

6.2   How effective is the party system in forming and sustaining governments in office?

6.3   How free are opposition or non-governing parties to organize within the legislature, and how effectively do they contribute to government accountability?

6.4   How fair and effective are the rules governing party discipline in the legislature?

6.5   How far are parties effective membership organizations, and how far are members able to influence party policy and candidate selection?

6.6   How far does the system of party financing prevent the subordination of parties to special interests?

6.7   To what extent do parties cross ethnic, religious and linguistic divisions?

7.0   Government effectiveness and accountability
Is government accountable to the people and their representatives?

7.1   How far is the elected government able to influence or control those matters that are important to the lives of its people, and how well is it informed, organized and resourced to do so?

7.2   How much public confidence is there in the effectiveness of government and its political leadership?

7.3   How effective and open to scrutiny is the control exercised by elected leaders and their ministers over their administrative staff and other executive agencies?

7.4   How extensive and effective are the powers of the legislature to initiate, scrutinize and amend legislation?

7.5   How extensive and effective are the powers of the legislature to scrutinize the executive and hold it to account?

7.6   How rigorous are the procedures for approval and supervision of taxation and public expenditure?

7.7   How comprehensive and effective is legislation giving citizens the right of access to government information?

8.0   Civilian control of the military and police
Are the military and police forces under civilian control?

8.1   How effective is civilian control over the armed forces, and how free is political life from military involvement?

8.2   How publicly accountable are the police and security services for their activities?

8.3   How far does the composition of the army, police and security services reflect the social composition of society at large?

8.4   How free is the country from the operation of paramilitary units, private armies, warlordism and criminal mafias?

9.0   Minimizing corruption
Are public officials free from corruption?

9.1   How effective is the separation of public office from the personal business and family interests of office holders?

9.2   How effective are the arrangements for protecting office holders and the public from involvement in bribery?

9.3   How far do the rules and procedures for financing elections, candidates and elected representatives prevent their subordination to sectional interests?

9.4   How far is the influence of powerful corporations and business interests over public policy kept in check, and how free are they from involvement in corruption, including abroad?

9.5   How much confidence do people have that public officials and public services are free from corruption?

3.   Civil Society and Popular Participation

10.0   The media in a democratic society
Do the media operate in a way that sustains democratic values?

10.1   How independent are the media from government, how pluralistic is their ownership, and how free are they from subordination to foreign governments or multinational companies?

10.2   How representative are the media of different opinions and how accessible are they to different sections of society?

10.3   How effective are the media and other independent bodies in investigating government and powerful corporations?

10.4   How free are journalists from restrictive laws, harassment and intimidation?

10.5   How free are private citizens from intrusion and harassment by the media?

11.0   Political participation
Is there full citizen participation in public life?

11.1   How extensive is the range of voluntary associations, citizen groups, social movements, etc., and how independent are they from government?

11.2   How extensive is citizen participation in voluntary associations and self-management organizations, and in other voluntary public activity?

11.3   How far do women participate in political life and public office at all levels?

11.4   How equal is access for all social groups to public office, and how fairly are they represented within it?

Chapter 10

Contract or Conversation? Conceptualizing Constitution-Making and Constitutional Identity at the Transnational Level

Patti Lenard and Luc Turgeon[1]

1. Introduction

Political issues that Canadians have dealt with over the past 40 years – including nationalism, multiculturalism, secession, citizenship, constitutional politics, and the politics of identity – have more recently made their way into the international social science community's research agenda. Canadian political theory in particular – for better or worse – has drawn the attention both of analysts who imagine that the 'Canadian' vocabulary is useful in clarifying political issues in other countries, as well as of those who argue that real-life politics show the limits of the 'Canadian model'.

This chapter deals with one theoretical issue that has garnered international attention, in spite of taking place at the Canadian domestic level: the theorization of a new constitutionalism, which emerged in connection with the Canadian constitutional crisis of the 1980s and 1990s and the recent ground-breaking decision of the Supreme Court on the right of secession for Québec. This new constitutionalism, we argue, 'finds its theoretical expression in the democratization of contract theory' (Chambers, 2001: 63). In particular, we ask whether 'Canadian' insights in constitutional theory are helpful in answering certain among the challenges posed by constitutionalism at the transnational level. We assess whether this new constitutionalism can help foster what James Tully refers to as a 'constitutional identity' – that is, 'the publicly recognized and accepted rules and procedures by which the members of the society recognize each other and coordinate their cooperation' – above the level of the nation-state (Tully, 2001: 11).

An understanding of the Canadian constitutional crisis, as well as its interpretation by political theorists, may prove useful for the consideration of transnational democracy, we argue, not only because Canada is composed of a multicultural and multinational population with divergent values and interests, but also because Canada's history reflects some of the constitutional uncertainty that characterizes the broader transnational case. As with transnational or cosmopolitan democracy, Canada has always been more akin to an evolving project than a concrete reality. As Peter Russell rightly argues, 'no other country in the world today has been engaged so intensively, and for so long in searching for the constitutional conditions of its continuing unity' (Russell, 1992: 193).

We begin this chapter with a discussion of cosmopolitan democracy and how it is related to issues of constitutional identity and constitution-making. We argue that the implicit model of constitutionalism in the writings of proponents of cosmopolitan democracy such as David Held replicates the conventional nation-state model of constitutionalism. It is the implicit model of nation-state constitutionalism, in particular, we argue, that makes cosmopolitan democracy subject to a number of criticisms from those who doubt both the feasibility and the desirability of cosmopolitan democracy. In the second section of the chapter we present a brief overview of Canadian constitutional history with an emphasis upon recent developments which have led to a new interpretation of constitutionalism – the activity-oriented (Tully, 2000) or conversational view (Chambers, 1998) of constitutional democracy. Both James Tully and Simone Chambers challenge the 'end-state' or 'contract' model of constitution making by arguing, in part, that it pays insufficient attention to the role that culture plays in determining the specific organization and policies of a liberal nation-state. Here, our disagreement with Katherine Fierlbeck (chapter 5 in this volume) will become clear. Whereas Fierlbeck is concerned that contemporary liberal nationalist theory overemphasizes the relevance of 'dignity' of nations and cultures, on the grounds that 'dignity' is overwhelmingly subjective and individualist in nature, we are more sympathetic to the empirical fact that culture is ultimately important to people, and people as they interact *as members of groups*. In the final section of the chapter, we will demonstrate the benefits of adopting a conversational perspective on constitutionalism as a way of making sense of current proposals for cosmopolitan democracy, even though the conversational model comes accompanied by certain limitations.

2. Obstacles to Constitution-Making at the Transnational Level

A constitution is essentially made up of the rules that create or embody a polity (see Stone, A., 1994: 444). From that perspective, any critical evaluation of the desirability and feasibility of developing a cosmopolitan model of democracy must investigate the conditions under which a constitutional order at the transnational level, that is, the 'codes of norms which aspire to regulate the allocations of powers, functions and duties among various agencies and of officers of governments and to define the relationships between these and the public' (Finer et al., 1995: 1), might be established.

In *Democracy and the Global Order* (1995), Held addresses a multitude of issues related to the development of a constitutional order, from the relationship between different orders of government to the entrenchment of different civic, political, and socioeconomic rights.[2] He proposes, in particular, that democratic cosmopolitan law 'be enshrined within the constitutions of parliaments and assemblies at the national and international level', and that the influence of international courts 'be extended so that groups and individuals have an effective means of suing political authorities for the enactment and enforcement of key rights and obligations, both within and beyond political associations' (Held 1995: 272). The list of rights that Held wishes to see entrenched is vast, ranging from basic political rights to potentially more controversial ones, including the right to 'control over fertility' and the right to a 'guaranteed minimum income'. In response, Michael Saward notes that, by removing such a large range of issues from the realm of domestic democratic politics, the 'cosmopolitan model appears to shift the balance between constitutionalism and democracy in favour of the former' (Saward, 2001: 562).

More so than other cosmopolitans, Held is sympathetic towards the difficulties associated with the political expression of cultural diversity in a cosmopolitan constitutional order (see Waldron, 1995). Held argues that, in a cosmopolitan democracy, 'citizens enjoy multiple citizenships. They should be citizens of their own communities, of the wider regions in which they live, and of a cosmopolitan, transnational democracy' (Held, 2000: 30). Still, Held offers no discussion of the basis for relations, at the cosmopolitan or international level, between cultural communities with radically different values and competing visions of the good. Held's depiction of politics is one in which rational (liberal) individuals interact at different levels (local, regional, national, international, and supranational), and in which different sets of political and social rights are relevant at each of these levels.

The project of cosmopolitan democracy has been widely criticized as both unfeasible and untenable (see Archibugi in this volume for an examination of these criticisms). Held himself has tried to deflect criticisms by presenting cosmopolitan democracy as a utopia towards which we should strive. We do not wish to insist, here, on the institutional feasibility of this project, but rather, with an eye to its treatment in the literature, to explore the desirability of this project. On this foundation, three analytically distinct but nonetheless interconnected criticisms of the cosmopolitan project become particularly relevant to attempts at developing a constitutional identity at the transnational level: the absence of a clear *demos*; the problems of domination and imposition; and, problems associated with existing institutional structures.

First, establishing constitutional rules and conventions is difficult when the nature of the community to be governed by them remains undefined. Those who express skepticism about the possibility of establishing some form of transnational democracy have been fond of insisting on the absence of a clear *demos* at the transnational level. Without this clearly defined community, the criticism runs, it is difficult, if not impossible, to establish democratic mechanisms capable of generating decisions perceived as legitimate by the citizens they are meant to affect. Many contemporary nation-states are able to point to a 'founding moment' of some kind, a moment in history when a diverse grouping of people was united in a decision to be governed as cohesive community.[3] The absence of symbols that a founding moment might provide prevents citizens from having a starting point to which they can refer in militating for a more just or democratic transnational society. As Bellamy and Jones argue, without a sense of community and a suitable founding moment, global democracy is unlikely even when it appears desirable and logically necessary (Bellamy and Jones, 2000: 211; see Markoff, Morgan, and Morrison, this volume, for further discussion).

The project of cosmopolitan democracy has been particularly strongly contested by analysts linking successful democracies with communities with strong cultural ties (see Kymlicka, 1999; Miller, D., 2000). When David Miller, for example, argues that shared national identity is a precondition for effective deliberative democracy, he is arguing against the feasibility of generating a transnational community. Instead, two conditions for deliberative politics tend to be more easily satisfied when national identities are shared: 'one is that the reasons given in political debate should be sincerely held', and 'the second condition is that citizens should be willing to moderate their claims in the hope that they can find common ground on which policy decisions can be based' (Miller, D., 1995: 96-7). According to Miller, having a shared national identity is precisely what generates the trust and shared understandings that underpin public discussions among citizens. The problem is articulated nicely, for example, by Margaret Moore, who writes that that liberal nationalists such as Miller take 'it as an empirical given that national identity is important for most people.... Cosmopolitanism is a possibility, but most liberal nationalists will claim that it is of limited sociological significance' (Moore, 2001: 56). The possible normative desirability of a transnational or cosmopolitan democracy, that is, is not as relevant for Miller as is the empirical fact that it is unlikely.

That democracy is linked somehow to a strong sense of community is not, however, uncontested, and we will point to two criticisms here. First, cosmopolitan critics claim that it is the existence of nation-state boundaries itself that prevents the development of a broader sense of attachment to human beings in general (Waldron, 1995; Buchanan, 1995). Second, cosmopolitans argue that the association between democracy and the nation-state is merely contingent, and that the prospects for transnational democracy are not, in principle, damaged by our current (ethical) attachment to nation-state arrangements (Weinstock, 2001). Yet, despite these criticisms, a central merit of both nationalist and communitarian critiques has been to remind proponents of cosmopolitan democracy that any democratic project must be based on a sense of belonging to some kind of common community. Janna Thompson writes, for example, that '[c]osmopolitans cannot be content with putting forward a moral position or with constructing blueprints for a cosmopolitan society. They must turn their attention to the creation of community' (Thompson, J., 1998: 193).

The second obstacle to the development of a constitutional order at the transnational level, the problem of domination and imposition, raises the issue of the legitimacy and the legitimation of the cosmopolitan project. This issue can be analyzed along two lines. First, there is the theoretical problem of whether a transnational constitutional order can be free of domination. Danilo Zolo, for example, rhetorically asks the following question: 'Can any cosmopolitan project ever be anything other than an inherently hegemonic and violent undertaking?' (Zolo, 1997: 15 quoted in Coates, 2000: 90). According to Zolo, the desire for a universal legal system that guides most proposals for cosmopolitan democracy, as well as current attempts to establish an overall legal and constitutional framework, can only reproduce existing patterns of economic and political domination. From a different perspective, Alexander Wendt has criticized proponents of cosmopolitan democracy for imposing on others what amounts to Western liberal values (Wendt, 1999). This is particularly relevant when considering the range of potentially controversial rights Held wishes to see entrenched in constitutional documents at the cosmopolitan level. Yet, rather than rejecting altogether the quest to extend democracy at the transnational level, Wendt argues that cosmopolitan democracy will succeed only if it manages to reassure 'individuals that the cultural attachments which give their lives much of their meaning will be respected at the global level' (Wendt, 1999: 132).

The last obstacle to constitution-making at the transnational level, and perhaps the most significant in terms of the feasibility of the cosmopolitan project, is the fact of existing institutional structures at the supranational level. For example, at the European level, pre-existing accords, as well as institutional structures created over the last fifty years, have seriously complicated attempts to establish a new European Community that might be guided by the principles of cosmopolitan/transnational democracy, that is, one where the needs of peoples' 'take precedence over the interests of states and their geo-political machinations' (McGrew, 2000). As Philip Schmitter argues, 'being a member of the EU does seem to make a significant difference, not just in the *acquis* of the supranational institutions and policies, but also in the performance of national political institutions, which means that its democratization, when and if it comes, must be accompanied by building upon existing institutions rather than in the classic federalist manner by drafting an entirely new constitution' (Schmitter 1999: 946).

The development of a constitutional order at the transnational level, considering the lack of an existing cosmopolitan community, the danger of domination and the quasi-impossibility of displacing current institutional structures to replace them with more democratic ones (chosen democratically), may seem both impossible and undesirable. Yet, these obstacles to the development of a constitutional identity are only insurmountable if we accept the logic of the contract theory of constitutionalism, with its emphasis on founding moments, pre-existing communities and the entrenchment of rights which binds present and future generations. This model of contract-making in the liberal tradition is that followed by Held and most proponents of cosmopolitan democracy. In the next section, we explore what some political theorists have presented as a new understanding of constitutionalism before evaluating it as a possible source of insights into constitution- and constitutional identity-making at the transnational level.

3. Canadian Constitutional Bickering: Exploring the New Constitutionalism

Constitutional politics is often said to be the national sport of Canada, and in a sense there is something that rings true in this popular (among politicians and political scientists!) saying. In many ways, Canada's history can be read as a series of constitutional moments: 1763 (Royal Proclamation), 1774 (Quebec Act), 1840 (Union Act), 1867 (British North America Act), 1982 (Constitutional Act), as well as a series of unsuccessful attempts to reform some of these accords in an effort to bring Québec back into the constitutional family, the most important of which have been the Meech Lake Accord (1987) and the Charlottetown Accord (1992). These continuous negotiations over the constitutional order show that Canada has never been governed by the rule of a clearly legitimated constitution. As Chambers argues, what is unique about 'the Canadian case is not that Canadians have failed to ratify their constitution: it is that they have continued to try' (Chambers, 2001: 65). In this section of the chapter, we first present a brief introduction to Canada's constitutional history, showing how some of the key problems that Canada has faced are in many ways similar to those faced at the transnational level. We then show how these developments have led to a new interpretation of constitutionalism in contemporary multicultural and multinational societies like Canada.

3.1 A Brief Introduction to Canada's Constitutional History   Canada's search for constitutional unity started right after the ratification of the British North America Act of 1867 which formally united Québec, Ontario, New Brunswick, and Nova Scotia into a federal union, with institutions 'similar in principle to those of the United Kingdom'. In many ways, it constituted what Janet Azjenstat has called a 'procedural constitution', that is, a constitution as the rulebook for the game of politics, detached as much as possible from specific ideology and political interests (Ajzenstat, 1995). This constitution contained no grand aspirations of the sort attached to the American or French constitutions. Yet, it is precisely this lack of a clear 'We the People' that allowed different interpretations of the Canadian constitution to co-exist (Gagnon and Turgeon, 2003). Not only was the original constitution unclear about what Canada was, it was also plagued by many omissions: the place of Aboriginals, the rights of citizens, and, importantly, a Canadian procedure for amending the constitution.

Although there were major tensions in Canada between French and English Canadians, as well as between provinces and the federal government, over the next hundred years, there were no major constitutional crises *per se*. Instead, this period of Canadian constitutional politics began with the rise of a territorially-based Québec nationalism in the 1960s which propelled the move from a French-Canadian to a Québécois identity (an identity not reflected in the BNA Act); a Québécois identity that was actively promoted by the Québec government.

Canada's original willingness to accommodate Québec's demands dampened following the election of Pierre Elliott Trudeau in 1968, who was deeply opposed to any form of accommodation of Québec nationalism (McRoberts, 1997). At the same time as the secessionist movement grew in Québec, Trudeau developed his own set of constitutional proposals. His main objectives included the repatriation of Canada's constitution from Britain, the inclusion in this constitution of a Charter of Rights and Freedoms and, by extension, the reinforcement of a strong loyalty to Canada over other subnational loyalties. The defeat of the 1980 referendum on Québec sovereignty allowed Trudeau to move forward with the project of developing a new constitutional order based on the supremacy of individual rights. The Constitution Act of 1982, adopted by the federal government and all provinces with the exception of Québec, established a new Charter of Rights and Freedoms that made it possible for citizens to contest federal government legislation. It also provided an amending formula that legitimated the contested notion of provincial equality. An equally controversial but interesting development was the inclusion of a notwithstanding clause (section 33) which allowed a legislature to override, for a period of five years, any court decision related to most articles of the Charter. According to Williams, this solution gives the Canadian system a way to resolve the inherent tension between representative democracy and the constitutional authority of judges:

> The Canadian solution thus resolves the problem in practice by refusing to dissolve the tension between fundamental law and democratic rule in theory. ... In declining to give the judges the last word on fundamental rights, it also makes the exercise of democratic power accountable to principle, and persistently so, by requiring the periodic review of legislation that conflicts with the Charter of Rights (Williams, 2001: 217).

For many Canadians the Constitutional Act of 1982 became a new founding moment for the Canadian community, a consequence of what Cairns referred to as the 'People's constitution' (Cairns, 1992). This 'new' founding act may in part explain the later rejection of the Meech Lake and Charlottetown Accords, which were viewed among their opponents as a dilution of the nation-building accomplished by the 1982 Constitution. Meech Lake failed, broadly speaking, because its exclusive focus on Québec had the felt effect of excluding a host of players in Canadian politics from the deliberations: Aboriginals, women, immigrants, etc. In order to respond to the claim that the Meech Lake Accord was centred exclusively on Québec's demands, a 'Canada Clause' was added to the Charlottetown Accord. This clause set out the various characteristics of the country that might serve as guiding principles in interpreting the Charter of Rights and Freedoms. Many of these eight characteristics were viewed by critics of the Charlottetown Accord as mutually antagonistic. Clause (c) that claimed that Québec was a distinct society, for example, seemed to conflict with clause (h) which confirmed the principle of provincial equality, while nevertheless recognizing their diverse characteristics. The proposal was rejected in a national referendum in October 1992, and was largely criticized as offering too little for Québec (according to Québec) and too much for Canada outside Québec.[4] The feeling of exclusion from the Canadian constitutional order, held by many Québécois, contributed to the 1995 referendum result on sovereignty, which featured a narrow victory for the 'No' forces, whose 50.6 per cent represented

54,288 more votes than were acquired by the 'Yes' camp. The main problems associated with Canada's constitutional odyssey of the 1980s and 1990s, we can see, arose not so much from the ongoing process of constitutional dialogue, as from the desire for the political class to settle once and for all, unambiguously, the terms of Canada's constitutional identity, that is, the conditions by which Canadians mutually recognize each other. Such an approach stood in stark opposition to the Canadian tradition of constitutional ambiguity which had been the basis of Canada's (largely successful) approach to the management of diversity for more than a century.

3.2 From Contract to Conversation in Constitution-Making   These multiple attempts at constitutional reforms have shown, according to Tully and Chambers, the limits of the contractual or modern model of constitution-making, associated in particular with the American constitution, but also more generally with the constitutions of modern democratic nation-states. In modern political theory, broadly understood, the making of the constitution has tended to be understood as a founding moment: 'contracts imply a privileged moment where constitutional essentials are unambiguously settled and made binding into the future' (Chambers, 1998: 149). Social contract versions of constitution-making, such as John Locke's and John Rawls', privilege individuals acting (ideally) unanimously to generate a legitimate constitution in which citizens' rights and privileges are formally codified, and so formally protected from encroachment by the state and by other individuals. In Tully's words, 'a constitution is presented as a written document which creates the foundations of government *de novo* by an act of the sovereign will and reason of the people' (Tully, 1995: 85). This perspective on constitution-making is indeed the one shared by both proponents and many of the critics of cosmopolitan democracy, with their emphasis on the founding moment, pre-existing communities and entrenchment of rights in binding documents.

According to both Tully and Chambers, this model of constitution-making is largely inadequate in light of new changes in contemporary multicultural and multinational societies.[5] There are two essential reasons, in light of contemporary developments, why the contract model of constitution-making and the modern form of constitutionalism are inadequate. First, in the framework of advanced industrial societies marked by a decline of deference to political elites (Nevitte, 1996), citizens are less willing to let a small elite speak for the people and establish new constitutional documents without their input. They want to feel a part of the process of discussion, so that the resultant constitutional document can be felt as 'their' document. Second, with the rise of multiculturalism and identity politics, people do not come to discuss constitutional issues as individuals, but rather as members of different groups with significant and distinctive conceptions of the goods to be gained by entering into a contract. Both developments make it extremely difficult to arrive at a final agreement that will produce a 'just' society that can speak as 'a people'. It is worth quoting Tully (2001: 5) at length here:

The politics of recognition of multiple nations and cultures within a constitutional democracy has reached a historical limit and is passing through a transition to a new orientation; a new self-understanding of the citizens, politicians and civil servants involved. The limit is an impasse caused by the inability to resolve the specific struggles definitively and permanently. The explanation of this inability is what I will call the 'plurality' of contests over recognition. This concept refers to two features of recognition politics: (1) struggles over the mutual recognition of identities are too complex, unpredictable and mutual to admit of definitive solutions, and (2) the intersubjective activity of striving for and responding to forms of mutual recognition is an intrinsic public good of modern politics which contributes to legitimacy and stability whether or not the form of recognition demanded is achieved.

The conversational or activity-oriented model proposed by Tully and Chambers focuses away from identifying abstract principles that we might all find acceptable and instead 'stress[es] the maintenance of a certain type of practice over time' (Chambers, 1998: 151). The emphasis here is on the process rather than the outcome, in an effort to achieve freedom (rather than perfect justice) under our constitutional order.[6] If we emphasize, in particular, the intercultural nature of dialogue that ought to occur among citizens and their representatives, our democratic politics will be revitalized. Tully offers three inter-related reasons why we need to revitalize democratic methods of making decisions around identity politics. The first two of these are: because the demands for recognition affect all members of a society; and 'democratic procedures of negotiation' are the only way in which 'disputes over contested norms' can be resolved. The third reason that Tully offers is critical, he claims, since it is the basis on which stability in a multinational society might be established. Because it 'is the people themselves who must experience the present system of recognition as imposed or unjust', they must have the freedom both to demand and grant recognition through democratic procedures. Stability is achieved, claims Tully, because the democratic processes by which demands for recognition are made and acknowledged are, in fact, part of the 'process of *citizenization*. Individuals and minorities *become* citizens of the nation demanding recognition by participating in these processes (Tully, 2001: 25).

Constitution-making, for proponents of the new constitutionalism, lies therefore in 'sustaining a conversation over time' (Chambers, 1998: 161). Such advocates therefore reject the idea of constitutional pre-commitment associated with modern constitutionalism (see Holmes, 1988), which is the idea that a constitution binds future generations by making it difficult to amend the constitution, and therefore by bringing a certain 'closure' to constitutional discussions. It is perhaps useful, at this point, to elaborate somewhat on Tully's 'activity-oriented' approach to generating a constitution: 'constitutional democracy must thus be seen as an activity, a system of discursive practices of rule-following and rule-modifying in which diversity is reconciled with unity through the continuous exchange of public reasons' (Tully, 2001: 17). This approach, both Tully and Chambers argue, is very different from the modern constitution's emphasis on closure, which 'locks contractors in and locks out those who come along later' (Chambers, 1998: 160). That is, by imagining constitution-making as an ongoing activity, we are able to see how members of present and future generations, representing a wide variety of cultural groups and value systems, may participate in structuring the constitutions that govern their lives. The constitution, moreover, contains written and unwritten rules, which stem from three sources: 'an understanding of the constitutional text itself, the historical context, and previous judicial interpretations of constitution-making' (Tully, 2000: 12). These unwritten rules, in particular, are ignored when we require strict adherence to the regulations established by the modern constitution. It is only an activity-oriented model of constitution-making with its emphasis on dialogue (or discourse, in Chamber's preferred terminology) that pays attention to the critically important role of these unwritten rules.

The importance of dialogue and unwritten rules link the proponents of the new constitutionalism, in fact, to the ancient view of the constitution. In Aristotle's words, the constitution is 'a certain organization of the inhabitants of a city-state' or 'a sort of life of city-state' (Aristotle, 1998: 1274b37-38, 1295a40-41). It is not a document, and so, by extension, it is not formally codified. It is meant, instead, to refer to the totality of laws, habits and customs that characterize a given people. Its informality allows for these laws, habits, customs to change flexibly, given changes in the makeup of the population, its needs or, indeed, in accordance with demands issuing from any number of sources. The constitution mirrors rather than transcends, therefore, the pluralism of a given society. Despite their explicit incorporation of the values of the ancient constitution, however, Tully and Chambers do not reject all the elements associated with the modern constitution. In fact, Chambers states clearly that we should not give up 'the Enlightenment ideals of human rights and universalizable principles' (Chambers 1998: 151). From this perspective, the conversational model should not be seen as displacing the contract model of constitutionalism, but rather as a way to democratize constitution-making in an age of diversity. In the next section, we explore how this conceptualization of constitution-making and the formation of a constitutional identity may help resolve some of the current obstacles to the development of a transnational constitutional identity.

4. Applying the New Constitutionalism at the Transnational Level: Some Implications

In the first section of the chapter, we identified three central problems for the development of a constitutional order at the transnational level. These are: the absence of a clear *demos*, the possibility of imposition and domination, and the existence of already functioning institutional structures. We could also view them as representing three analytically distinct but nonetheless overlapping challenges: that of building a community, that of ensuring the legitimacy of the constitutional order and, finally, that of developing a framework of rights and political institutions that reflect the different forms of attachment and loyalties of citizens of different communities. In this section, we argue that the conversational approach, although to some extent limited as we will show, offers valuable insights when considering the development of constitutionalism at the transnational level.

The first challenge is to build democratically a new political community. In our democratic society, the public policies associated with the birth of the nation-state – which transformed 'peasants into Frenchman' within a generation – are no longer viable.[7] The recognition of people's diversity and the value of preserving this diversity must therefore be part of any cosmopolitan approach to constitutionalism. As Michael Ignatieff (2000: 41) recently argued:

> What we have in common as human beings is the very way we differentiate ourselves – as peoples, as communities, and as individuals. So it is not the naked body we share in common, but the astoundingly different ways in which we decorate, adorn perfume, and costume our bodies in order to proclaim our identities as men, women, members of this tribe or that community.

We are thus stuck with the following problem: we need a sense of community to develop a transnational constitutional identity at a time when the intellectual and political climate makes it next to impossible to create a sense of 'We the People'. The conversational response to the challenge of defining the community is connected to Tully's definition of 'citizenization' noted above. Members of a community, that is, self-define through dialogue – the very fact of engaging in dialogue creates the sense of belonging that is critical to democratic politics at the national level, and ideally, the same will be true at the transnational level. A central claim of the conversational perspective is, indeed, that communities are essentially constructed over time through acts of politics. Chambers refers, for example, to Bernard Crick who argues that

> Diverse groups hold together because they practice politics – not because they agree about 'fundamentals'. ... The moral consensus of a free state is not something mysteriously above politics: it is the activity (the civilizing activity) of politics itself (Crick, 1962: 24, quoted in Chambers, 1998: 151).

Too often, proponents of cosmopolitan democracy develop a list of goods to be secured and then develop institutional mechanisms in accordance with these goods, presupposing in advance the results of political debates (Morgan develops this point in the following chapter). It is paradoxical that proponents of cosmopolitan democracy, who base their conception on the model of the rational liberal individual, presuppose most of the rules and rights that will constitute the basis of our constitutional identity. Since we cannot identify, in an age of diversity, universal goods that would satisfy all participants *a priori*, these must instead be identified through a process of dialogue or conversation. As Bellamy and Castiglione argue, 'if no objective or universal standpoint can be identified *a priori*, then it will be necessary to construct common grounds by encouraging each person to adapt his or her viewpoint to accommodate as far as possible those of everyone else concerned' (Bellamy and Castiglione, 1997: 613). A transnational community will not develop, therefore, because people have been granted universal, liberal rights that provide them with a constitutional identity, but rather because they feel they have been a part of and are still a part of, through their representatives, a political conversation that matters. It is the deliberative aspect of democracy which allows citizens to transcend the current limitations imposed by the existence of national political boundaries. As Dryzek argues, 'deliberation and communication, in contrast, can cope with fluid boundaries. For we can now look for democracy in the character of political interaction, without worrying about whether or not it is confined to particular territorial entities' (Dryzek, 1999: 44).

The Canadian case provides reason for optimism in attempts to create or sustain the development of a transnational community living under the rule of a constitutional apparatus. Despite the fact that the constitutional order has been widely contested for most of the country's history, it is still holding together and people have generally followed the rules established by the constitution. That it is holding together is in large part because, although Canadians have disagreed about its meaning and whether it is a just document, there has been, for most of Canada's history, a sense that the constitution could be challenged and transformed to adapt to a new reality.[8] We should be wary, therefore, of attempts to find *a* just solution at the transnational level.

The second challenge we identified is to develop a constitutional order that is perceived, despite the likelihood of some amount of disagreement, to be legitimate, and not as a tool of hegemony imposed by a specific group or country. There are two ways in which a conversational approach, with its recognition of the (evolving) plurality of voices and values, is useful, particularly in relation to the contractual model of constitutionalism. First, the conversational model makes an attempt to take seriously the affiliations of the participants in constitution-making and, second, it recognizes that a genuinely free society is one in which the rules of association are open to challenge from generation to generation (and even within one generation). No rules are set in stone, save the human rights that allow for deliberation in the first place.

The contract model, it is alleged, assumes an individualist perspective, one consequence of which is that it fails to account for the cultural diversity of the parties to the original contract. The conversational model, on the other hand, does not require that the participants in constitution-making adopt an individualist starting point, and, by extension, participation is opened to a larger, and more diverse, constituency. Participants are not required, in Chambers' words, to subscribe to the 'individual as rights-possessor model' that is at the heart of modern constitutionalism (Chambers, 1998: 150). The conversational model, in addition to allowing that there is a range of possible self-conceptions other than the individualist one, does not presuppose cultural uniformity in the same way the contract model does. Those who participate in the creation of the original contract, in past expositions, have been presumed to be white, rational, and autonomous men. In more contemporary versions of contract theories, the participants are less obviously these same types of people, but, Rawls' original position, for example, is still criticized on the grounds that the characteristics of the participants are not possessed by the majority of the population (see Young, 1989: chapter 1). The key problem of the contract model, however, that the conversational model imagines itself to be rectifying, is that it allows for the expression of cultural differences (this is distinct from the recognition of cultural differences). Chambers writes: 'the creation of a people, however, must be achieved without erasing differences.... [I]t has become more difficult to claim that only those people who think of themselves and their claims in liberal individualist terms may come to the negotiating table' (Chambers 1998: 151).

One key advantage of the conversational model is its willingness to think more expansively about the affiliation of participants to the constitutional conversation. This is one critical way in which the conversational model is helpful at the transnational level. At the national level, conversationalists tend to emphasize the cultural and national affiliations of the participants. The potential participants, that is, who occupy attention in the conversational model, tend to be those who demand recognition based on cultural/ethnic/national attributes which they identify as key to their own sense of self, in the sense that they would feel *personally* marginalized if their claims were ignored. As is clear, both in Canada and at the transnational level, more and more people with a range of affiliations are demanding consultation on constitutional matters. In Canada, women's groups, labour unions, and 'charter' groups have been expressing their dissatisfaction with the current constitution (as well as proposed constitutional amendments), and are thereby expanding the concerns that an amended constitution might consider (Archibugi also examines the implications of such expanded rights claims in chapter 12). At the transnational level, the range of participants in the process of constitution-making must be thought of in similarly expansive terms. These participants are typically said to belong to 'civil society' at the national level and, although the analogy is imperfect, similarly motivated participants at the transnational level are occasionally said to belong to some kind of 'global civil society'.[9]

The second way in which the conversational perspective is useful in dealing with problems connected to domination is in its willingness to view a constitutional order as an evolving reality, rather than as the definitive statement of a just society. On an activity-oriented view of constitutional democracy, the objective is not so much to arrive at a '"just" ordering of the members and their relations once and for all', but one in which primary concern is 'to discuss and modify any prevailing ordering of the members and their relationships, on the grounds that any ordering will be less-than-perfect and will always harbour anticipated or unanticipated elements of injustice' (Tully 2000: 4). This view of constitutionalism may deflect resentment over the constitutional structure not only by making it open to both dissent and punctual adaptations to new realities, but also by encouraging constant reassessment of the constitutional structure.

And yet, an acceptance that reassessment is possible and welcome does not dissolve the problem faced by the conversational model at the transnational level (and, indeed, the national level), that is, its failure to deal adequately with the tensions between constitutionalism and democracy. It may be easier to encourage a conversational model of constitutional amendment, connected to issues of recognition in liberal democracies, in which basic civic and political rights are generally secured in an at least partially viable constitution, and hence one in which opening the discussion about constitutional change does not necessarily pose the risk that basic rights might be infringed by transient majorities. But where a constitution does not yet exist, or where an existing constitution is perceived to be wholly without legitimacy, the conversational model of constitution-making leaves unanswered a host of questions connected to the lexical order of constitutionalism and democracy. For example, how can a constitution, which will formalize the democratic arrangements by which we decide on rules, be formulated in such a way as to be consistent with our democratic principles, which themselves must be articulated in a constitution in order to be protected? There is plenty of evidence, from the claims made by marginalized groups themselves, that effective ground rules must be in place in order that the conversation proceeds fairly, and indeed, it is only because of successes in this area that they have been able to further press their claims for recognition (Williams, 1998). It is, therefore, only because of the effectiveness of modern constitutions in settling, if only in the short term, the rules by which a community must abide, that we may have the discussion about the conversational approach at all (Elster, 1998: 6). Andrew Mason offers a telling example: 'in order to be in a position to refuse consent [to the constitution], individuals must be able to speak against any proposed constitutional settlement, so they must at least possess freedom of expression' (Mason, 2000: 79). The conversationalists fail to acknowledge that we may need closure on certain elements and that certain protections must be offered, full-stop, before the conversation, and its tendency to amend, may proceed.

How then might we think about developing a constitutional order which protects civil and political rights, and so which provides the basic conditions that must be satisfied so that a conversation might take place? And, to complicate the question, how will we think about the added difficulty that this conversation must allow for us to pursue the conditions of our constitutional identity *itself*, and this while nevertheless respecting the diversity of the world we live in? Some recent developments in the recent Canadian constitutional history provide, we believe, some avenues that ought to be explored.

The constitutional crisis of the last twenty years in Canada has shown us that it may be better to have a deficient constitution – with omissions, limited objectives and conflicting interpretations – than an 'ideal' constitution which tries either to delineate all the rules, which is an impossible task, or to create a new all-encompassing communal identity that marginalizes a significant portion of the population. Michael Foley (1989: 10) refers to these omissions and limited objects as 'constitutional abeyances', which,

> refer to those parts of a constitution that remain unwritten and even unspoken not only by convention, but also by necessity. More precisely, abeyances represent a way of accommodating the absence of a definitive constitutional settlement and of providing the means of adjusting the issues left unresolved in the fabric of a constitution.

Our argument is more than that these 'abeyances' are critical to the functioning of a stable constitutional democracy at the transnational level. In particular, we wish to highlight the danger inherent in attempts to generate a clear and well-defined constitutional democracy in the short term at the transnational level. It is better, we would argue, to hold a conversation within an existing framework, despite, such as in the case of the EU, its obvious shortcomings (see also Bellamy and Castiglione, 1998).

Finally, and potentially more provocatively, the existence of a 'notwithstanding' clause in the Canadian constitution may provide a mechanism by which we might avoid the potentially destabilizing effects of judicial interpretations of rights at the regional level. The fact that certain political communities, in specific cases, may use such a clause may provide a way to foster dialogue between the courts and the elected representatives of the population (thus resolving the problem of the adaptation of 'universal' laws to local realities). Because such a clause must constantly be re-enacted, the dialogue about whether certain rights must be constricted in order to protect the cultural interests in the community remains open. In short, such a clause may be a precondition for communities to allow the development of a new regional or transnational constitutional order (as was indeed the case in Canada). Likewise, it may be a key factor in maintaining the system's stability in the face of controversial interpretations of founding constitutional documents at the transnational level.

5. Conclusions

Constitution-making at the transnational level is riddled with dilemmas, both empirical and normative. Our objective in this chapter has been to evaluate the extent to which one constitution-making model – the activity-oriented or conversational model – now applied to understand Canadian constitutional bickering over time might also be useful at the transnational level. From a theoretical point of view, the primary benefit in applying the conversational model (as indeed as already been done to a certain extent) to the transnational level is that it throws into relief the importance that we should place on pre-constitutional discussions at the transnational level. The goods that are to be secured at the transnational level, if we ought to develop a legitimate and stable form of cosmopolitan democracy, ought to be object of deliberation, not decided *a priori* as elements of a just community.

Yet, the most important lesson from current developments in societies as different as Canada and South Africa is that the new understanding of constitutionalism that we have outlined here is gaining ground. Citizens are demanding the opportunity to participate in constitutional affairs and are making clear the requirement that previously meaningful 'founding moments' be open to renegotiation. This is a new reality that proponents of cosmopolitan democracy as well as its critics must take into consideration when evaluating the feasibility and the desirability of establishing a constitutional order at the transnational level.

Notes

1 The authors of this paper would like to thank the following people for helpful comments: Nicholas Cheeseman, Terry Macdonald, David Miller, Melissa Williams, the participants of the Graduate Seminar Series of the Department of Political Science at the University of Toronto, the participants at the Nuffield Graduate Student Workshop in Political Science, and the participants at the Nuffield International Normative Theory Workshop, and of course the participants at the conference that gave rise to this volume.

2 Yet, in large part, Held is silent as to the mechanism by which this constitutionalism would developed concretely.

3 We leave aside, here, the obvious fact that many of these 'moments' which attain historical significance are often the result of military conquest or loss which by no means are a clear indication of any kind of 'unity' of a political community.

4 For an account of this 'blindness' to other groups point of view, see Tully (1994).

5 Chambers has also started to apply her model to other societies such as South Africa and Germany (Chambers, 2002).

6 In fact, the emphasis on freedom rather than justice is on that is generally attributed to the contemporary republican position. See Pettit (1997).

7 We have in mind, for example, the educational policy of the Third French Republic which had, among its various objectives, the cultural and linguistic homogenization of France. The expression turning 'peasants into Frenchman' is Eugen Weber's (1976). The broad economic development that, arguably, spawned the development of nations is described, for example, in Ernest Gellner (1994b) and Benedict Anderson (1983).

8 The reaction of Americans to their constitution, for example – to generate and justify policies almost exclusively in relation to their constitutionality rather than arguing for changes to the constitution itself – is precisely what we hope does not arise in the transnational arena.

9 Let us emphasize that we are aware that the analogy is imperfect and potentially of very little use in the sense that it may, on occasion, obfuscate rather than clarify what is going in these arenas. For an argument criticizing this analogy, see Brown, 2001b. We would like to suggest, however, that as revealed for instance in Chadwick Alger's contribution to this volume, the strivings in this direction are significant and growing.

Chapter 11

Democratic Equality, Transnational Institutions, and the Constraints of Modernity

Glyn Morgan

It is widely believed that transnational institutions pose a special challenge to democracy (Markoff, this volume). This belief forms a central premise, for instance, in the debate in Europe over the legitimacy of European political institutions. Proponents of European integration commonly concede that Europe's current political arrangements suffer from something of a democratic deficit. But they believe that democratic political institutions can be constructed that will satisfy all plausible criteria of democratic legitimacy (Habermas, 1998: 2001a, 2001b; Schmitter, 2000). Euroskeptics maintain that this project is either impossible or undesirable. From the Euroskeptics' perspective, democratic governments presuppose *national* institutions embodying *national* political traditions (Judt, 1996; Malcolm, 1994).

This disagreement between Europhiles and Euroskeptics is mirrored, at a more theoretical level, in the debate amongst contemporary political theorists over the possibility of transnational democracy. Some political theorists – such as Robert Dahl (1999), Will Kymlicka (1999), and David Miller (1996, 1998) – are deeply skeptical of the prospects for democratizing transnational institutions. Others – including John Dryzek (1999), Daniele Archibugi (1998, 2000, 2002), and David Held (1992, 1995, 1999) – are more sanguine. Indeed, Archibugi and Held – the principal architects of something they call 'cosmopolitan democracy' – believe that the new era of globalization provides an opportunity to revivify democracy at the local, national, and transnational levels.

Notwithstanding the important disagreements between proponents and critics of transnational democracy, the various parties to the debate tend to share one general assumption: transnational institutions pose a special, distinctive, or unique challenge to democracy. The negative part of my essay challenges this assumption. The essay argues that the challenge transnational institutions pose is ordinary, familiar, and endemic to all modern, socially complex, political systems. This challenge forms part of – and cannot be comprehended in isolation from – a more general trend: the rise of regulatory agencies staffed by technical experts overseen by courts and the consequential decline in the authority of democratically elected legislatures.

Having cleared away this confusion, the chapter tackles the more important questions: What policy issues ought to be settled by democratically elected legislatures? And what policy issues are better delegated to non-majoritarian institutions like courts and regulatory agencies? The positive part of my essay argues that while democratically elected legislatures ought to settle the most controversial moral questions, we would be better off delegating many scientific and technical issues to regulatory agencies, some of which belong at the national level, others at the transnational level. Viewed from this perspective, the recent proposals of some 'cosmopolitan democrats' for a constitutional legal order are deeply problematic. Their effect would be to give the courts authority over issues that ought to be settled by democratically elected parliamentary institutions.

The argument of the chapter proceeds in five sections. Section one defends a normative conception of democracy. Section two identifies certain basic constraints that the conditions of modern society impose upon democracy. Section three defends the claim that the most important moral issues ought to be settled by democratically elected legislatures. Section four draws on the conceptions of democracy and modernity defended in the preceding sections to criticize Archibugi's and Held's argument for 'cosmopolitan democracy'. Section five offers an alternative perspective of a desirable future, a perspective premised on the idea that the state retains certain advantages as a unit of political membership.

1. The Idea of Democracy

In its original sense, democracy meant 'rule by the *demos*'. For most political theorists up until the nineteenth century, democracy called to mind the distasteful prospect of being ruled by an erratic, unwashed mob. Leibniz had this thought in mind, when he stated that 'today there is no prince so bad that it would not be better to live under him than in a democracy' (Riley, 1979: 186). The story of how 'democracy' went from being a term applied to the worst form of government to a term that today defines the minimum condition of any legitimate polity is long and interesting (Dunn, J., 1992). The full details of that story need not concern us here. But it is important to recognize that the term 'democracy' has undergone some important conceptual transformations since the days it was associated with 'rule by the *demos*'.

Two of these conceptual transformations are worthy of comment. First, under the influence of Madison and Sieyès, democracy lost its link to direct popular rule and gained a link to the much safer practice of electing representatives (Forsyth, 1987, Hont, 1994, Morgan, 1988). Thus by the nineteenth century when political theorists like Mill (both father and son) wrote in defense of democracy, it was a democracy of representatives that they had in mind. Indeed, for John Stuart Mill (1975) the central task for democratic theory was to identify the mechanisms sufficient to ensure the election of a representative with the right intellectual furniture. The second conceptual transformation is more recent. Under the influence of sociologists like Weber, Michels, and – perhaps most important of all – Schumpeter, democracy has reconciled itself to the exigencies of bureaucratic and oligarchic domination. Schumpeter's famously deflationary definition of democracy says it all: 'that institutional arrangement for arriving at political decisions in which individuals acquire the power to decide by means of a competitive struggle for the people's vote' (Schumpeter, 1976: 269). From this sociological perspective, a democratic government is nothing but a government chosen by citizens in a competitive election.

In addition to its role as an adjective attached to the noun 'government', the term 'democracy' also plays a more general evaluative role in our political language. Most people in Western industrial societies today take it as axiomatic that any legitimate polity – which is to say any polity worthy of allegiance – must be democratic. To label a polity 'undemocratic' is thus to deny that it is legitimate. Arguments of this sort go on all the time with respect to the EU. Euroskeptics commonly complain that the EU suffers from a 'democratic deficit,' and as such lacks legitimacy. To complain about a 'deficit,' however, presupposes some measure of adequacy. Here there is considerable disagreement about the features that must be present in a polity or political institution for it to be democratically adequate.

My own view, which I can only stipulate for the moment, is that the democratic ideal is best conceptualized as a fair egalitarian procedure. This view assumes that the idea of the moral equality of citizens entails that they are able to participate as equals in a procedure to elect and remove those who govern them. This egalitarian procedure is worthy of support regardless of the outcomes that the procedure yields. The value of such a procedure derives, in part, from the fact that the egalitarian procedure of voting is one of the few significant institutions in a modern industrial society where all members participate as equals. Applied to the question of the democratic adequacy of a legitimate polity, this egalitarian procedural approach requires only that a legitimate polity possess a fair electoral procedure that allows citizens to elect and remove the government.

To appreciate the distinctiveness of this procedural approach to democracy, it might be helpful to contrast this approach with two influential alternatives:

a. Democracy as a Procedural Value. A decision, policy, or institution is democratic when it results from a fair electoral procedure that aggregates the votes of citizens;

b. Democracy as a Substantive Value. A decision, policy, or institution is democratic when it yields outcomes that protect or advance the equality, autonomy, or well-being of citizens;

c. Democracy as a Participatory Value. A decision, policy, or institution is democratic when it permits citizens to participate on equal terms in the decision-making procedure.

The procedural approach to democracy demands less than either the substantive or the participatory approaches to democracy. The procedural approach focuses solely on what might be termed the inputs rather than the outputs of politics (Scharpf, 1999). Those who favour the substantive approach to democracy, in contrast, think that a democratic output must measure up to some substantive requirements. Thus Ronald Dworkin (1996) – perhaps the most influential contemporary proponent of a substantive conception of democracy – argues that a democratic decision, policy or law must be compatible with the principle of equal concern and respect. Indeed, Dworkin (1996) goes so far as to say that a court that strikes down majoritarian decisions that conflict with this principle is democracy-affirming. For Dworkin and other substantivists, the procedural approach to democracy is too permissive of governmental outputs that are, in one dimension or another, inegalitarian (Cohen, 1991).

The participatory approach to democracy shares with the procedural approach an emphasis on the input side of decision-making process. At first glance, it might seem that, given the account provided above of the importance of egalitarian procedures, then the more active participation of citizens in the process of government would be desirable. The mere act of voting in elections, so it might seem from the perspective of the participatory approach, is insufficient. To vindicate the claim that the democratic ideal is best conceptualized as an egalitarian procedure, it is necessary to say something about the constraints that modernity imposes upon normative conceptions of democracy.

2. The Constraints of Modernity

Whatever measure of democratic adequacy we employ in our political language, it is important that that measure of adequacy acknowledge the constraints imposed by what might pretentiously be termed *the condition of modernity*. The assumption here is that whatever evaluative conception of democracy we choose to employ, that conception must be relevant to the world we live in. Perhaps it would be possible to enjoy a more participatory democratic regime if we did not have bureaucratic organizations, liberal constitutions, and capitalist economies, but that is not a realistic option for us. With this point in mind, I want to identify three conditions of modernity that constrain not just the type of democracy we can enjoy, but political life in general.

2.1 The Condition of Disagreement   In modern industrial societies, people disagree about the ultimate ends or purposes of human existence (Rawls, 1991; Waldron, 1999). Some people are religious; others are not. Some people structure their lives in accordance with inherited traditions and customs; others lead lives of radical experimentation. Some people set a high value on communal and public life; others pursue individualistic goals. This 'fact of disagreement' – as the late John Rawls famously termed it – constrains the type of arguments that can be legitimately deployed in public life. If we take seriously the condition of disagreement, then the arguments we deploy to justify fundamental political decisions ought to avoid thick, substantive conceptions of the good. Instead, we ought to rely on strategies of justification that any citizen can accept regardless of his or her ultimate ends or purposes. What Rawls and other liberals have in mind when they draw attention to the condition of disagreement is not the commonplace sociological observation that it will be difficult to get people in modern society to agree on substantive ends or purposes. What they have in mind is a normative commitment – a quintessentially liberal normative commitment – to respecting the diversity of opinions and ways of life in a modern society. In other words, to acknowledge that the condition of disagreement provides a constraint on the conduct of politics is to pay due respects to this underlying normative principle.

2.2 The Condition of Social Complexity By historical standards, late modern industrial societies sustain extremely high levels of material welfare for the vast majority of their citizens. This material welfare is made possible by a highly complex social organization. This complex social organization involves: (i) a rationalized system of administration; (ii) functionally-differentiated systems of knowledge; and, (iii) a trained scientific and technical elite. Together, these three features make it impossible to direct or micro-manage modern society in accordance with a popular, democratic, or collective will. These features impose, in other words, limitations on the extent to which a modern polity can permit citizens to share in power or in key decision-making processes.

A rationalized system of administration requires an elaborate network of administrative offices that focus on a single task. There is a vast number of such offices in a modern industrial society: passport offices; driving license offices; offices that regulate prisons; offices that administer the health system; and so on and so forth. The operating procedure of these offices will, if they are to be efficient, approximate the account given by Max Weber in his famous work on bureaucracy.

Functionally differentiated systems of knowledge are equally crucial to the maintenance of the material welfare of late modern industrial societies. These functionally specific systems – engineering science, electronics, law, medicine, education – must operate more or less according to their own inner logic, if they are to provide modern societies with that complex cluster of goods – including material well-being, security, long-term predictability, and equity – that their citizens have come to expect.

These two features of modern society – a rational system of administration and functionally differentiated systems of knowledge – require the creation, reproduction, and cooperation of a scientific and technical elite. Absent this elite, the key features of modern society will not work effectively. The scientific and technical elite must, moreover, be accorded a certain degree of authority, if they are to do their jobs. What this implies, in effect, is that an important range of decisions affecting the lives of all citizens will be decided not by democratic methods, but by an elite that relies upon specialized knowledge incomprehensible to the ordinary citizen.

The account provided here of the condition of social complexity, much like the description given earlier of the condition of disagreement, contains a number of normative assumptions. It takes for granted, for instance, the desirability of a productive, dynamic economy. It also takes it for granted that democracy must accommodate itself to this condition. These normative assumptions will be rejected by those who believe that a strong, participatory form of democracy has a merit beyond that of a modern rationalized society (Loomis, 1997). In other words, the condition of social complexity, as described here, forms part of a normatively loaded conception of modernity.

2.3 The Insufficiency of Private Action   Some libertarian political theorists hold out the hope of a society where all action is private and, as far as possible, unregulated by governmental (or public) authorities (Hayek, 1973; Murray, 1998). The free market serves, for these theorists, as a model. The coordination of human activities takes place, in this idealized view, by the promptings of a freely-formed, information-rich, price mechanism. This aspiration is at odds with the third condition of modernity: the insufficiency of private action.

In a modern rationalized society, publicly coordinated action will be necessary, for a wide number of reasons. The idea of a self-regulating market, a fantasy that inspires libertarians, is belied by the need for governmental action to provide the legal framework that a market needs; to ensure the production of public goods that the market fails to supply; and to redress inequities in the market's distribution of material benefits. In response to these needs, all modern industrial societies have a bureaucratic state apparatus that absorbs anywhere from nearly a third (Japan) to more than a half (Scandinavian countries) of GDP.

The centrality of the state in the landscape of modern industrial societies is difficult to ignore. For better or worse, the state is the agency that the public employs to solve problems that its members cannot solve acting alone or through the market. The sovereign territorial state owes much of its success – and indeed its historical emergence – to the fact that it proved better able to protect its citizens, against domestic and international predators, than rival forms of political organization (McNeill, 1963, 1987; Mann, 1993a; Spruyt, 1994). Much of this success can be attributed to the fact that it possessed a centralized decision-making authority that enabled it to make decisions more rapidly than rival forms of political organization. Put differently, the sovereign territorial state was better able to overcome *the insufficiency of private action* than any other form of political organization. If the sovereign territorial state is to be replaced, as some political theorists now suggest, then the replacement must perform at least as well in those areas of social life where private action is insufficient.

Much in the same way that the two previous conditions of modernity presupposed a set of normative commitments, the same holds true for *the insufficiency of private action*. As described here, the insufficiency of private action assumes the value of personal security, material well-being, and some form of social justice. If none of these things mattered then private action might be thought of as sufficient. By the same token, it might be argued that a simpler, less technologically entranced society would permit greater scope for private action. The account given here of the insufficiency of private action, so it might be objected, simply takes for granted the necessity and desirability of a productive, technologically advanced industrial society. This criticism is exactly on the mark. The account of modernity provided here is a normative account. It provides an interpretation of modern society, which picks out what it takes to be the desirable and indispensable achievements of modernity, achievements that include a productive, technologically advanced industrial society.

2.4 Conclusions Regarding the Constraints of Modernity For the purposes of this chapter, the account provided here of the constraints of modernity serves two purposes. First, it provides a further justification for the claims made in the previous section concerning democracy as a procedural value. And second, it lays down certain parameters that proposals for extending democracy beyond the nation-state must heed. For the moment, it will be enough to explain how this account of the constraints of modernity supports the idea of democracy as a procedural value.

The fact of disagreement provides a sufficient justification for rejecting all substantive approaches to democracy that designate as 'democratic' outputs a controversial list of rights. In modern industrial societies, we disagree about such issues as whether abortion and euthanasia should be recognized as rights. To identify these rights – as, for instance, Ronald Dworkin (1996) has done – as essential components of any desirable conception of democracy is to make democracy more controversial than it actually is. The procedural conception of democracy is, in this respect, more attentive to the fact of disagreement.

The participatory conception of democracy conflicts with another feature of modernity: the fact of social complexity. Proponents of participatory democracy seem to think that citizens can participate in all the major decision-making processes that affect their lives. In a modern complex society, this is simply not possible. In a wide range of policy areas, citizens have no choice but to rely upon experts. Even if it were possible for citizens to participate, it would not be desirable. Indeed, as I intend to show in the next section, modern democracies are often right to delegate decision-making authority to various administrative agencies.

3. Democracy and Delegation

While Schumpeter's sociological conception of democracy seeks to reconcile us to the actual nature of democratic government, his account remains, in at least one important way, unduly flattering to the modern democratic citizen. For Schumpeter, the modern democratic citizen could not be expected to be self-governing, but could nonetheless cast a vote for one or another competing political elite. This conception of democracy remains misleading, however, in its suggestion that elites competing for elective office – democratically elected legislative representatives, in other words – are in full control of the processes of government. In modern industrial societies, however, this no longer holds true. Today, a large number of the rules and regulations that structure our daily life emanate not from democratically elected legislatures but from a variety of non-parliamentary public agencies. These agencies include the higher courts, the executive, the central bank, and such regulatory bodies as (to confine myself to US examples) the Security Exchange Commission (SEC), the Nuclear Regulatory Commission (NRC), the Food and Drugs Administration (FDA), the Environmental Protection Agency (EPA), and countless others. For better or worse, we are now governed, at least in part, by various non-parliamentary agencies that exercise discretionary power delegated to them by legislatures.

There are two important conclusions to be drawn from the fact that democratically elected legislatures have delegated so many important decisions to non-parliamentary bodies. First, it forces us to reject the idea that transnational institutions pose an especially urgent or distinctive threat to our capacity for democratic self-government. The threat (if that's the right word) posed by transnational institutions – such as the EU, the World Trade Organization (WTO), the International Monetary Fund (IMF) and so forth – is not very different from the threat posed by nationally-based central banks, supreme courts, and other regulatory bodies. The importance of this point has been nicely captured with respect to the EU by Andrew Moravcsik (2002: 661-2):

> EU decision-making procedures, including those that insulate or delegate certain decisions, are very much in line with the general practice of most modern democracies in carrying out similar functions.... As long as political procedures are consistent with existing national democratic practice and have a *prima facie* normative justification, I conclude, we cannot draw negative conclusions about the legitimacy of the EU from the casual observation of the non-participatory nature of its institutions – a dictum that could usefully be applied in many contexts outside the EU.

The second conclusion to be drawn about the current power of non-parliamentary bodies concerns the task of normative democratic theory. A democratic theory relevant to the world we inhabit must have something to say about the division of responsibility between democratically elected legislatures and non-parliamentary agencies. Democratic theory must, at a minimum, be able to answer the following questions: What policy issues should be left in the hands of democratically elected legislatures? And what policy issues (if any at all) should be delegated to one or another non-parliamentary agency? The answers reached on these questions will, as will be seen in the next section, partly determine our assessment of the democratic legitimacy of transnational institutions.

Some democratic theorists – let's call them *parliamentarians* – take the view that political authority should be concentrated in democratically elected legislative bodies (Saward, 1998; Schoenbrod, 1993, 1999; Waldron, 1999). From this perspective, delegation – whether to courts or regulatory agencies – is democratically undesirable. While it would be impossible to consider all the arguments that parliamentarians advance against delegation, three of their arguments stand out. First, parliamentarians contend that if we take seriously the value of democracy, we must allow democratic procedures to settle the most important moral and political issues that confront us. Any alternative – such as turning the matter over to the higher courts – fails to respect our capacity for self-government (Waldron, 1999). Second, parliamentarians contend that unless policies are enacted by our elected representatives, citizens will not be able to hold decision-makers accountable for policy failures. Elected representatives, in turn, will constantly seek to pass the buck to politically insulated administrative agencies (Schoenbrod, 1993). And thirdly, parliamentarians argue that delegation is elitist, because it elevates experts above citizens (Schoenbrod, 1999).

Against these arguments, other theorists – let's call them *public administrators* – argue that delegation improves the quality of government (Majone, 1996, 1998; Mashaw, 1997; Schuck, 2000). Again they offer many arguments in support of this position, so I can mention here only a few of the most important. First, they contend that social complexity makes it impossible for legislatures to decide many policy issues. Turning the formulation of policies over to experts is, in many cases, unavoidable. Second, they contend that the quality of the policies that result from non-parliamentary agencies will often be superior to the statutory laws enacted by parliaments. Third, they contend that citizens will often have greater scope to participate in the formulation of policy, when it takes place in non-parliamentary agencies. And fourth, they contend that it will often be easier to hold these agencies accountable, to force them to be transparent, and to ensure that they act on the deliberative basis of shared public reasons. Summarizing the strengths of the public administrators' position, Peter Schuck (2000: 252) concludes that:

> delegation – when backed (as it is in our [US] system) by many powerful institutional and informal controls over agency discretion – constitutes one of the most salutary developments in the long struggle to instantiate the often competing values of democratic participation, political accountability, legal regularity, and administrative effectiveness.

The most extreme poles in the debate between parliamentarians and public administrators represent, at least at first glance, untenable positions. The idea that parliament should enact a strict non-delegation doctrine would simply founder on the fact of social complexity. Parliaments are simply not equipped to regulate many of the technically complex issues that arise in an advanced industrial society (Moran, 2002). The idea that courts and administrative agencies should be the site of all major laws and policies faces a different problem: it would not be democratic. In so far as we think of democracy as an egalitarian procedure that permits citizens to elect and remove those individuals that govern them, it is crucial that parliamentary bodies retain a preponderance of legislative authority.

Yet while a procedural conception of democracy rules out those extensive forms of delegation that undermine the status of parliament as the principal locus of government, a procedural conception of democracy does not preclude more limited, policy-specific, forms of delegation. It is difficult to say anything in the abstract concerning the boundary between legitimate and illegitimate forms of delegation. But broadly stated, the boundary ought to be drawn in such a way that it represents the best solution to the problem of maximizing the role of parliament consistent with the constraints of modernity (disagreement, complexity, and insufficiency of private action). From this democratic proceduralist perspective, it would be desirable for many of the most controversial issues of the day to be settled by parliament. Questions such as the place of religion in public life; abortion; euthanasia; the weight and scope of minority rights: these ought to be settled, if we value procedural democracy, by our democratically elected representatives in parliament. When this happens, people will be able to retain a sense of themselves as free and equal citizens whose vote matters. With parliament in control of the controversial moral issues, the delegation of many of the more technical policy issues to national or transnational non-parliamentary agencies would be of little consequence.

Substantive democrats find this parliamentary solution to the problem of delegation deeply disturbing. For substantive democrats – including Ronald Dworkin (1996), Joshua Cohen (1991), and, as we shall see, David Held (1995) – democracy, properly understood, entails a rights-protecting outcome. To give a democratic majority rather than a higher court the final word is to open the possibility that the majority will enact rights-violating policies. Against this line of argument, some procedural democrats point out that we disagree about the substantive rights that democracy ought to protect (Waldron, 1999). Given this fact of disagreement, it would be better, so procedural democrats contend, not to seek a final, irreversible solution that makes one side of the disagreement permanent losers. For this reason, it would be better to keep controversial issues on the parliamentary agenda, amenable to reversal by the sway of electoral majorities, rather than to take these issues off the agenda – as, say, the United States has done with abortion and Canada has done with its minority rights (Lenard and Turgeon, this volume).

It would be fully consistent to agree here with the procedural democrats concerning the nature of democracy – which they correctly, I think, define as a fair egalitarian procedure rather than a procedure that necessarily yields a rights-protecting outcome – while disagreeing with them concerning the importance of democracy. Earlier, I noted that the term 'democratic deficit' suggested a corresponding conception of 'democratic adequacy'. I further noted that most people in modern industrial society assume that 'democratic adequacy' is a necessary condition of political legitimacy. I now want to consider the possibility that this assumption is wrong. Perhaps, in other words, it is an error to think that democracy is a necessary condition of political legitimacy. Some political theorists have recently questioned the link between democracy and legitimacy. Richard Arneson, for instance, has argued that the procedural rights of democracy are only valuable insofar as they secure 'more fundamental rights ... better than do alternative feasible arrangements' (Arneson, 1993: 118). Fareed Zakaria (1997) has drawn a similar conclusion after observing the extent to which many new democratic governments fail to protect liberal rights and the rule of law. Zakaria thinks that US foreign policy should favour regimes that protect liberal rights even if those regimes are undemocratic. These arguments would fit nicely into the worldview of the public administrators described above. They support the conclusion that in a modern complex society, technical decisions should be left in the hands of experts, and moral questions should be settled by judges. Democratically elected parliaments would exercise an oversight role; they might select the people to serve in agencies and on the bench. But the idea that a democratically elected parliament could remain at the centre of political life is a dangerous anachronism (Zolo, 1994).

In light of the anti-democratic spirit of arguments like these, it is important to remind ourselves why democracy, conceived as a fair procedure, matters. It matters, so I have argued here, because it provides political-institutional recognition of the fact of our moral equality as citizens. That fact is one of the key achievements of modernity. It was hard won and can be easily lost. In modern societies that depend heavily on a highly educated scientific-technical elite, there is a tendency towards growing income inequality. When education and income differences are further reinforced by marital patterns, as seems to be increasingly the case in advanced industrial societies, there is always the danger that inequalities will sediment into caste-like social strata (Kaus, 1991; Brooks, 2000). Democratically elected parliaments that control the major issues of the day provide a prophylactic against the most egregious caste-like forms of social inequality. Parliaments that merely oversee the courts and other regulatory agencies – where the real action, as it were, takes place – will not suffice. When a democratic majority can settle the great moral issues of the day, the defining activity of citizens – voting – matters a great deal. Such is not the case in the world envisaged by the public administrators (and, for that matter, the substantive democrats). In their world, the appropriate political-institutional recognition of our equality will be lacking. Moreover, when voting is everything, each citizen will have a strong incentive to ensure that each other citizen is as well-informed and knowledgeable as possible. It will not be possible, as is now the case in some democracies, to rely on judges to strike down the ill-informed preferences of a majority.

A further advantage of the proposal to make parliament the arbiter of controversial moral questions is that it enables parliament to delegate without losing its position in the political life of the community. Here it is important to recognize that the constraints of modernity are such that regulatory agencies are an inescapable feature of any complex society (Moran, 2002). This is not to say, however, that there is any uncontroversial way of distinguishing between 'the moral' issues that belong in the parliamentary arena and 'the technical' issues that can be delegated to regulatory agencies. What in one community will be a moral issue will be a technical issue in another. Such is the case, for instance, with 'stem-cells', scientific research on which is deeply controversial in the United States but not in Europe. There are a number of ways of responding to this difficulty. It may be possible, for instance, to employ referenda to contest the designation of an issue as technical rather than moral, an issue to be regulated by an agency rather than legislated by parliament. In other words, citizens should be allowed some institutional mechanism that allows them, when they have sufficient supporters, to place an issue on the legislative agenda.

There remains one final point to be made in this discussion of democracy and delegation. The difficult questions that we have been wrestling with in this section – what issues belong in the hands of parliaments? What issues should be delegated to non-majoritarian institutions? – are questions that crop up in national arenas. It just so happens that some courts and administrative agencies are now located at the transnational rather than the national level. From the perspective of majoritarian democracy, the location of these non-majoritarian issues matters less than the range of important issues that remain up for grabs in democratically contested elections. It is with this cautionary point in mind that I now wish to consider the claims of some recent advocates of transnational democracy.

4. Some Difficulties with Transnational Democracy

For a number of democratic theorists writing today, globalization poses both the greatest threat to democratic government today and the greatest opportunity. The *threat* comes in the form of increasing cross-border flows of goods and people, capital and cultural fashions. These flows, so it is thought, have weakened nation-states to such an extent that democratically elected governments are not in a position to control the economic and social forces that shape their citizens' lives (Habermas, 1998). The *opportunity* comes in the shape of new forms of political membership located at local, national, and transnational levels of human community. Some democratic theorists look hopefully towards the EU which, if properly organized, might serve as a model of a postnational, multi-tiered polity (MacCormick, 1999; Shaw, J., 1999).

The difficulty with many arguments for transnational democracy is that they tend to underestimate the constraints of modernity and overestimate the desirability of replacing national parliamentary institutions with supranational legal institutions. To further justify this rather pessimistic assessment of the transnational democracy literature, I want to consider some of the central arguments put forward by Daniele Archibugi and David Held, perhaps the most influential theorists of transnational democracy writing today. The premise of their work, as I understand it, is a sociological observation concerning the increasing level of 'regional and global interconnectedness' (Held, 1995: 16). They have in mind here two somewhat different phenomena: one, 'regional and global economic relations which stretch beyond the control of any state' (Held, 1995: 20); and two, the increasing number and importance of transnational political organizations and social movements. Theorists of 'cosmopolitan democracy', to put it crudely, hope to build on the latter to control the former.

The idea that transnational social movements – or, more generally, a nascent global civil society – can 'democratize' the various processes of globalization forms a central element in the writings of many cosmopolitan democrats. While there is much to be applauded in the efforts of various activists to ensure that the processes of globalization are not steered exclusively by, and in, the interests of one particular segment of global society, the notion that transnational social movements provide the basis for a radical democratic transformation of global politics seems both unlikely and undesirable. The problem that confronts transnational social movements is the problem that was identified earlier in the discussion of *the insufficiency of private action*. Under conditions of modernity, large-scale social change tends to require great concentrations of power. The greatest agent of social change in modern times is the state, a consequence of the fact that the state can wield tremendous amounts of many different types of power (Mann, 1993a). It is difficult to see how transnational social movements can play any comparable role. At best, they can bring specific issues to the attention of statal authorities; they can assist in the effective delivery of state services; and they can organize protests against actions of states. Beyond performing these worthy subaltern roles, transnational social movements are largely irrelevant.

If it is unrealistic to expect transnational social movements to take over functions performed by the state, what about the suggestion that transnational social movements represent something akin to a global public interest? Consider here, for instance, the following remarks by Martin Köhler (1998: 232):

> Though they have received no formal mandate from any political community or authority, civil society organizations and their transnational networks are increasingly recognized by governments as legitimate representatives of a global sphere of public interest which acts on its own behalf.

This description of the role of transnational social movements brings into focus an aspect of these movements that is frequently overlooked: they lack any democratic mandate. In other words, transnational social movements cannot claim to represent anyone other than their own members. In this respect, transnational social movements are no different from multinational corporations. Neither General Motors nor Greenpeace can claim a genuine democratic mandate. Perhaps it might be said that Greenpeace acts on behalf of a higher good – a conception of the global public interest – but this claim is untenable, if only because the 'global public interest' is itself a matter of fundamental disagreement. Some critics of transnational social movements have amplified this point to suggest that these movements seek to enact policies at the global level because they cannot win support for them at the national level (Rabkin, 1999). From this perspective, transnational movements seek to circumvent the democratic will of national majorities. Even if this point is overdrawn, the fact remains that there is nothing obviously democratic in transnational movements, no matter how worthy their aims. A world in which such movements exercised greater power would be less rather than more democratic.

To their credit, theorists of 'cosmopolitan democracy' do not rely exclusively on transnational social movements. In addition, they advocate two important institutional reforms: one, a cosmopolitan legal order; and two, a set of political institutions operating at the global level. David Held's writings contain the fullest account of this cosmopolitan legal order. Held envisages a legal framework that establishes the rule of law at all levels of political community – local, national, and transnational. This framework limits the scope of popular mandates in the name of a cluster of basic rights, including not only the standard civil and political rights, but also 'control over fertility', 'universal childcare', and 'a guaranteed minimum income' (Held, 1995: 192-3). Held justifies this extensive list of rights with reference to an underlying conception of personal autonomy. For Held, autonomy – 'the ability to deliberate, judge, choose, and act … upon different possible courses of action in private as well as public life' – is an uncontroversial good, which can be defended as neutral, impartial, and acceptable to all (Held, 1995: 225-7).

Not content with the creation of a cosmopolitan legal order, cosmopolitan democrats also seek to create political institutions at the transnational and global levels. Thus Archibugi (1998, 2002, 2003) constantly stresses the need for democracy at three levels – within the state; among states; and above states at the global level. Broadly stated, Archibugi seems to offer two different arguments in support of the creation of global democratic institutions. First, he notes that some problems simply cannot be solved by national governments. They can only be solved by transnational or global political authorities which, if we value democracy, must themselves be democratic (Archibugi, 1998: 211-12).

The second argument Archibugi offers in support of global democracy concerns the problem of what might be termed 'democratic externalities'. In a world of separate territorial states, decisions reached in one country will sometimes negatively impact the well-being of people outside that country (Archibugi, 1998: 204). To remedy the problem of democratic externalities, both Archibugi and Held propose creating decision-making jurisdictions at the transnational and global levels that enable 'all-affected' by a decision to have a voice. More specifically, Archibugi expects intergovernmental institutions, including international judicial institutions, to settle the disputes that emerge from democratic externalities (Archibugi, 1998: 218-19). He also wants to turn the UN into a democratic organization by creating an 'elective parliamentary assembly with consultative powers' (Archibugi, 1998: 221).

The institutional reforms envisaged by cosmopolitan democrats amount to a radical transformation of the international state system. While these reforms fall short of the creation a fully federal global polity, they would involve something more substantial than a loose confederation of sovereign states. The EU writ large is probably the closest approximation to what the cosmopolitan democrats have in mind (Archibugi, 1998: 219-20). For some of Archibugi's and Held's critics, these aims are simply unrealistic (Gilbert, 1999; Hawthorn, 2001; Urbinati, 2003). My own view is that they are both unrealistic and undesirable, not least because they ignore what I described above as the constraints of modernity.

Proposals to create a cosmopolitan legal order – or 'democratic cosmopolitan law', as Held puts it – are especially problematic in light of what I called earlier 'the fact of disagreement'. Held's willingness to link autonomy, rights, and democracy together in an overarching legal framework bears comparison with

Dworkin's 'constitutional conception of democracy', which would enable judges to strike down majoritarian decisions whenever those decisions conflict with the rights deemed necessary to secure 'equality of concern and respect' (Dworkin, 1996). Since Held's list of rights is even more specific and extensive than those Dworkin favors, Held must confront the criticism that his cosmopolitan democratic framework leaves too little for citizens to deliberate and vote upon (Thompson, D., 1999). More generally, Held must answer objections put forward by some procedural democrats, who argue that there is a form of democratic disrespect involved in taking fundamental decisions out of the hands of ordinary citizens and embedding them, permanently and untouchably, in a legal framework (Waldron, 1999). From the perspective of procedural democracy, Held's project of constructing a cosmopolitan legal order amounts to the triumph of a liberal legal system at the expense of democracy and politics.

Turning now to the second major institutional reform proposed by Archibugi and Held: the creation of international political and judicial institutions to remedy the problem of democratic externalities. The hope here is that when states enact policies detrimental to those people outside the state's jurisdictional boundaries, an international body will step in and remedy the situation. Archibugi and Held both cite the example of one state setting its interest rates at a level detrimental to other countries. But the problem runs much deeper than this. One of the most harmful examples of a 'democratic externality' arises in the case of the citizens of wealthy countries (the US and the EU, in particular) protecting their agricultural and manufacturing sectors from cheaper products from poor countries. It would doubtless be a very good thing if the WTO (or some other organization) had the power to bring this type of protectionism to an end. But this would require the victory of an undemocratic international organization over the democratic will of national communities. The proposal of 'cosmopolitan democrats' to democratize international organizations – either by opening them up to inputs from transnational social movements or by bringing them under the control of a global parliament – simply fails to recognize the role of democracy in causing the problem in the first place. If international organizations were under the control of interest groups and regional factions, these organizations would likely become even more ineffectual than they already are. Put bluntly, any genuinely democratic solution to the problem of democratic externalities requires the development of global fellow-feeling. In the absence of this fellow-feeling, people in one country will continue to care more about 'their' farmers and 'their' textile workers than the invisible misery of millions many miles away.

5. The Persisting Advantage of the State

For many proponents of transnational democracy, the nation-state has lost much of its problem-solving capacity (Habermas, 1998). They look forward to new modes of political organization that can solve the problems that now exceed the capacities of the state. These new modes of political organization – democratic cosmopolitan law, democratic international organizations, and a global representative parliament – will, so they hope, transform the current international state system. The state will still exist, but in much the same way as California and Texas exist within the United States, or Bavaria and Saxony exist within the Federal Republic of Germany. Cosmopolitan democrats, in other words, aim neither for a world state nor a weak confederation, but for something in between.

The claim that the state is now obsolete, that its once-great problem-solving capacities are now largely vestigial, faces one very large problem: the United States. The cosmopolitan democrats' critique of the state is not directed at particular difficulties that some specific states face. Their critique applies to this very type of polity. Indeed, Held sometimes seems to suggest that the modern state is likely to go the same way as the *polis*, the medieval *regnum*, and the absolutist monarchy (Held, 1992). The difficulty with this argument is that these earlier types of polity failed, because they were unable to meet the challenge of more effective rivals. There is no obvious analogy to this situation today. The United States remains the dominant political power in the modern state system. For the first time in the modern era, we live in a 'unipolar world'. Moreover, the United States provides a classic example of a nation-state (see John Hall, this volume). In the areas that matter – foreign and security policy – it centralizes decision-making in the hands of the executive; and it can call upon the animating ideology of something called 'the American way of life' to mobilize its citizens behind *grands projets*. The EU, which the cosmopolitan democrats like to cite as the model for the new cosmopolitan order, suffers in comparison. It lacks a centralized decision-making body; it remains deeply divided on many key constitutional questions; and it cannot call upon any European-wide loyalties. As a result, the EU is utterly dependent on the US for its security.

In this context, the cosmopolitan democrats' suggestion that the United States reconstitute itself and the international order on the model of the EU seems bizarre in the extreme. This is to draw precisely the wrong lesson from the current state of the world. The right lesson to draw, surely, is that the EU should become politically more like the US. The EU, in other words, ought to centralize decision-making in an institution that is capable of making decisions quickly and effectively. For this to be possible, the EU will need to give more power to both its executive and legislature. The losers here will be national executives and legislatures. But the only alternative is for the EU and its member states to remain permanently dependent on the United States. Any steps towards the creation of a European 'superstate', which is essentially what this proposal amounts to, will have to proceed in tandem with the emergence of European political loyalties. Despite the fact that these loyalties are, at the moment, either very weak or wholly absent, there is no necessary reason why such loyalties cannot be created, on which point I am in agreement with Archibugi (see next chapter). National political loyalties were based, at least in their initial stages, on a common educational system and the military (for more on this, see Markoff and Morrison, this volume). Europe is, in some respects, in a more advantageous position than the nascent European nation-state, for Europe's business and political elites already share a common language (English). Moreover, modern communications make it very easy to link all Europeans in a common public sphere.

Given the argument of the preceding two sections, the principal difficulty facing the construction of a European 'superstate' lies in the problem of ensuring that parliamentary institutions remain at the centre of the political life of the community. If a European superstate becomes a Europe dominated by an appointed Commission, the Courts, and regulatory agencies, then Europe will fail to provide its members with the political-institutional recognition commensurate with their status as free and equal citizens. Voting in democratic elections will lose its importance; the status of citizen will decline in value. To protect against these outcomes, European, member-state, and regional parliaments must be the site where the great moral issues of the day are settled. The division of responsibility between these parliaments will become one of the most difficult questions. At the moment, many pro-Europeans support the so-called 'principle of subsidiarity', which privileges decentralized decision-making bodies (MacCormick, 1999). But if Europe is to become a superstate, it will need a European parliament strong enough and prestigious enough to control Europe's executive institutions. For this reason alone, we can expect the European Parliament to assume an ever larger role in the political life of Europe.

Needless to say, the creation of a European superstate is not likely to happen any time soon. The current European convention, under the Chairmanship of Valéry Giscard d'Estaing, looks likely to bring the idea of 'an ever closer union' to a halt. Some observers think that the EU in its present intergovernmental form represents the final destination of the European project (Moravcsik, 2002). But the question of a likely future is, in the present context, less germane than that of a desirable future. The cosmopolitan democrats have done us all the service of forcing us to take up this question. Their account of a desirable future differs from other accounts. They are, for instance, much more willing to impose limitations on external sovereignty than, say, the proposals for a desirable future entertained by John Rawls (1999).

In contrast to either the cosmopolitan democrats or the Rawlsian *Law of Peoples*, the argument presented here in support of a European superstate is premised, in part, on the idea that under the constraints of modernity the state remains an indispensable institution. But there is another part to this argument in support of a European superstate. To call for the creation of a European superstate is to take seriously the overall distribution of power in the international state system. It is to assume that the current unipolar state system is not the best point of departure for the creation of a more eirenic international order. In such a system, the dominant power faces very little incentive to support multilateral norms and institutions, at least outside of those areas in which it is their direct beneficiary. It can simply act alone. In the last few years, we have seen ample evidence of this. The United States has vetoed international agreements – such as the Kyoto Accords and the International Criminal Court – that it considers incompatible with its own national interest. The United States has also used its power to ensure that international institutions reflect its own values. Thus the US has sought to ensure that UN agencies do nothing to encourage abortion as a method of family planning. In acting in this way, the United States is acting in precisely the way one would expect any dominant or hegemonic power to act (Hall, 1996).

Now it might be argued that the best hope for a peaceful international order is to rely upon the United States to act as global policeman, global lender of last resort, and global role model. But this vision of the future is unlikely to work. Forceful displays of American power, even when effective in the short term, tend to provoke counter-reactions (Johnson, 2000). The level of anti-Americanism in the world today must give pause to any hope of the world falling in line behind US leadership. A European superstate that was able to match America's strengths both economically and strategically provides a better way forward. Not only would Europe be able to balance the United States' role in international organizations, but Europe would present to the world a somewhat different model of modernity than that found in the United States (Habermas, 2001b). As a result of their very different histories, Europe and the United States possess somewhat different understandings of the boundary between state and market, public and private, sacred and profane. The realization that modernity can come in different forms will be an asset in the effort to spread the values of modernity around the world. Insofar as a European superstate serves the cause of modernity, it will benefit not just Europeans but the world at large.

These remarks concerning the desirability of a European superstate fall a long way short of providing a convincing justification for such a polity. They are meant only to serve as a reminder that the desirable future found in the writings of cosmopolitan democrats must be compared to alternative desirable futures. It is possible to construct a new international order, which brings the benefits of modernity to the world, without jettisoning the sovereign state. Since the United States, the unrivalled power in the international state system, remains a quintessential nation-state, it is premature to speak of the obsolescence of this type of political unit. In this respect, the EU has more to learn from the US than vice-versa. A European superstate would temper US inclinations to act unilaterally. A European superstate would, moreover, be easier to democratize than the complex multi-tiered political system envisioned by cosmopolitan democrats. At the very least, the onus is on cosmopolitan democrats to explain why their vision of a desirable future requires such an extensive transformation of the current international state system.

Chapter 12

Cosmopolitan Democracy and Its Critics

Daniele Archibugi[1]

1. The Origins of Cosmopolitan Democracy

Fewer than fifteen years have passed since we witnessed the fall of the Berlin Wall, and yet we get the feeling that the event already belongs to a distant past. Today, we find ourselves in an entirely new global political era, and the dreams of a world founded on the rule of law, cooperation among people, and even democratic public participation in global decision-making, have dissolved as can only happen to the boldest of utopias. Meanwhile, we continue to die because of wars, political violence, and famine, just as we did two decades ago.

It is not the first time that humanity has cherished dreams of justice that have suddenly been put aside. Following the *prise de la Bastille*, for instance, the many new expectations that emerged from the revolution in France continued to be nourished throughout even the Napoleonic wars. The Battle of Waterloo, however, put an end to the dreams of the revolution – moreover so badly pursued – of freedom, equality, and fraternity. In our time, there are those who hold the belief that the fall of the Twin Towers marked the ending of the hopes raised by the fall of the Berlin Wall. Despite the radical effects that the events of 11th September 2001 have had on worldwide politics, a new political order has not yet emerged to suppress the hope for a global society keen to the values of democracy and legality. The collapse of the Soviet Union and the parallel victory of the West, combined with the new wave of democracy and the accentuation of economic and social globalization, have brought profound changes to global politics. The idea of a cosmopolitan democracy, also one of the products of this era, may yet be the beneficiary of these developments. Neither Waterloo, nor the fall of the Twin Towers, could entirely and enduringly suppress the aspirations for a New World Order.

The victory of the West, understood here as that *ensemble* of advanced capitalist states governed by liberal-democratic regimes, is not unprecedented: the allies brought a similarly thorough defeat to the fascist regimes during the Second World War. Rather, what is entirely new is the resolution of the Cold War without resort to armed conflict. The liberal-democratic and capitalist bloc had simply grown powerful enough to prevent a violent confrontation with its post-World War

II rival. Thus, the strength of liberal democracies has not been measured exclusively in military terms – a physical confrontation between the two major nuclear powers would have spared no winners – but rather also in terms of their political, economic and cultural abilities.

The West's hegemony has only grown since the end of the Cold War. What effect was this victory to have on the rest of the world? Would the triumph of Western democracies generate similar political systems in the remaining part of the globe? Some positive effects were observed at the beginning of the 1990s, when a new wave of democracy permeated countries in the South as well as in the East. Nelson Mandela and Vaclav Havel left their prison cells to rule from the presidential palaces of their respective countries. Free elections became a positive tool for the legitimation of governments in a steadily increasing number of states. The United Nations, after decades of dullness imposed by the superpower rivalry, appeared to rediscover the ambitions nurtured by its founders: the establishment of a political locus where the most important global issues could be condensed.

These examples are by no means an attempt to dismiss the despicable behaviour that Western democracies have all too often assumed outside their national borders. Colonial adventures and the many battles fought for them find their echo in the brutality exerted by Western states over the Third World. Moreover, on far too many occasions the United States has supported bloody and despotic regimes in the South, with the sole intention of gaining their loyalty and using it against their communal enemies, the Soviet Union and its allies. With this menace dissolved, one could have hoped that the West would choose more cautiously its friends and partners, favouring the consolidation of democratic movements within developing countries rather than supporting those elites that, although loyal to them, were nonetheless despotic in nature. Within the West, the United States' foreign policy had been dominated by the slogan, 'the enemies of my enemies are my friends'; but could it have been replaced with the more promising maxim, 'the friends of my rights are my friends'?

Putting aside the political vicissitudes, economic and social processes have increasingly connected the various parts of the globe. Globalization – a word that nobody likes but everybody uses – has become the emblem of our times. As David Held notes (1995: 17), mortgage repayments, the spread of a contagious disease, or employment – all examples of factors that directly affect our daily lives – can be dependent upon decisions taken far from some or all of the affected parties. So is it with an American Federal Reserve increase in interest rates, for instance, or the intent of a tropical government to keep secret the development of a new epidemic, or the choice of a Japanese firm to invest abroad. It is only fair to question how such a pronounced globalization could proceed in spheres as different as finance, trade, fashion, and the mass media without exerting repercussions also upon the international political system.

2. The Necessity of a Cosmopolitan Democracy

The historical events mentioned above have led to the idea of cosmopolitan democracy: broadly speaking, the attempts to globalize not only the economic model that won the battle, but also its political model (the necessity of democracy beyond the state has been discussed in Archibugi and Held, 1995; Held, 1995; 1997; 2002; Falk, 1995; 1998; McGrew, 1997; 2002; Archibugi and Köhler, 1997; Archibugi, Held and Köhler, 1998; Kaldor, 1998; Linklater, 1998; Habermas, 1998; 2001a; Dryzek, 1999; Thompson, D., 1999; Holden, 2000; Archibugi, 2003). However, the expression 'to globalize democracy' hides a trap: must we read the maxim as the application of a democratic system in every state in the world, or as a worldwide democracy? The most tenacious defenders of democracy *within* states often become skeptics, if not outright cynics, when confronted with the hypothesis of a global democracy. Dahrendorf (2001: 9) settled the issues by hastily declaring that to propose a global democracy is to 'bark at the moon'. With a more elegant argument, Dahl (1999: 21) concluded that 'the international system will lie below any reasonable threshold of democracy'. Nonetheless, cosmopolitan democracy continues to take upon itself the risks of proposing the globalization of a democracy both at the level of state institutions – present and future – and at the level of global society. Cosmopolitan democracy aspires simultaneously to the pursuit of democratic values *within*, *among*, and *beyond* states.

The pursuit of such a goal is dependent on a combination of assumptions, to be examined in turn:

2.1 Democracy is to be Conceptualized as an Historical Process Rather Than as an Agglomeration of Norms and Procedures
Democracy cannot be understood in static terms. Those states with the most grounded traditions are today attempting to sail into uncharted waters. For example, in the most fully established regimes, the number of rights-holders is on the increase: minorities, immigrants, future generations, even animals, have today been granted a particular set of rights. Modalities for decision-making are once again under dispute, as indicated by the debate over deliberative democracy (Habermas, 1998; Dryzek, 2000; Bohman, 1998), while the issue of the aggregation of political preferences, initially raised by Condorcet, is once again at the centre of the debate.[2]

Never before has the debate within democratic theory been as vigorous as during the last decade of the twentieth century, the same decade that also witnessed the victory of democracy. What conclusions could we possibly draw from all this? First of all, that the idea of democracy as an unaccomplished mission is gaining new support (Dunn, 1992). More generally, democracy is increasingly seen as an endless journey, such that we lack today the ability to predict the direction in which future generations will push the forms of contestation, participation, and management (see John Markoff, in this volume and 1996, for elaboration).

Such assumptions place democracy not only in a world-historical context, but also within the history specific to each political community. The way in which the evaluation of political systems is effectively configured thus becomes decisive: each and every political system can be evaluated more effectively on the basis of a scale relative to its own development, rather than through a simplistic democracy/non-democracy dichotomy. This would imply that, in order to evaluate a state's arrangements, it becomes necessary to take into account both the level of, and path to, democracy (see Beetham, 1994; and chapter 10 in this volume; UNDP, 2002).

2.2 A System of States Based on Conflict Impedes Democracy Within States The absence of a peaceful international climate has the effect of blocking dissent, modifying opposition, and inhibiting freedom of information within states. Citizens' rights are limited and, in order to satisfy the need for security, civil and political rights are therefore wounded. This is all too familiar. Back in the sixteenth century, Erasmus noted that 'I am loth to suspect here what only too often, alas!, has turned out to be the truth: that the rumour of war with the Turks has been trumped up with the purpose of mulcting the Christian population, so that being burned and crushed in all possible ways it might be all the more servile towards the tyranny of both kind of princes (ecclesiastical and secular)' (Erasmus, 1536: 347-8). In the eighteenth century, Jean-Jacques Rousseau elucidated the connection between internal/external by reminding that war, or its menace, was but a method employed by tyrants as a means to control their subjects: 'war and conquest without and the encroachment of despotism within give each other mutual support.... Aggressive princes wage war at least as much on their subjects as on their enemies, and the conquering nation is left no better off than the conquered' (1756: 91). These observations took on a new meaning during the Cold War: in the East the foreign menace was being employed as a tool to inhibit democracy, whilst in the West to limit its potential (Kaldor, 1990). At the same time, leaders were fuelling the confrontation – the democratic ones no less than the autocratic leadership of the old Soviet Union – as an instrument to maintain internal dominion.

The Cold War has ended, but the need to find scapegoats has not ceased. Extremist parties – even in democratic states – still reinforce their power by fanning the flames of international conflict. The development of democracy has thus been influenced by both the lack of external conditions and the will to create them. Even today, the dangers of terrorism have led to an imposed limitation on civil rights in many states. It is, therefore, undoubtedly significant that the recent project of the International Institute for Democracy and Electoral Assistance (see Beetham, chapter 10 in this volume) evaluates the democratic status of a state, possibly for the first time, also on the basis of its external conditions. Thus, an international order, founded both on peace and the rule of law, is a necessary condition for the progress of democracy within states.

2.3 Democracy Within States Does Not Univocally Influence a State's Foreign Policy Democratic states do not necessarily apply to their foreign policy those same principles and values on which their internal system is built. Already in his day, Thucydides narrated with disenchanted realism how citizens of the *polis* voted with enthusiasm, 'amongst a pile of other fascinating nonsense' (1954: Book VI, 8. See also 1 and 24 in the same book), in favour of the campaign against Sicily, despite the fact they were totally oblivious to both the island's location and its size. The analogies between Athens' foreign policy and the United States' are many (cfr. Gilbert, 1999: chapter 4). Of course, realist theorists would not expect a democratic regime necessarily to imply a more virtuous foreign policy. The calamity of US engagement in Vietnam, purportedly in democracy's name, should still torment the consciences of democrats. Cosmopolitan democracy, therefore, takes for granted the lesson imparted by realists regarding the absence of consistency between domestic and foreign policies. It is, however, through further investigation of two hidden virtues of democratic regimes that it may become possible to bridge the 'real' and the 'ideal' elements of their foreign policies. The first of these two virtues is the interest of states in generating and participating in inter/transnational associations (Russett and Oneal, 2001). The second one is the tendency of states to nourish a greater respect for rules when these are shared amongst communities that recognize each other as analogous.

2.4 Global Democracy is Not Just the Result of Generalizing Democracy Within the State The debate that has flourished over the hypothesis that 'democracies do not fight each other' (Doyle, M., 1983; Russett, 1993; Russett and Oneal, 2001) suggests a connection, causal and precise, binding the system internal to states to peace at the international level. According to a syllogism that is never made explicit, the persistence of war is ascribable to the presence of non-democratic states. Consequently, it is simply by acting upon the internal political system of states that one can guarantee a peaceful community at the international level.

Although the attainment of democracy within states does strengthen the international rule of law and might also reduce the tendency to resort to war, we do not consider this sufficiently strong to serve as the basis for the reform of international relations (see Franceschet, 2000, for a comparison between democratic peace and cosmopolitan democracy). There is an added specific dimension that requires consideration, and that is how to extend democracy also to a global level, which cannot be understood solely in terms of the 'absence of war'.

2.5 Globalization Limits the Political Autonomy of a State It would be hard to imagine nowadays a state's political community that is both autonomous and independent. Each state's political choices are bound to a set of obligations and formalities (as for example those determined by agreements undersigned between states) and, even more so, to informalities (see, after Held, 1995, the flourishing debate on the matter: Clark, I., 1999; Cerny, 1999a; Keohane, R.O., 2003). Whilst the traditional internal/external dichotomy of international relations assumes the existence of a defined separation between the two areas, these two dimensions appear progressively connected, as has been highlighted by the literature on international regimes (Rosenau, 1997). The chances of a national political community taking decisions autonomously are thinning, which consequentially leads us to the question: via what kind of structures will the various political communities be able to deliberate in a democratic fashion on matters that are of interest to them?

2.6 Stake-Holders' Communities Do Not Always Respect National Borders

We can identify two sets of interests that bypass states' borders. On the one hand, we can find matters that involve all inhabitants of the planet. Many environmental problems are authentically global, since they influence the destiny of both men and women irrespectively of their state of origin (Gleeson and Low, 2001), though we must not think that only issues of such breadth cross a state's borders. Borders are also crossed by circumscribed communities which share communal interests on a limited number of aspects, all equally important to them. The management of a lake surrounded by five different states, the existence of a religious or linguistic community with members scattered in remote areas of the world, the dependence of workers in more than one state on the strategic choices of a single multinational firm, the ethics of a specialized and professional society, are all issues that are not faced democratically within a state's political community. In most cases, such 'overlapping communities of faith' (Held, 1995: 136) lack the means necessary to influence those political choices that affect their destiny. Governments have put in place specific intergovernmental organizations, but these are dominated by government officials rather than by a stake-holders' majority, causing in turn the adoption of a statist perspective. Even in cases where all participating states are democratic ones, the deliberative process on these matters does not follow the democratic principle according to which everyone involved should benefit from the right to take part in the decision-making process, which should hold even if not all participating states are democratic.

Take the striking example of the nuclear experiments conducted by the French government in 1996 in Mururoa, in the Pacific: the decision to undertake the experiment was based on the procedures of a state with a long-standing tradition of democracy. Evidently, though, the stake-holders' community was substantially different, since the French public was not exposed to eventual nuclear radiation, but was receiving the (supposed) advantage in terms of national security and/or nuclear energy. The French public would certainly have had a different reaction if those same experiments had been conducted in the Parisian region. Instead, the communities in the Pacific experienced the full environmental consequences. The Mururoa case is certainly one of the most outstanding, but the occasions in which a state's political community diverges from the stake-holders' community are increasing in number.

The role of stake-holders in a democratic community has long been recognized: democratic theory attempts to take into account not only the sum of individual preferences, but also the number of times each individual is involved in making a specific choice. In a similar fashion, a significant part of contemporary democratic theory, inspired by Rousseau, is committed to the analysis of the process concerning the *production* of preferences rather than their *aggregation* (Young, 2000: 23). This is just one of many fields in which the theory and practice of democracy are developing, but without any recognizable effects at the level of international affairs. Can the issues affecting stake-holders alien to a particular state continue to be overlooked in a democratic order?

2.7 Global Ethical Participation It is not only a common interest that brings populations closer together. Already, Kant (1795: 107) noted that 'in reference to the association of the world's populations one has progressively come to such an indication, that the violation of a right in any one point of the Earth, is adverted in all of its points'. Along with the violation of human rights, natural catastrophes, conditions of extreme poverty, and environmental risks also tend increasingly to unite the various populations of this planet.

Human beings are capable of a solidarity that often extends beyond the parameters of their state. Surveys have revealed that approximately 15 per cent of the Earth's inhabitants already perceive themselves as global citizens, against the 38 per cent who identify themselves nationally and 47 per cent locally (Norris, 2002; for a discussion, see Marchetti, 2002). If we take these data *prima facie*, it emerges that only a minority of the world's population considers its own identity to reside in those institutions that depend upon the Weberian monopoly of the legitimate use of force. The emergence of a multiple identity could also lead to multiple layers of governance. If we add to this the increasing global identity on the part of young people as well as those at a higher cultural level, it becomes possible to ask: what results will these surveys yield in ten, 50, or 100 years time?

This desire to participate in global issues is expressing itself also via the formation of an increasing number of non-governmental organizations and global movements (Anheier et al., 2001; 2002; Pianta, 2003). Although there is a tendency to exaggerate the extent to which citizens participate in matters that do not directly affect their political community, the feeling of belonging to a planetary community is nevertheless growing and assuming a political dimension.

It has been observed that the need to form a political association out of various populations would hold even in the absence of a process of globalization (Saward, 2000: 33). If globalization strengthens the need to coordinate interstate politics, as a result of the changed interests of states, then the dynamic tension favouring global ethics would not dissipate even if it were possible to re-establish the autonomous condition of each state.

3. The Structure of Cosmopolitan Democracy

These issues are both old and new: old, because they belong to that journey to democracy that has yet to be accomplished, and re-emerge periodically in theory as much as in practice; new, because worldwide economic, social, and cultural transformations are exerting pressure upon the cradle – the *polis* and now the nation-state – from which democracy originated and developed. It is not the first time that democracy, in an attempt to survive, has had to undergo a transformation (Held, 1997). Throughout its history, however, democracy has held to certain values: the juridical equality of citizens, the majority principle, government's duty to act in the interest of everyone, the need for majorities to be transitory and not perpetual, and the idea that deliberation must be the result of a public confrontation between various positions. The crucial question, then, is how can democracy's core be preserved whilst adapting it to new circumstances and issues?

We believe that the best way to conceptualize cosmopolitan democracy is to view it in terms of its different levels of governance. These levels are not to be considered hierarchically, but rather in terms of a series of functional relations. We have schematically indicated five paradigmatic dimensions: local, statewide, interstate, regional, and global. At the end of this exercise it will be possible to distinguish the similarities and differences that exist between the present system of representative democratic states and a potential global democratic system.

3.1 The Local Dimension   It is difficult today to imagine a national democracy without a local network of democratic institutions, associations and movements. Already, however, the local and global dimensions are becoming interrelated. The creation of organizations – both governmental and non-governmental – that connect together communities and local bodies that may not belong to the same state is becoming an increasingly frequent phenomenon (see Alger, chapter 6 in this volume). Since states seldom devolve competency on issues specific to inter-local institutions, this often involves the relevant actors extending beyond their assigned jurisdictions. Cosmopolitan democracy suggests, therefore, strengthening, where possible, the structure of local government, even if this might require crossing state borders.

3.2 The State Dimension   To date, approximately half of the world's states have still not adopted a political system that corresponds to the contemporary understanding of democracy (UNDP, 2002). Although the ideal of democracy has proselytized even yesterday's opponents, its worldwide affirmation is still far from realized. New democracies are constantly in danger and face a daily struggle for the consolidation of a democratic regime. After all, not even the most advanced democratic regime should be satisfied with their domestic arrangements.[3] In expanding democracy from the state to the global level, it becomes possible that each of the existing (incompletely) democratic states could be a laboratory as much as an agent of cosmopolitan democracy. In fact, states are today called upon to grant rights to individuals – such as refugees and immigrants – who had traditionally been denied these rights. Much still needs to be done before these individuals are able to benefit from the same rights granted to indigenous populations (see Rubio-Marin, 2000). Revealingly, however, democratic states are now being confronted with the dilemma of whom to consider as their own citizens: those who are born in a specific community? Those who live and pay taxes? Those who would simply like to be citizens of a particular democratic community?

Even within a particular community, the rights of various groups and citizens are being differentiated. One of the most important developments of modern citizenship theory concerns the acknowledgement of the community's right to identify on the basis of a variety of religious, cultural, and ethnic values. A democratic state, we are told, is not exclusively based on equality, but also on the acknowledgement and even the valorization of diversity (Young, 1990; Kymlicka, 1995). To acknowledge the diversity that exists within a given political community causes the community's boundaries to lose clarity. Why should we consider as members of our community people who speak a language, profess a religion and have a cultural background different from our own but hold the same passport, and then consider as members of a different community those who are much more similar to us but hold a foreign passport? To find good reasons to be cosmopolitans we need not cross the borders of our states; it is enough to look at our schools and neighbourhoods.

Along with its domestic arrangements, a state is also characterized by its membership of the international community. What is it, then, that distinguishes a good member from a bad member? Extending beyond common reliance upon narrow sovereignty, we feel that a liberal state must distinguish itself not only by the substance of its foreign policy, but also by its willingness to follow shared procedures. A good citizen of the international community (Linklater, 1992) is thus distinguished by the will not only to be actively involved in the production of norms, but also in respecting them, or at least incorporating and reflecting them, within the state's own foreign policies.

3.3 The Interstate Dimension The presence of intergovernmental organizations (IGOs) is an indicator of the willingness to expand at the interstate level the application of a number of democratic principles (formal equality between member states, public accountability, rule of law) but, at the same time, it is also an expression of the difficulties involved in achieving this. It not necessary to be a partisan of democracy, nor particularly of its cosmopolitan version, to support the work of IGOs; it is their duty to facilitate the work of states – democratic and autocratic – at least as much as to limit their sovereignty. Statists, functionalists, and federalists are all equally in favour of IGOs, although they may wish to see them grow in different ways.

However, could we consider IGOs democratic institutions? And, if not (Dahl, 1999), could they ever become so? The issue of democratic deficit is appearing with increased frequency not only in reference to the European Union, but to other organizations as well, beginning with the United Nations. The fiftieth anniversary of the UN, for instance, brought demands to make this body not only more powerful, but also more transparent, more respectful of the rule of law and, overall, more democratic (see, for instance, Commission for Global Governance, 1995).

However, the UN does not require members themselves to be democracies, thus making it unclear that the introduction of the majority principle would constitute an increase in democracy. In many of these organizations, starting from the UN, there are no specific entry requirements concerning the character of a state's internal regime. Would basing decision-making on the majority principle lead to an increase in democracy? A democratic state can have various motivations for hesitating before accepting, for instance, the majority principle when many of the representatives of these IGOs may not have been elected democratically, especially if the organization's competencies are extended to matters that touch upon issues of domestic politics. Even if the membership of IGOs were to include democratic states only, as is the case for the European Union, there would be no guarantee that the decision-making process would respect the preferences of the majority of stake-holders. Most IGOs are founded on the formal equality of their member states, and this in turn guarantees each state the right to one vote independently of its population, its political and military power, and its level of involvement in the decisions to be taken. In the UN General Assembly, those member states whose total number of inhabitants represents just 5 per cent of the planet's entire population dispose of the Assembly's majority. Would it then be more democratic to base decisions on the preferences of just six states (China, India, United States, Indonesia, Brazil and Pakistan) representing more than half of the world's population?[4]

On the other hand, the veto power held by the five permanent members of the UN Security Council goes against all traditional principles of democracy. Within the International Monetary Fund and the World Bank, the decision-making power of a state is measured on the basis of its wealth. Within the G7 and G8 summits, not formally IGOs due to the absence of a charter, it is rare for a government to deliberate in favour of an option that is of interest to the planet as a whole. Meanwhile, the main contemporary military alliance, NATO – almost entirely composed of democratic states – has been on several occasions more of an obstacle to, than a facilitator of, democratic relations among states.

Moreover, the participation of individuals in decision-making processes within IGOs, if not absent, is often simply decorative in nature. With the exception of the European Union, which possesses an elected parliament, no other IGO envisages for its citizens a participatory role within the discussions over the choice of available options. Dahl (1999) is certainly right in pointing out the number of difficulties that IGOs encounter in their attempts to reach a decision-making process that satisfies the prerequisites of democracy, although this should also be taken as an incentive for IGOs to place this *problématique* at the core of their agenda. The projects and campaigns for the reform and democratization of the UN and other IGOs are many (for a review see Patomaki et al., 2002). These choices are much more political than theoretical. Thus, where should the partisans of democracy stand when the abolition of the veto power within the UN Security Council, a more substantial weight for those states with lower quotas within the International Monetary Fund, or an increased level of transparency with the World Trade Organization is under consideration?

3.4 The Regional Dimension Problematic issues that slip by at the state level can be dealt with also at the regional level. In many cases, in fact, the regional level of governance is the most appropriate. The most striking historical example of this has been integrated Europe, in which the first six states slowly but more or less continuously developed a political system capable of growing not only in strength, but also in the domestic democratic character of the members. The presence of a parliament elected through universal suffrage, coupled with the ability to associate, initially six states, now 15, and possibly 27 in the near future, distinguishes Europe from any other regional organization. It is nonetheless of interest that this past decade has witnessed both an increase in and intensification of regional organizations almost everywhere, with a particular focus on trading agreements (Telò, 2001; McDougall, in this volume, addresses the prospect that Europe may represent the model for the new regionalisms).

The regional dimension can also become an important promoter of stability in areas where its components are far less familiar with the procedures of democracy, areas where for instance the state's political unity has proven incapable of preserving on the one hand the exclusive use of legitimated violence within its borders, and on the other hand peaceful relationships with its neighbours. Take for instance the case of the Great Lakes Region in central Africa (for more, see Shaw, this volume): the formation of states has replaced more archaic communities, as in the case of the village, the extended family, and the ethnicity of local populations. Many of the conflicts within this region could be better managed through an organization that operated at a regional level, one that included both state representatives as well as representatives of the various local communities. This is not to say that we should expect from a hypothetical regional organization of central Africa institutions as sophisticated as those in the European Union. Still, even a less fully developed regional organization could be helpful in managing problematic issues such as endemic conflicts between rival ethnic groups.

3.5 The Global Dimension It is undoubtedly bold to think that global decisions could also be part of a democratic process, given that in realms such as armaments, financial flows, and trade, governance has proven extremely difficult to establish (for an analysis of global governance, see Rosenau, 1997; Keohane, R.O., 2001; Held and McGrew, 2002; Koenig-Archibugi, 2002). However, the proposition of a global governance may, in actual fact, be less bold that it initially appeared to be. For the past decade or so, non-state subjects have benefited from the ability to make their voice heard at various UN summits, as well as within such agencies as the IMF and WTO, although, to date, their participation has been limited to a mere advocacy role deprived of any deliberative powers. But a level of governance that goes beyond the state's ray of action is gradually imposing itself politically. The United Nations and other international organizations, in spite of their inter-governmental character, have for the most part gone beyond their original mandate and opened their floor to non-governmental players.

As a matter of fact, the revendication of a global level of governance is strong in many areas, such as financial flows, immigration, environmental concerns, human rights, and development aid (cfr. Held and McGrew, 2002). The list is extensive. Each one of these specific regimes provides for autonomous rules; though it is surprising to note how in the field of global governance, whose emergence was a response to growing interdependence, one can still observe such a wide separation between the various regimes (for an attempt to map the levels of global governance, see Koenig-Archibugi, 2002). It is not astonishing therefore that, in each one of these regimes, one can find initiatives and campaigns that push for greater accountability and democratization (a comprehensive literature on the subject includes Holden, 2000; Edwards and Gaventa, 2001; Patomaki et al. 2002; Anheier et al., 2002). Moreover, these initiatives often proceed independently of each other, though all aim at a greater democratization: every day it is possible to act concretely in pursuit of the increased accountability of global governance. However, it is equally important to bear in mind the goal that has here operated as premise – cosmopolitan democracy – from which perspective a framework can be developed which connects up the diversity of issue areas on which citizens and global movements are strenuously working.

During the G8 summit in Genoa in July 2001, protesters were displaying banners with the slogan, 'you G8, we 6 billion'. These protesters were expressing the spirit of many groups' and global movements' concerns about environmental issues, human rights, and economic inequalities. They believed – and rightly so – that such issues are often neglected within the formal expression of politics. However, would it not be easy for heads of state to retort by asking (as in Morgan, this volume): 'we got elected, who elected you?' As noted by Wendt (1999: 129), meanwhile, the *demos* as it stands is not necessarily prepared to support a global democracy.

Overall, there is no single criterion by which global legitimacy can be established. To build a level of democracy valid for the entire planet requires the pursuit of many different criteria. A cardinal institution of democratic *governance* – which therefore distinguishes itself by the absence of central *government* – is a world parliament. This is an ancient and utopian proposition that has never been fully appeased (cfr. Archibugi, 1993; Heater, 1996; Falk and Strauss, 2001). A level of global governance must also rest on a more stringent international juridical foundation.

3.6 The Relationship Among the Various Levels of Governance

As both the levels and institutions of governance are on the increase, the question that arises is: how can the competencies of these different bodies be shared? Is there a risk of creating a new division of bodies, in which every one claims to have sovereignty but in reality no one has it effectively? Would new conflicts originate from the existence of institutions endowed with overlapping competencies, where each institution could claim its own sovereignty?

The key concept is of course sovereignty, the foundation of the system of international law since the Restoration. Sovereignty has been responsible for limiting both the state's competencies and its constraints, at least formally, to its geographical boundaries. Ideally, the concept of cosmopolitan democracy belongs to that school of thought that from Kelsen (1920) onwards has regarded sovereignty as a dogma to be overcome. The assumption that a political or institutional subject should be exempted from responsibility for its actions is incompatible with the essence of democracy. Each political actor, whether a tyrant or a 'sovereign' people, must come to terms with other actors when competencies overlap. From an historical point of view, the concept of sovereignty has been the artificial basis of an 'organized hypocrisy' (Krasner, 1999), and in very few instances has it succeeded in limiting a state's extraterritorial interests. Nevertheless, we must face the challenge of finding a replacement that is effective, since still today the revendication of sovereignty is used to curb the prevalence of the strong over the weak.

Our proposal is to replace, within states as much as between states, the concept of sovereignty with that of constitutionalism (Ferrajoli, 1995). The content of this proposal is similar to the idea of the vertical dispersion of sovereignty, as suggested by Pogge (1992: 61), and to the cosmopolitan model of sovereignty proposed by Held (2001: 23). However, we feel that the use of the term 'sovereignty', in itself, ought to be removed. Therefore, conflicts concerning the issue of competence, arising as a result of the different levels of governance, must be resolved within the domain of global constitutionalism, and referred to jurisdictional bodies which, in turn, must act on the basis of an explicit constitutional mandate, as Kelsen (1944) had foretold.

To think that conflicts could be resolved at the global level by means of constitutional and juridical procedures, rather than by means of force, is certainly utopian. The project of a cosmopolitan democracy is thus identified with a much broader ambition: that of turning international politics from the realm of *antagonism* into the realm of *agonism* (competitive spirit; see Bobbio, 1995). This process has gradually affirmed itself within democratic states, as it is common practice that different institutions engage in disputes over their competencies. Reaching the same result on a global level would mean taking a decisive step towards a more progressive level of civilization.

4. The Critics of Cosmopolitan Democracy

After more than a decade from its first formulation, the idea of cosmopolitan democracy is being discussed within the domain of political theory, though unfortunately it has met with much resistance within the sturdy sphere of *realpolitik*. In spite of this, what is encouraging is that many new thinkers, including young ones, have begun sharing ideas advanced originally by a scanty group of scholars. Of course, criticisms have not been spared, and to these the rest of this essay is dedicated.

4.1 Realist Critics The disenchanted realists remind us that the world's mechanisms are very different than the way cosmopolitan dreamers imagine them to be. Ultimately, they argue that force and interest are the principal elements regulating international relations. Every effort to tame international politics through institutions and popular participation is pure utopia (Zolo, 1997; Hawthorn, 2000). We do not disagree with the importance attributed to force and interest, but it is excessive to consider them, not only as the sole moving force behind politics, but also as being immutable. Meanwhile, it would also be incorrect to think that the interests of all actors involved in international politics are opposed to democratic management of the decision-making process. More appropriate is the idea that there are opposite interests that are in tension with each other: on the one hand, a strong pressure exerted over the decision-making process by the few (a few governments, military centres, and large enterprises); and, on the other, the demands of interest groups to increase their access to the decision-making table. Whether peripheral states, global movements, or national industries, these interest groups are not necessarily pure at heart. They stand in opposition to other powers because, as subjects, they have their own interests to follow, and therefore an attitude that is anti-hegemonic. To support these interests is not a matter of theory, but rather of political choice.

Realists reject not only the feasibility of the cosmopolitan project but also its desirability. These two critiques are quite different and should not be confused. It is certainly relevant that, in order to construct his critique, Zolo must continuously force the position taken by his adversaries. In his book, Zolo often criticizes the prospect of a global government, but none of the authors he cites – Bobbio, Falk, Habermas, Held – ever argued in its defence. These scholars simply limited their support to an increase in the rule of law and integration within global politics; they never argued in favour of the global concentration of coercive power. Cosmopolitan democracy is not to be identified with the project of global government – necessarily reliant upon the concentration of forces in one sole institution – but, on the contrary, it is a project that invokes voluntary and revocable alliances between governmental and meta-governmental institutions, where the availability of a coercive power, *in ultima ratio*, is shared between actors and subjected to juridical control.

4.2 American Hegemony   Some realist critics have begun to look upon contemporary political reality with disenchantment. These critics have embraced a definition of today's world in terms of the hegemonic bloc dominated by a single state, the United States, endowed with extraordinary powers and the mandate to defend very confined economic interests (Chandler, 2001; Gowan, 2001). This hegemony goes so far as to resort to the threat of military power in order to penetrate economic and political activities. These authors have also described how many international organizations – such as the International Monetary Fund, the World Trade Organization, and NATO – serve the purpose of maintaining and preserving the interests of this new hegemonic bloc. Basing observation on real world conditions, these critics argue that a project that aims to increase the intergovernmental management of national policies leads *de facto* to a decrease in the independence of the various states and, ultimately, reinforces the ideology behind hegemony (the critiques of Hall and Morgan in this volume have some of this flavour). Authors such as Zolo, Gowan, and Chandler have noted how those same years that witnessed the contemplation of the possibilities of UN reform and the debates over the issue of global governance also witnessed the significant military engagement of Western states. In their resort to conflict, these states made use of a rhetoric that dangerously resembles those discourses based on a longing for a global order founded on the values of lawfulness and democracy.

We agree that the amount of power concentrated within the hands of the United States is excessive, and that its domestic democracy is no guarantee of the wise or lawful application of such power. However, the key is to find a strategy that can effectively oppose US hegemony. Contrarily to these critics, we dispute the ability of the old sovereignty dogma to provide a satisfactory alternative to US hegemony, or to any hegemony, as a matter of fact. Until this moment, sovereignty has served the purpose of aiding governments in abusing their citizens, rather than offering protection to the weaker states from the greed of the stronger ones. The strengthening of international institutions, especially if inspired by the values of democracy, would most probably produce the desired effect of obliging the United States, as well as its allies, to engage in a foreign policy that adhered much more coherently to their internal constitution. Barricading ourselves behind the notion of sovereignty merely for the sake of counterbalancing America's hegemony may cause us to forget the millions of people who are everyday subjected to the oppression of their own governments.

4.3 The Marxist Critique I (Karl) It has become commonplace to believe that the US's hegemonic power, and that of its closest allies, is a consequence of the present international economic system (Gowan, 2001). If cosmopolitan democracy were to focus on the institutional aspects of the international order without taking into consideration the economic dynamics, it would disregard the importance of crucial centres of power. International democracy, taken solely as an institutional project, would thus be impossible (Görg and Hirsch, 1998), whilst the transformation global politics could only be brought about by a new economic regime.

We believe that it is not easy to establish well-defined links of cause and effect between politics and economics. Indeed, many economic interests are more than satisfied with the present mechanisms of control and have no interest in increasing the democratic control over the flows of capital or international trade. However, there are many other interests, maybe more widespread, that are pushing for greater accountability. The financial speculation that is of advantage to some groups is an obstacle to others, and many economic powers are now looking forward to altering the current structure of international finance (Soros, 2002).

4.4 After Proletarian Internationalism There are those critics who believe that we have made improper use of the notion of cosmopolitanism. Brennan (2001: 76) maintains that to talk about 'internationalism' would be much more exact. Of course, concepts, not words, are what really matter. Nevertheless, we maintain that it is more precise to qualify our version of democracy as cosmopolitan rather than international. The term 'international', coined by the Abbot of Saint-Pierre and Jeremy Bentham, recalls a relation between governments and a type of organization that is characterized by two levels of representation: the definition of governments within states; and the creation of an 'international' community based on governments (Anderson, P., 2002). Bentham's position graduates from that school of thought that maintains the existence of democratic governments, within states, as the fundamental guarantee of the democratization of society at the international level. The adoption of the notion of 'cosmopolitanism', instead, allows for the introduction of a third level of governance, one that evokes from citizens a more active participation in political matters. Citizens should therefore play a twofold role: that of citizens of the state, and that of citizens of the world.

Gilbert (1999) and Brennan (2001) evoke the internationalism of another glorious tradition of which we are very fond: the workers' movement and, in particular, the international associations of workers in the nineteenth and early twentieth centuries. The famous slogan, 'proletarians of the world, unite!' anticipated the essence of this spirit. Although this slogan still represents today the guiding flame in the fight for a fairer global society, it should nevertheless be revised. Within this perspective, the use of 'internationalism' is no longer used to refer to representatives of the state. Internationalism refers rather to the political subjects, within the state, who are in conflict with governments because they are believed to be the expression of the antagonist class, the bourgeoisie. The Marxist view maintains the assumption that proletarians in different states hold interests that are so much in common with each other that conflicts between proletarian states would be resolved much more effectively than conflicts between bourgeois states. The fratricidal dispute of the European bourgeoisie in the First World War confirmed the incapacity of the old ruling class to resolve conflicts through peaceful mechanisms.

However, this Marxist definition of 'internationalism' was built upon the belief that the defeat of the ruling class – brought about by the proletariat – would result in the cessation of all conflicts between organized groups, since proletarian communities would never cherish the desire to subjugate any other (worker's) community. Consequently, there would be no need to organize an international political system that could mediate conflicts, simply because there would not be any. Sovereignty would dissolve together with its holder, the bourgeois state.

What needs to be revised is the political programme – not the spirit – of proletarian internationalism. Cosmopolitan democracy therefore suggests the creation of institutions and representative channels, not limited to a specific social class, but aimed at all individuals. Its aim is not to bypass social classes, but to follow the modest objective of offering a channel of direct representation to all people, at the global level, regardless of their social status. This implies basing deliberation over global issues on the preferences of a majority, rather than on those of a single class. Paraphrasing the *Communist Manifesto*, Ulrich Beck (1999: p.18) invoked: 'Citizens of the world , unite!'.

Marxist analysis suggests the existence of an eternal conflict of interests between rival social classes; interests that – now more than in the past – are in conflict not only *within* states, but also *between* states. The creation of a global citizenship will not put an end to this conflict of interests, nor does it intend to. Its goal is simply to find institutional *loci* where these conflicts of interests could possibly be managed. If the prolonged civil war in Sierra Leone were somehow linked to the diamond trade, and the traders from Anvers, Moscow, or New York were thought to have played an effective role in instigating the hostilities, what kind of institutional channels might prove effective in resolving the dispute? Possibly, international institutions and the politics they alone could generate – such as the required certification of the diamonds' origins – could offer the possibility of mitigating the conflict. In other words, global institutions may constitute channels of effective conflict resolution.

Transnational campaigns have already succeeded in influencing the choices of political decision-makers: take the decision of the UK government to follow environmentally friendly procedures for the disposal of the Brent Spar (Prins and Sellwood, 1998); the institution of the International Criminal Court (Glasius, 2002); the persuasion of some multinationals to recede from their profit-making interests and allow for the free diffusion of the AIDS drug (Seckinelgin, 2002); or even the case of obtaining military interventions to protect human rights (Kaldor, 2001). Overall, the actions of an emerging global civil society have already produced substantial results (Pianta, 2003).

4.5 The Marxist Critique II (Groucho) Groucho Marx once said that he would never wish to be part of a club that accepted him amongst its members. Groucho was anticipating what became one of the most frequent criticisms of the European Union: 'if the EU were to apply for membership in the EU, it would not qualify because of the inadequate democratic content of its constitution' (Zürn, 2000: 183). Many critics make go beyond this comment to argue the inability of the EU ever to become a democratic institution (for an in-depth discussion of the case of the EU see, Pogge, 1997; Bentham and Lord, 1998; Schmitter, 2000; Bellamy and Castiglione, 2001; Moravcsik, 2002). Since the EU is the most democratic of all current international organizations, the argument would involve the position that it is difficult, if not impossible, to extend democracy beyond the state system. Robert Dahl (1999) has produced a list of criteria for the evaluation of democracy within a state and, following this methodology, he demonstrates the impossibility of a global democracy.

International organizations, including the European Union, are far less democratic than many of their member states, but we do not believe that international organizations can be judged according to the same criteria that apply to states (the issue is discussed in Beetham, this volume). In our view, it is more a question of evaluating the ability of different assets to increase democratic participation, particularly at a time when many complain about the lack of control over the decisions taken by state-level executives.

Dahl does not appear to be hostile to the idea of international organizations, nor does he deny the usefulness of increasing their transparency and accountability. What he considers improper is the use of the word 'democracy'. However, if one shares the view that decisions over issues that cross national borders are to be taken within appropriate institutions (i.e., international institutions), and that these should respond at least to the criteria of transparency and accountability, one will observe that the discrepancies are mainly an issue of terminology. Possibly, it would prove far more useful to debate possible courses of action, rather than to argue over the choice of words.

We cannot refrain from asking ourselves to what extent a critic like Dahl would object to a substantial reform of the various international organizations, such as for example the creation of a parliamentary assembly within the United Nations (cfr. Falk and Strauss, 2001), or a compulsory jurisdiction of the International Court of Justice (Archibugi, 1993). We must avoid finding ourselves in a situation in which the best is the enemy of the good. Given the difficulty of constructing state-like democracy beyond the level of the state, we often neglect the possibility of pushing for greater legitimacy of the decision-making process, even in those areas where it would be feasible to do so.

4.6 The Dangers of a Global Technocracy There is always the fear that a level of governance beyond the state may ultimately deprive states of their hard-won democratic content. It is not purely by chance that those small communities with the highest level of participation, and which are tenaciously and generously committed also to global issues, are often those which most object to the adhesion to international organizations. Switzerland, homeland of Rousseau, country of origin of the Red Cross, seat of the League of Nations and of many other UN agencies, became a formal member of the UN only in 2002, and still maintains its independence from the European Union, despite being entirely surrounded by it. The Norwegian people have twice voted against the adhesion to the EU, while both the Swedes and the Danes have refused to exchange their currency for the Euro. We are not here to judge this behaviour, as much as to understand it, especially since these communities, in the matter of democracy, have more to teach than to learn. The most convincing account has come from Wolf (1999: 343), who points to governments' propensity to use their obligations towards international organizations to limit the sovereignty of their citizens. There is a widespread concern that international organizations might become the Trojan horse that will allow technocrats to prevail over democratic control.

The parameters of Maastricht have become in Europe the religion that has forced states to resort to restrictive economic policies. The directives of the International Monetary Fund have forced particular political choices upon many developing countries and, moreover, have reduced the possibility of reaching a satisfactory level of democratization. We share the worries related to the ability of international organizations even to limit the political autonomy of a state, but does the absence of international integration sustain these political communities at a higher degree of autonomy? Take the examples of three neighbouring states: Finland, Sweden, and Norway. The first of these is fully integrated within the European Union, the second has decided not to introduce the Euro, whilst the third has chosen to opt out. Could we thus conclude that Norway benefits from a greater degree of autonomy than Finland? At least Finland has the possibility of expressing its concerns within institutions at the European level. At present, the autonomy of Norway appears to be more at risk than that of Finland. To integrate within supranational democratic organizations helps to preserve states' democracy far more than it obstructs it.

To refuse to extend democratic decision-making beyond the state's territory not only leaves decisions within no-man's land, but it also jeopardizes democracy within the state. It may therefore be preferable to go the opposite way and push for more accountability and transparency within international organizations, introducing within each one of these different mechanisms of control and public participation (Pogge, 1997; Zürn, 2000).

4.7 The Communitarian Approach   A similar critique has been proposed by communitarian authors, such as Will Kymlicka (1999) and Craig Calhoun (2003). These authors have gone so far as to maintain that a political system can only be either democratic or cosmopolitan, since a democracy cannot be cosmopolitan, and a cosmopolitan system cannot be democratic. Kymlicka encourages democratic states to take responsibility also for novel issues such as immigration, financial flows, multi-ethnic communities, and minority rights, while at the same time providing a positive contribution to global human society, for example by strengthening internationally the protection of human rights and development aid. Exonerating the state of these responsibilities, in view of an imprecise global order, may result in an 'under-lapping' of responsibilities between the state political system – which although insufficient is nevertheless extensible – and a global system that is not yet existent.

Kymlicka's concerns are understandable. We are not confronted with the rejection of global responsibility, but with the idea that this kind of responsibility may be better managed through existing state institutions rather than through institutions under development and founded on global citizens. We have argued before that the state is not alien to cosmopolitan democracy, and that, on the contrary, it holds the ability to become a cosmopolitan laboratory. However, when Kymlicka (1999: 121) maintains that 'democratic politics is politics in the vernacular', he appears to be oblivious to the fact that far too many aspects of our daily lives escape the vernacular dimension, at the global level as much as at the state level. What is the vernacular political dimension of China or India? Or even of tiny Switzerland? What part of the population is excluded from vernacular politics in countries such as the United States or Canada?

The absence of a vernacular dimension of politics is an issue that is confined not only to a developing global democracy, but also to the democracy within states. Therefore, either we reduce democratic politics to a exclusively tribal dimension, leaving all other issues to be dealt with non-democratically, or we invent a political dimension that is also meta-vernacular (for one version of such a response, see Lenard and Turgeon, this volume).

Many parliaments, at the moment of being institutionalized, have resented the effects of the lack of a common language. Today, the issue has shifted to other locations, such as the UN General Assembly and the European Parliament. Undoubtedly, this will be a problem in the event of the creation of a global government. To date, democracy has been quite ductile in allowing these transformations to manifest themselves, and we have faith in its ability to do so also in the future. The validity of Kymlicka's argument holds for any form of democracy, whether within a multicultural community or a multilingual one.

4.8 Searching for the Global Demos   It is often argued that a cosmopolitan democracy would not be democratic because of the lack of a global *demos* (Axtmann, 2002; Calhoun, 2003; Urbinati, 2003; Thaa, 2001; Morgan, this volume. The issue is also discussed to opposite effect, in Zürn, 2000, and Habermas, 2001a). We too share this view, and we also hold that the notion of a global civil society has often been exaggerated, because – unfortunately – minorities and elites are still the primary participants in discussions relative to global politics. However, we also believe that it is not possible to think of the *demos* as antecedent to institutions. In many cases, the same institutions give birth to the *demos* (see Morrison, this volume). We see today a unique American *demos* because, over two centuries ago, there were colonials who fought for the United States of America despite the diversity of languages and religious beliefs. Had there not been that subjective choice, today's states would probably be very different, each one proud of its own identity, just as there are very different identities in the United States and Canada. To think that the *demos* is independent of institutions is equal to thinking that the *demos* could ever be independent of history.

There is also the belief that democracy cannot exist without a *demos*. Once again, we share this belief. However, there appears to be no agreed set of criteria to judge what makes of a multitude of people a *demos*. Populations can be interpreted as the inhabitants of a village, a city, or a country; but they can also be formed of members of religious movements, or even fans of a football team. Calhoun (2003) has noted how the solidarity of a community does not necessarily coincide with the state's exact boundaries. It seems more logical to try and understand which elements bring individuals together. This question has led us to support the idea that, in many functional areas, there are different *demoi* which are not always clearly distinguished by their state's borders. If communities *de facto* overlap, it is regressive to anchor in a static manner a political community to a 'population'.

Others, though, still hold an elitist view of cosmopolitanism (Brennan, 2001; Calhoun, 2003; Urbinati, 2003). According to Collins Cobuild English dictionary's definition: 'Cosmopolitan is someone who has had a lot of contact with people and things from many different countries and as a result is very open to different ideas and ways of doing things'. However, already within Kant's philosophy of history there emerged a view of cosmopolitanism that was not to be understood exclusively in terms of the privileges of a few, but rather as an aim to which the entire humanity should aspire. To marry the cosmopolitan ideal to the notion of democracy allows for this aspiration to become explicit. This demands a sense of responsibility that is developed by citizens *of* the world, *for* the world.

4.9 The Rule of Law and Democracy   Other critics, including Dahrendorf (2001), Urbinati (2003) and Morgan (chapter 12, this volume), have distinguished between democracy and the rule of law, remarking how, within the context of a political system beyond the state, it is more logical to refer to the generalization of the rule of law than to democracy. The modern notion of democracy comprehends the rule of law as well as the majority principle (see for instance the essay 'On the Internal Relation between the Rule of Law and Democracy', in Habermas, 1998). We welcome, however, the suggestion of separating the two aspects the moment it faces the expansion to a different scale.

The strengthening of citizen participation within global politics necessarily requires a more stringent rule of law, as argued already by Kelsen (see for instance, Archibugi, 1993; Held, 1995; Falk, 1998). It is known, though, that the rule of law, as an international or transnational phenomenon, is left in practice to the discretion of states. State representatives, in fact, often successfully characterize international norms as lacking democratic legitimacy in order to disregard them. It is therefore necessary to strengthen the rule of law in its legislative aspects as much as in its juridical components. However, the institutions that promote and apply it – whether it is the UN General Assembly or the World Court – require a greater popular legitimacy. The same juridical bodies, if they are not legitimated by a democratic mandate, risk turning into a new juridical aristocracy (this risk, in the context of *ad hoc* Courts for crimes carried out in the ex-Yugoslavia and Romania, has been remarked upon by Chandler, 2001, and Zolo, 1997).

It is not a coincidence that Dahrendorf's violent critique of global democracy was soon joined by a robust criticism of democracy in general, even at the state level. Dahrendorf's proposition was to attribute greater weight to those institutions on which the *demos* exerted less influence, such as those institutions whose membership is perpetual. He cites, as examples of bodies necessitating institutional reinforcement, the American Supreme Court and the House of Lords (but he spares us the Cardinals' Assembly). So, the objective of his polemic is democracy itself, not its potential global dimension. Dahrendorf's critique is therefore antithetical to those of Dahl and Kymlicka.

Nevertheless, we can derive from the work of Dahrendorf, Morgan, and Urbinati the idea that the rule of law can precede democracy; after all, this was the spirit of Kelsen (1944) and of many projects aimed at juridical pacifism (see Clark and Sohn, 1966; Falk and Black, 1969). In the case of the development of liberal states, it has often been the case that the formation of courts has preceded the formation of parliament. Before we ever reached a clear separation between the executive, legislative, and juridical powers, courts sometimes exerted coercive powers. The examples that are of main interest to us are those that witnessed courts of law operating in the absence of coercive powers and even against the executive power (Ferrajoli, 2001). Though international laws and tribunals are devoid of coercive powers, they still serve a decisive function in forcing major players to assume more virtuous behaviour.

One could object that a rule of law is legitimated by the mere fact it is assimilated by single states and, as the number of democratic states increases, the popular consensus also experiences an increase. We do not deny the importance of this channel of legitimation, but it is not always sufficient, for the reason explained in the first part of this essay. The United States, among the early promoters of the

United Nations, has on several occasions openly breached international agreements and obstructed the course of the law by making use of violence. Probably, the violation of international norms would prove more difficult if the global rule of law and the institutions in charge of its application were to be ratified by all citizens of the world, North Americans included.

4.10 Global Ethics and Cosmopolitan Democracy   Another debate that has bloomed recently, especially among philosophers, has focused on the ethics of international relations, as well as global ethics. The virtue of this debate resides in its ability to identify not only the institutional aspects but also the distribution of global resources (see Pogge, 2001; for a review, see Caney, 2001). This debate has many aspects in common with the idea of cosmopolitan democracy, though these features have not yet been fully developed. All we need to note is that determinate objectives, such as a redistribution of revenue between rich and poor countries, require the presence of institutions especially dedicated to them. The welfare state is not the result of the compassion of the upper classes, but the consequence of social battles that gave rise to equal political rights for individuals. Only once the workers had gained political weight did it become possible to bargain over social and economic rights.

Today, a similar agenda is forcing itself on the international scene: to establish the responsibility of richer countries (and democratic too) towards poorer countries (often non-democratic) means identifying institutional channels (possibly democratic ones) that will connect these two areas. While the richer states are in the advantaged position of unilaterally deciding how much of their own national income to devolve to development aid, this will continue to be limited and reversible. It is indeed emblematic that, following the collapse of the Berlin Wall, development aid on behalf of democratic states has experienced a substantial reduction (Soros, 2002).

5. Concluding Remarks

Although a long chapter, I have been able to discuss only some of the elements raised within the debate surrounding the issue of cosmopolitan democracy. The role of cosmopolitan citizenship (see Hutchings and Dannreuther, 1999; Carter, 2001; Dower and Williams, 2002; Heater, 2002), of an emerging global civil society (Anheier et al., 2001, 2002; Pianta, 2003), and of sovereignty (Brown, 2002) have merely been mentioned, rather than receiving the more detailed discussion they deserve.

Urbinati (2003) has noted how, for the most part, the proponents of cosmopolitan democracy are European. This fact should not surprise the reader, if one considers that in Europe we are experiencing an integration between states founded upon consensus and, contrarily to the experiences of many other unions of states, in the absence of a foreign menace and of a co-active communal power. Cosmopolitan democracy is, however, substantially different from the European example, and it is not possible, unfortunately, to generalize from the European case to the rest of the world (see McDougall, this volume). First of all, the homogeneity of EU members, present and future, surpasses that of the members of the United Nations. The European Union is a union of democratic states; cosmopolitan democracy, on the contrary, aims also the participation of non-democratic states, based on the assumption that integration will act as a strong stimulus to their internal democratic development.

An increasing number of critics with an interest in cosmopolitan democracy originate from those states that are themselves examples of cosmopolitanism, such as Canada and Australia, in spite of such North American exceptions as Richard Falk and his collaborators. To date, American critics have placed more weight on the issue of global governance than on the issue of institutional reform in the democratic sense.

The criticisms of the idea of a cosmopolitan democracy have been far too benevolent for such an ambitious project. For the most part, these critiques help us to better articulate our position and to clarify the more complex aspects of our arguments. The essential problem we face today involves connecting the theoretical viewpoint of cosmopolitan democracy to a realistic transformation of society.

The theoretical debate does not always reflect the progressive transformation of society. Cosmopolitan democracy – on a foundation laid by its most eminent Enlightenment ancestors – goes so far as to suggest a journey through which the human race could come closer together, and one whose final destination we can not yet determine. On the other hand, an increasing number of campaigns have recently developed around very specific and relevant objectives, such as those organized by the new global movements, although perhaps without sufficient clarity as to how to use these campaigns to transform society (see, for example, Edwards and Gaventa, 2001; Prokosch and Raymond, 2002).

Let us hope that the next generation of studies concerning the prospect of a cosmopolitan democracy will attempt to combine theoretical matters with more practical aspects (examples include Patomaki et al., 2002; Coleman and Porter, 2000). We do not expect to see the creation of a global democratic system as a result of the unique and massive transformation; quite the opposite. We hold that it is more feasible to take little steps forward that can yield tangible results. Discrete and feasible objectives, such as the banning of chemical weapons and landmines, must also be backed by institutional reforms. Each step towards a cosmopolitan democracy is in itself a desirable objective. For the first time in history, states with democratic regimes are concentrating an amount of economic, technological, military, ideological, and political resources sufficient to ensure control over the entire world. Despite this, we are running the current risk that brutal military force will once again rule international politics. Cosmopolitan democracy will be nothing more than a consolation amidst misery if it proves incapable of restraining the consolidation of this increasing hegemonic power.

Notes

1   Mathias Koenig-Archibugi has been a tireless and generous provider of criticism, suggestions and references. Bruce Morrison provided very detailed comments and feedback on an earlier draft. I also wish to thank David Beetham, Kim Bizzarri, Raffaele Marchetti, and Satu Sundstrom for comments on a previous draft. The debate held at the Conference in London, Ontario (March 2001), provided inspiration for the whole paper as well as for much of my future research. I express my sincere gratitude to all the participants.

2   On the one hand, it has been stressed that democracy cannot be expressed solely in terms of the majority principle (see, for example, Beetham, 1999: chapter 1). On the other hand, it is often proposed that one should consider not simply the arithmetical sum of individual preferences, but also how different individuals are affected by a given decision. This has led to the introduction of the concept of stake-holders.

3   For an assessment of national democracies, see, among others, Shapiro and Hacker-Cordon (1999) and Carter and Stockes (2002).

4   IGOs are a typical case where the majority principle proves insufficient in guaranteeing democratic outcomes. See Beetham (1999), chapter 1.

Bibliography

Abbott, F.M. (1995), *Law and Policy of Regional Integration: the NAFTA and Western Hemispheric Integration in the World Trade Organization System*, Martinus Nijhoff Publishers, Dordrecht, Netherlands.

Abrahamsen, R. (2000), *Disciplining Democracy: Development Discourse and Good Governance in Africa*, Zed, London.

Adams, M., and Lennon, M. J. (1992), 'Canadians, Too, Fault Their Political Institutions and Leaders', *Public Perspective*, vol. 3, pp. 6-21.

Adler, G., and Steinberg, J., eds. (2000), *From Comrades to Citizens: the South African Civics Movement and the Transition to Democracy*, Macmillan for Albert Einstein Institution, London.

Ajulu, R. (2001), 'Uganda's Flawed Presidential Election Bodes Ill for the Future', *Global Dialogue*, vol. 6, no. 2, July, pp. 20-22.

Ajzenstat, J. (1995), 'Decline of Procedural Liberalism: the Slippery Slope to Secession', in J. Carens, ed., *Is Québec Nationalism Just?*, McGill-Queen's University Press, Montréal-Kingston.

Albrow, M. (1997), *The Global Age: State and Society Beyond Modernity*, Stanford University Press, Stanford.

Alger, C.F. (1995), 'The United Nations in Historical Perspective', in C.F. Alger, G. M. Lyons and J. Trent (eds.), *The United Nations System: The Policies of Member States*, United Nations University Press, Tokyo.

Alger, C.F. (1997), 'Transnational Social Movements, World Politics and Global Governance', in Jackie Smith, C. Chatfield and R. Pagnucco (eds.), *Transnational Social Movements and Global Politics*, Syracuse University Press, Syracuse.

Alger, C.F. (1999a), 'The Future of Democracy and Global Governance Depends on Widespread Public knowledge About Local Links to the World', *Cities*, vol. 16, no. 3, pp. 195-206.

Alger, C.F. (1999b), 'Strengthening Relations Between NGOs and the UN System: Toward a Research Agenda', *Global Society*, vol. 13, no. 4, pp. 393-409.

Alger, C.F. (2002a), 'The Emerging Roles of NGOs in the UN System: From Article 71 to a People's Millennium Assembly', *Global Governance*, vol. 8, pp. 93-117.

Alger, C.F. (2002b), 'What are the Implications of the Regional and Global Activities of Local Authorities for Future Global Governance?', *Futurbili* ('Special Issue on 'Urban Systems and the Future'), Trieste, Italy.

Alger, C.F. (2003), 'Evolving Roles of NGOs in Member State Decision-Making in the UN System', *Journal of Human Rights, vol. 2, no. 3, September (in press)*.

Alger, C.F., ed. (1998), *The Future of the United Nations System: Potential for the Twenty-First Century*, UN University Press, Tokyo.

Anderson, B. (1983), *Imagined communities: Reflections on the Origin and Spread of Nationalism*, Verso, London.

Anderson, P. (2002), 'Internationalism: A Breviary', *New Left Review*, second series, no. 14, March-April, pp. 5-25.

Anena, C. (2001), 'Participation of Civil Society in Policy-Related Advocacy for Poverty Reduction in Uganda: an experience from the Uganda Debt Network', presented at Fifth

Gender Festival, September, *Tanzania Gender Networking Programme*, available at: www.tgnp.co.tz/plenary_participation.htm.

Anheier, H., Glasius, M., and Kaldor, M. (2001a, 2002), *Global Civil Society*, Oxford University Press, Oxford.

Anheier, H., Glasius, M., and Kaldor, M. (2001b), 'Introducing Global Civil Society', in H. Anheier, M. Glasius and M. Kaldor (eds.), *Global Civil Society*, Oxford University Press, Oxford.

Anthony, J.O. (2002), 'Ethnicity, State Power and the Democratisation Process in Uganda', Occasional paper no. 33, May, IGD, Johannesburg.

Appadurai, A. (1996), *Modernity at Large: Cultural Dimensions of Globalization*, University of Minnesota Press, Minneapolis and London.

Appendini, K. and Bislev, S., eds. (1999), *Economic Integration in NAFTA and the EU: Deficient Institutionality*, St. Martin's Press, New York.

Archibugi, D. (1993), 'The Reform of the United Nations and Cosmopolitan Democracy', *Journal of Peace Research*, vol. 30, no. 3, pp. 301-315.

Archibugi, D. (1995), 'From the United Nations to Cosmopolitan Democracy', in D. Archibugi and D. Held (eds.), *Cosmopolitan Democracy: An Agenda for a New World Order*, Polity Press, Cambridge.

Archibugi, D. (1998), 'Principles of Cosmopolitan Democracy', in D. Archibugi, D. Held, and M. Köhler (eds.), *Re-imagining Political Community: Studies in Cosmopolitan Democracy*, Polity Press, Cambridge.

Archibugi, D. (2002), 'Demos and Cosmopolis', *New Left Review,* no. 13, pp. 24-40.

Archibugi, D., and Held, D. eds. (1995a), *Cosmopolitan Democracy: An Agenda for a New World Order*, Polity Press, Cambridge.

Archibugi, D. and Held, D. (1995b), 'Editors' Introduction', in D. Archibugi and D. Held, *Cosmopolitan Democracy. An Agenda for a New World Order*, Polity Press, Cambridge.

Archibugi, D., and Köhler, M., eds., 'Global Democracy', special issue, *Peace Review*, vol. 9, no. 3, pp. 309-393.

Archibugi, D., ed. (2003), *Debating Cosmopolitics*, Verso, London.

Archibugi, D., Held, D., and Köhler, M. (1998), 'Introduction', in D. Archibugi, D. Held, and M. Köhler (eds.), *Re-imagining Political Community: Studies in Cosmopolitan Democracy*, Polity Press, Cambridge.

Archibugi, D., Held, D., and Köhler, M., eds. (1998), *Re-imagining Political Community: Studies in Cosmopolitan Democracy,* Polity Press, Cambridge.

Aristotle (1998), *Politics*, Hackett Publishing Company, Cambridge.

Arndt, S. W., and Kierzkowski, H., eds. (2001), *Fragmentation: New Production Patterns in the World Economy*, Oxford University Press, Oxford.

Arneson, R.J. (1993), 'Democratic Rights at National and Workplace Levels', in D. Copp (ed.), *The Idea of Democracy*, Cambridge University Press, Cambridge.

Arrighi, G. (1994), *The Long Twentieth Century: Money, Power, and the Origins of Our Time*, Verso, London and New York.

Arrighi, G. (2002), 'The African Crisis: World Systemic and Regional Aspects', *New Left Review*, no. 15, May/June, pp. 5-36.

Asea, P.K, and Kaija, D. (2000), 'Impact of the Flower Industry in Uganda', Working Paper no. 148, January, International Labour Organization, Sectoral Activities Programme, Geneva.

Axtmann, R. (2001a), 'Introduction II: Between Polycentricity and Globalization: Democratic Governance in Europe', in R. Axtmann (ed.), *Balancing Democracy*, Continuum, London.

Axtmann, R., ed. (2001b), *Balancing Democracy*, Continuum, London.

Axtmann, R. (2002) 'What's Wrong with Cosmopolitan Democracy?', in N. Dower and J. Williams (eds.), *Global Citizenship.A Critical Reader*, Edinburgh University Press, Edinburgh.

Aykac, A. (1994), 'Transborder Regionalisation: An Analysis of Transborder Cooperation Structures in Western Europe Within the Context of European Integration and Decentralization Toward Regional and Local Governments', *Libertas Paper 13*, Europaisches Institute GmbH, Sindelfingen, Germany.

Bailyn, B. (1968), *The Origins of American Politics*, Vintage, New York.

Baker, W.G. (2001), 'Uganda: the Marginalisation of Minorities', Minority Rights Group International, London.

Barber, B. (1996), *Jihad vs McWorld*, Ballantine, New York.

Barry, B. (1998), 'The Limits of Cultural Politics', *Review of International Studies*, no. 24, July, p. 308.

Barry, B. (2001), *Culture and Equality: An Egalitarian Critique of Multiculturalism*, Harvard University, Cambridge.

Beck, U. (1996), *The Reinvention of Politics: Rethinking Modernity in the Global Social Order*, Polity Press, Cambridge.

Beck, U. (1999), *World Risk Society*, Polity Press, Cambridge.

Becker, E. (2002), 'On World Court, US Focus Shifts to Shielding Officials', *New York Times*, September 7, p. A4.

Beetham, D. (1999), *Democracy and Human Rights*, Polity Press, Cambridge.

Beetham, D., and Lord, C. (1998), *Legitimacy and the European Union*, Longman, London.

Beetham, D., Bracking, S., Kearton, I., and Weir, S. (2002a), *Handbook on Democracy Assessment*, Kluwer Law International and International IDEA, Stockholm.

Beetham, D., Bracking, S., Kearton, I., Vittal, N., and Weir, S., eds. (2002b), *The State of Democracy*, Kluwer Law International and International IDEA, Stockholm.

Beetham, D., Byrne, I., Ngan, P., and Weir, S. (2002c), *Democracy Under Blair*, Politicos, London.

Beetham, D., ed. (1994), *Defining and Measuring Democracy*, Sage, London.

Beik, W. (1997), *Urban Protest in Seventeenth-Century France: The Culture of Retribution*, Cambridge University Press, New York.

Beiner, R.S. (1998), 'National Self-Determination: Some Cautionary Remarks Concerning the Rhetoric of Rights', in M. Moore (ed.), *National Self-Determination and Secession*, Oxford University Press, Oxford.

Bellamy, R., and Castiglione, D. (1997), 'Review Article: Constitutionalism and Democracy – Political Theory and the American Constitution', *British Journal of Political Science*, vol. 27, pp. 595-618.

Bellamy, R., and Castiglione, D. (1998), 'Between Cosmopolis and Community: Three Models of Rights and Democracy within the European Union', in D. Archibugi, D. Held, M. Kohler, eds., *Re-imagining Political Community*, Polity Press, Cambridge.

Bellamy, R., and Castiglione, D. (2000), 'The Uses of Democracy. Further Reflections on the Democratic Deficit in Europe', in E.O. Eriksen and J.E. Fossum (eds.), *Integration through Deliberation? On the Prospects for European Democracy*, University of City London Press, London.

Bellamy, R., and Jones, R.J.B. (2000), 'Globalization and Democracy – an Afterword', in B. Holden (ed.), *Global Democracy: Key Debates*, Routledge, London.

Berman, S., and McNamara, K. (1999), 'Banking on Democracy', *Foreign Affairs*, vol. 78, no. 2, March/April, pp. 2-8.

Bibangambah, J.R. (2001), *Africa's Quest for Economic Development: Uganda's Experience*, Fountain, Kampala.

Bien, D.D. (1994), 'Regime Origins of Democratic Liberty', in D. Van Kley (ed.), *The French Idea of Freedom: The Old Regime and the Declaration of Rights of 1789*, Stanford University Press, Stanford.

Black, S. (1991), 'Individualism at an Impasse', *Canadian Journal of Philosophy*, vol. 21, no.3, pp. 347-77.

Blackbourn, D., and Eley, G. (1984), *The Peculiarities of German History: Bourgeois Society and Politics in Nineteenth-Century Germany*, Oxford University Press, Oxford.

Blank, S., and Haar, J. (1999), *Making NAFTA Work: U.S.. Firms and the New North American Business Environment*, North-South Center Press, University of Miami.

Bobbio, N. (1995), 'Democracy and the International System', in D. Archibugi and D. Held (eds.), *Cosmopolitan Democracy: An Agenda for a New World Order*, Polity Press, Cambridge.

Bodin, J. (n.d.), *Six Books of the Commonwealth*, Basil Blackwell, Oxford.

Bohman, J. (1998), 'The Coming Age of Deliberative Democracy', *Journal of Political Philosophy*, vol. 6, no. 4, pp. 400-425.

Bond, P., ed. (2002), *Fanon's Warning: a Civil Society Reader on the New Partnership for Africa's Development (NEPAD)*, Africa World Press, Trenton.

Bosher, J.F. (1970), *French Finances 1770-1795: From Business to Bureaucracy*, Cambridge University Press, Cambridge.

Bratton, M. and Lambright, G. (2001), 'Uganda's Referendum 2000: the Silent Boycott', *African Affairs*, vol. 100, no. 400, July, pp. 429-452.

Brennan, T. (2001), 'Cosmopolitanism and Internationalism', *New Left Review*, second series, no. 7, January-February, pp. 75-84. Reprinted in D. Archibugi, ed. (2003), *Debating Cosmopolitics*, Verso, London.

Breuilly, J. (1982), *Nationalism and the State*, University of Chicago Press, Chicago.

Brewer, J. (1990), *The Sinews of Power: War, Money and the English State, 1688-1783*, Harvard University Press, Cambridge.

Brock, M. (1973), *The Great Reform Act*, Hutchinson, London.

Brooks, D. (2000), *Bobos in Paradise*, Simon and Schuster, New York.

Brown, C. (2001a), 'Africa in Canadian Foreign Policy 2000: the Human Security Agenda', in F.O. Hampson, N. Hillmer and M.A. Molot (eds.), *Canada Among Nations: The Axworthy Legacy*, Oxford University Press, Oxford.

Brown, C. (2001b), 'Cosmopolitanism, World Citizenship, and Global Civil Society', in P. Jones and S. Caney (eds.), *Human Rights and Global Diversity*, Frank Cass, London.

Brown, C. (2002), *Sovereignty, Rights and Justice*, Polity Press, Cambridge.

Bryce, J. (1921), *Modern Democracies*, Macmillan, New York.

Buchanan, A. (1995), 'The Morality of Secession', in W. Kymlicka (ed.), *The Rights of Minority Cultures*, Oxford University Press, Oxford.

Byers, M. (2002), 'The world according to Cheney, Rice and Rumsfeld', *London Review of Books*, 21 February, pp. 14-15.

Cairns, A. (1992), *Charter versus Federalism: the Dilemmas of Constitutional Reform*, McGill-Queen's University Press, Montréal-Kingston.

Calhoun, C. (2003), 'The Class Consciousness of Frequent Travellers: Towards a Critique of Actually Existing Cosmopolitanism', in D. Archibugi, ed., *Debating Cosmopolitics*, Verso, London.

Callaghy, T.M. (2001), 'Networks and Governance in Africa: Innovation in the Debt Regime', in T. Callaghy, R. Kassimir and R. Latham (eds.), *Intervention and Transnationalism in Africa: Global-Local Networks of Power*, City University of New York, New York.

Callaghy, T.M., Latham, R., and Kassimir, R., eds. (2001), *Intervention and Trasnnationalism in Africa: Global-Local Networks of Power*, Cambridge University Press, Cambridge.

Cameron, M.A., Lawson, R.J., and Tomlin, B. (1998), *To Walk without Fear: The Global Movement to Ban Landmines*, Oxford University Press, Toronto.

Caney, S. (2001), 'Review Article: International Distributive Justice', *Political Studies*, vol. 49, pp. 974-997.

Cannadine, D. (1997), 'Imperial Canada: Old History, New Problems', in C. Coates (ed.), *Imperial Canada, 1867- 1917*, Centre for Canadian Studies, Edinburgh.

Cannon, J. (1973), *Parliamentary Reform 1640-1832*, Cambridge University Press, Cambridge.

Canovan, M. (1996), 'The Skeleton in the Cupboard: Nationhood, Patriotism, and Limited Loyalties', in S. Caney, D. George, and P. Jones (eds.), *National Rights, International Obligations*, Westview Press, Boulder.

Canovan, M. (2001), 'Sleeping Dogs, Prowling Cats and Soaring Doves: Three Paradoxes in the Political Theory of Nationhood', *Political Studies*, vol. 49, pp. 203-215.

Carothers, T. (2002), 'The End of the Transition Paradigm', *Journal of Democracy*, vol, 13, no. 1, pp. 5-21.

Carter, A. (2001), *The Political Theory of Global Citizenship*, Routledge, London.

Carter, A., and Stokes, G., eds. (2002), *Democratic Theory Today*, Polity, Cambridge.

Casper, G., and Taylor, M. (1996), *Negotiating Democracy: Transitions from Authoritarian Rule*, University of Pittsburgh Press, Pittsburgh.

Castells, M. (1994), 'European Cities, International Society, and the Global Economy', *New Left Review*, no. 204, pp. 18-32.

Centeno, M.A. (2002), *Blood and Debt: War and the Nation-State in Latin America*, Pennsylvania State University Press, University Park.

Cerny, P. (1999a), 'Globalization and the Erosion of Democracy', *European Journal of Political Research*, vol. 36, pp. 1-26.

Cerny, P. (1999b), 'Globalization, Governance, and Complexity', in A. Prakash and J.A. Hart (eds.), *Globalization and Governance*, Routledge, London.

Chambers, S. (1998), 'Contract or Conversation? Theoretical Lessons from the Canadian Constitutional Crisis', *Politics and Society*, vol. 26, pp. 143-72.

Chambers, S. (2001), 'New Constitutionalism: Democracy, Habermas, and Canadian Exceptionalism', in R. Beiner and W. Norman (eds.), *Canadian Political Philosophy*, Oxford University Press, Toronto.

Chandler, D. (2000), 'International Justice', *New Left Review*, second series, no. 6, November-December, pp. 55-66. Reprinted in D. Archibugi, ed. (2003), *Debating Cosmopolitics*, Verso, London.

Childers, E., and Urquhart, B. (1994), *Renewing the United Nations System*, Dag Hammarskjold Foundation, Uppsala, Sweden.

Clark, G., and Sohn, L. (1966), *World Peace through World Law*, Harvard University Press, Cambridge, Massachusetts.

Clark, I. (1999), *Globalization and International Relations Theory*, Oxford University Press, Oxford.

Clark, J.D. (2002), 'NGOs and the State', in V. Desai and R.B. Potter (eds.), *The Companion to Development Studies*, Arnold, London.

Clark, J.F (2001), 'Foreign Policy Making in Central Africa: the Imperative of Regime Security in a New Context', in G.M. Khadiagala and T. Lyons (eds.), *African Foreign Policies: Power and Process*, Lynne Rienner, Boulder.

Clarke, H., Jenson, J., LeDuc, L., and Pammett, J. (1995), *Absent Mandate: Canadian Electoral Politics in an Era of Restructuring*, Gate, Toronto.

Coates, T. (2000), 'Neither Cosmopolitanism Nor Realism', in B. Holden (ed.), *Global Democracy: Key Debates*, Routledge, London.

Cohen, J. (1991), 'Review Symposium on *Democracy and Its Critics*', *Journal of Politics*, vol. 53, pp. 215-231.

Cohen, J., and Arato, A. (1994), *Civil Society and Political Theory*, MIT Press, Cambridge and London.

Coleman, W.D., and Porter, T. (2000), 'International Institutions, Globalization and Democracy: Assessing the Challenges', *Global Society*, vol. 14, no. 3, pp. 377-398.

Collier, D., and Levitsky, S. (1997), 'Democracy With Adjectives: Conceptual Innovation in Comparative Research', *World Politics*, vol. 49, no. 3, pp. 430-451.

Collier, R.B. (1999), *Paths Toward Democracy: The Working Class and Elites in Western Europe and South America*, Cambridge University Press, Cambridge.

Commission for Global Governance (1995), *Our Global Neighbourhood*, Oxford University Press, Oxford.

Commonwealth Foundation (1999), 'Citizens and Governance: Civil Society in the New Millennium', London.

Commonwealth Human Rights Initiative (2001), 'Human Rights and Poverty Eradication: a Talisman for the Commonwealth', CHRI, New Delhi.

Conze, W., and Koselleck, R., eds. (1972-1984), *Geschichtliche Grundbegriffe. Historisches Lexikon zur Politisch-Sozialen Sprache in Deutschland*, Klett Verlag, Stuttgart.

Cooper, R.N. (1968), *The Economics of Interdependence: Economic Policy in the Atlantic Community*, McGraw-Hill, New York.

Copp, D., ed. (1993), *The Idea of Democracy*, Cambridge University Press, Cambridge.

Council of Europe (2001), *Case of Refah Partisi and others v. Turkey*, Strasbourg, 31 July 2001.

Cousins, C. (1999), *Society, Work and Welfare in Europe*, Macmillan, Houndmills.

Cowles, M.G., and Smith, M., eds. (2000), *The State of the European Union, Volume 5: Risks, Reform, Resistance, and Revival*, Oxford University Press, Oxford.

Cox, R.W. (1999), 'Civil Society at the Turn of the Millennium: Prospects for an Alternative World Order', *Review of International Studies*, vol. 25, no. 1, January, pp. 3-28.

Cranston, M. (1973), *What Are Human Rights?*, Bodley Head, London.

CRIC Papers (2001), 'Trade, Globalization and Canadian Values', Montreal.

Crick, B. (1962), *In Defense of Politics*, Penguins, Harmondsworth.

Crook, M. (1996), *Elections in the French Revolution: An Apprenticeship to Democracy, 1789-1799*, Cambridge University Press, Cambridge.

Culpepper, R. (2001/2), 'Introduction: Building a Fairer World', *Canadian Development Report*, North-South Institute, Ottawa.

Dahl, R. (1999), 'Can International Organizations be Democratic? A Skeptic's View', in I. Shapiro and C. Hacker-Cordón (eds.), *Democracy's Edges*, Cambridge University Press, Cambridge.

Dahl, R., and Tufte, E.R. (1973), *Size and Democracy*, Stanford University Press, Stanford.

Dahrendorf, R. (1967), *Society and Democracy in Germany*, W.W. Norton and Co., New York.

Dahrendorf, R. (2001), *Dopo la democrazia*. Intervista a cura di Antonio Polito, Laterza, Roma-Bari.

de Sola Pool, I. (1952), *Symbols of Democracy*, Stanford University Press, Stanford.

de Tocqueville, A. (1990 [1835-1840]), *De la Démocratie en Amérique, vol. 1, Librairie Philosophique*, J. Vrin, Paris.

de Vanssay, X. and Mahant, E. (1996), 'Three's Company and Fifteen's a Union: The Comparative Political Economy of NAFTA and the European Union – Integration or Liberalization?', in T. Geiger and D. Kennedy (eds.), *Regional Trade Blocs, Multilateralism, and the GATT: Complementary Paths to Free Trade?*, Pinter, London.

Desai, V. (2002), 'Role of NGOs', in V. Desai and R.B. Potter (eds.), *The Companion to Development Studies*, Arnold, London.

Desai, V., and Potter, R.B., eds., (2002), *The Companion to Development Studies*, Arnold, London.

Di Palma, G. (1990), *To Craft Democracies*, University of California Press, Berkeley.

Diamond, L. (1999), *Developing Democracy: Toward Consolidation*, Johns Hopkins University Press, Baltimore.

Diamond, L., Linz, J., and Lipset, S. (1995), 'Introduction: What Makes for a Democracy?', in L. Diamond, J. Linz, and S. Lipset (eds.), *Politics in Developing Countries: Comparing Experiences with Democracy*, 2nd ed., Lynne Rienner, Boulder.

Dicklitch, S. (1998), *The Elusive Promise of NGOs in Africa: Lessons from Uganda*, Macmillan, London.

Dicklitch, S. (2000), 'The Incomplete Democratic Transition in Uganda', in R. Bensabat-Kleinberg and J.A. Clark (eds.), *Economic Liberalization, Democratization and Civil Society in the Developing World*, Palgrave, London.

Dogan, M. (1997), 'Erosion of Confidence in Advanced Democracies', *Studies in Comparative International Development*, vol. 32, no. 3, pp. 3-29.

Donnelly, E.A. (2002), 'Proclaiming Jubilee: The Debt and Structural Adjustment Network', in S. Khagram, J.V. Riker, and K. Sikkink (eds.), *Restructuring World Politics: Transnational Social Movements, Networks, and Norms*, University of Minnesota Press, Minneapolis and London.

Dower, N., and Williams, J., eds. (2002), *Global Citizenship. A Critical Reader*, Edinburgh University Press, Edinburgh.

Downing, B. (1992), *The Military Revolution and Political Change: Origins of Democracy and Autocracy in Early Modern Europe*, Princeton University Press, Princeton.

Doyle, M. (1983), 'Kant. Liberal Legacies and Foreign Affairs', *Philosophy and Public Affairs*, vol. 12, nos. 3 and 4, June and October, pp. 205-35 and 323-53.

Doyle, W. (1996), *Venality: The Sale of Offices in Eighteenth-Century France*, Clarendon Press, Oxford.

Dryzek, J.S. (1999), 'Transnational Democracy', *Journal of Political Philosophy*, vol. 7, no. 1, pp. 30-51.

Dryzek, J.S. (2000), *Deliberative Democracy and Beyond*, Oxford University Press, Oxford.

Duffield, M. (2001), *Global Governance and the New Wars: the Merging of Development and Security*, Zed, London.

Dunn, J., ed. (1992), *Democracy: The Unfinished Journey*, Oxford University Press, Oxford.

Dunn, K.C., (2001), 'MadLib #32: the (*Blank*) African State: Rethinking the Sovereign State in International Relations Theory', in K.C. Dunn and T.M. Shaw (eds.), *Africa's Challenge to International Relations Theory*, Palgrave, London

Dunn, K.C., and Shaw, T.M., eds. (2001), *Africa's Challenge to International Relations Theory*, Palgrave, London.

Dworkin, R. (1996), *Freedom's Law: The Moral Reading of the American Constitution*, Harvard University Press, Cambridge, Massachusetts.

Edwards, M., and Gaventa, J., eds. (2001), *Global Citizen Action*, Earthscan, London.

Edwards, M., and Hulme, D., eds. (1996), *Beyond the Magic Bullet: NGO Performance and Accountability in the Post-Cold War World*, Kumarian, West Hartford.

Egret, J. (1970), *Louis XV et l'opposition parlementaire*, Librairie Armand Colin, Paris.

Ehrhart, C., and Ayoo, S. J. (2000), 'Conflict, Insecurity and Poverty in Uganda: Learning from the Poor, *UPPAP Briefing Paper No. 4*, MFPED and Oxfam UK, Kampala.

Ehrlich, E. (1936), *Fundamental Principles of the Sociology of Law*, Harvard University Press, Cambridge.

EIU (2000/1) Uganda Country Profile/Country Report, annually/quarterly, London.

Elliott, L. (2002), 'Global Environmental Governance', in R. Wilkinson and S. Hughes (eds.), *Global Governance: Critical Perspectives*, Routledge, London and New York.

Elster, J. (1998), *Delibarative Democracy*, Cambridge University Press, New York.

Engel, M. (2002), 'How Americans See Us', *The Guardian, Review*, 26 February, pp. 1-3.

Erasmus of Rotterdam (1964 [1536]), *The 'Adages' of Erasmus*, M. Mann Phillips (ed. and transl.), Cambridge University Press, Cambridge, 1964.

Eriksen, E.O., and Fossum, J.E., eds. (2000), *Integration through Deliberation? On the Prospects for European Democracy*, University of City London Press, London.

Erlanger, S. (2002), 'A Jumpy, Anti-Immigrant Europe is Creeping Rightward', *New York Times*, January 30, p. A3.

Ertman, T. (1997), *Birth of the Leviathan: Building States and Regimes in Medieval and Early Modern Europe*, Cambridge University Press, Cambridge.

Eschle, C. (2001), 'Globalizing Civil Society? Social Movements and the Challenge of Global Politics from Below', in P. Hamel, H. Lustiger-Thaler, J. N. Pieterse, and S. Roseneil (eds.), *Globalization and Social Movements*, Palgrave, Houndmills.

Evans, P. B., Rueschemeyer, D., and Skocpol, T., eds (1985), *Bringing the State Back In*, Cambridge University Press, Cambridge.

Falk, R. (1995), *On Humane Governance: Towards a New Global Politics*, Pennsylvania State University Press, University Park, Pennsylvania.

Falk, R. (1997), 'Resisting "Globalization-From-Above" Through "Globalization-From-Below"', *New Political Economy*, vol. 2, pp. 17-24.

Falk, R. (1998), *Law in an Emerging Global Village. A Post-Westphalian Perspective*, Ardsley, Transnational Publishers.

Falk, R. (2002), 'The United Nations System: Prospects for Renewal', in D. Nayyar (ed.), *Governing Globalization: Issues and Institutions*, Oxford University Press, Oxford.

Falk, R. and Strauss, A., (2001), 'Toward Global Parliament', *Foreign Affairs*, vol. 80, no. 1, Jan/Feb, pp. 212-220.

Falk, R., and Black, C.E., eds. (1969), *The Future of the International Legal Order*, Princeton University Press, Princeton.

Ferrajoli, L. (2001), *Diritti fondamentali*, Laterza, Roma-Bari.

Ferrajoli, L. (1995), *La sovranità nel mondo moderno*, Anabasi, Milano.

Fierlbeck, K. (1998), *Globalizing Democracy*, Manchester University Press, Manchester.

Finer, S.F., Bogdanor, V., and Rudden, B. (1995), *Comparing Constitutions*, Clarendon Press, Oxford.

Fischer, D. H. (1989), *Albion's Seed*, Oxford University Press, Oxford.

Fitzsimmons, M.P. (1994), *The Remaking of France: The National Assembly and the Constitution of 1791*, Cambridge University Press, Cambridge.

Flick, C. (1978), *The Birmingham Political Union and the Movements for Reform in Britain 1830-39*, Archon Books, Hamden.

Florini, A.M., and Simmons, P.J. (2000), 'What the World Needs Now?' in A.M. Florini (ed.), *The Third Force: The Rise of Transnational Civil Society*, Japan Center for

International Exchange and Carnegie Endowment for International Peace, Tokyo and Washington.

Florini, A.M., ed. (2000), *The Third Force: The Rise of Transnational Civil Society*, Carnegie Endowment, Washington.

Fold, N., Gibbon, P., and Ponte, S. (2003), *Globalisation and Economic Change in Africa*, Palgrave, London.

Foley, M. (1989), *The Silence of Constitutions: Gaps, 'Abeyances' and Political Temperament in the Maintenance of Government*, Routledge, New York.

Forsyth, M.G. (1987), *Reason and Revolution: The Political Thought of the Abbé Sieyès*, Leicester University Press, Leicester.

Fowler, A. (2002), 'NGO-Donor Relationships: the Use and Abuse of Partnership', in V. Desai and R. B. Potter (eds.), *The Companion to Development Studies*, Arnold, London.

Fowler, A., ed. (2001), 'Special Issue: NGO Futures Beyond Aid' *Third World Quarterly*, vol. 21, no. 4, August, pp. 587-699.

Fox, J., and Brown, D. L., eds. (1998), *The Struggle for Accountability: the World Bank, NGOs and Grassroots Movements*, MIT Press, Cambridge.

Franceschet, A. (2000), 'Popular Sovereignty or Cosmopolitan Democracy? Liberalism, Kant and International Reform', *European Journal of International Relations*, vol. 6, no. 2, pp. 277-302.

Franceschet, A. (2002), 'Justice and International Organization: Two Models of Global Governance', *Global Governance*, vol. 8, no. 1, pp. 19-34.

Frankman, M. (2002), 'Beyond the Tobin Tax: Global Democracy and a Global Currency', *The Annals of the American Academy of Political and Social Science*, vol. 581, pp. 62-73.

Fukuyama, F. (1989), 'The End of History?', *The National Interest*, vol. 16, pp. 3-18.

Fukuyama, F. (1992), *The End of History and the Last Man*, Macmillan, New York.

Furetière, A. (1970 [1690]), *Dictionnaire Universel, Contenant Généralement Tous les Mots Français, Tant Vieux Que Modernes, et les Termes de Toutes les Sciences et des Arts*, Slatkine Reprints, Geneva.

Furley, O. (2000), 'Democratization in Uganda', *Commonwealth and Comparative Politics*, vol. 38, no. 3, November, pp. 79-102.

Gagnon, A., and Turgeon, L. (2003), 'Managing Diversity in 18th and 19th Century Canada: Québec's Constitutional Development in Light of the Scottish Experience', *Journal of Commonwealth and Comparative Politics*, vol. 31, no. 1, forthcoming.

Ganley, G. (1992), *The Exploding Political Power of Personal Media*, Ablex, Norwood, New Jersey.

Gans, C. (2001), 'Historical Rights: the Evaluation of Nationalist Claims to Sovereignty', *Political Theory*, vol. 29, no. 1, February, pp. 58-79.

Gariyo, Z. (2002), 'Civil Society and Global Finance in Africa: the PRSP Process in Uganda', in J. A. Scholte and A. Schnabel (eds.), *Civil Society and Global Finance*, Routledge, London and New York.

Garrett, G. (1998), *Partisan Politics in the Global Economy*, Cambridge University Press, Cambridge.

Gellner, E. (1994a), *Conditions of Liberty: Civil Society and Its Rivals*, Penguin Books, London.

Gellner, E. (1994b), *Encounters with Nationalism*, Blackwell, Oxford.

George, D. (1996), 'National Identity and National Self-Determination', in S. Caney, D. George, and P. Jones (eds.), *National Rights, International Obligations*, Westview Press, Boulder, Colorado.

Gereffi, G., and Kaplinsky, R., eds., (2001) 'The Value of Value Chains: Spreading the Gains from Globalisation', *IDS Bulletin*, vol. 32, no. 3, pp. 1-136.

Gibbon, P. (2001) 'Civil Society, Locality and Globalization in Rural Tanzania: a Forty-Year Perspective', *Development and Change*, vol. 32, no. 5, November, pp. 819-44.

Gilbert, A. (1999), *Must Global Politics Constrain Democracy?*, Princeton University Press, Princeton.

Gills, B. K., ed. (2000) *Globalization and the Politics of Resistance*, Palgrave, London.

Gilpin, R. (2001), *Global Political Economy: Understanding the International Economic Order*, Princeton University Press, Princeton.

Glasius, M. (2002), 'Expertise in the Cause of Justice: Global Civil Society Influence on the Statute for an International Criminal Court', in H. Anheier, M. Glasius, and M. Kaldor (eds.), *Global Civil Society*, Oxford University Press, Oxford.

Gleeson, B., and Low, N., eds. (2001), *Governing for the Environment: Global Problems, Ethics and Democracy*, Palgrave, Houndmills.

Global Policy Forum (1999), 'NGOs and the UN: Comments for the Report of the Secretary General', available at: www.globalpolicy.org/ngos/docs99/gpfrep.htm.

Go-Between, October/November 1995, UN Governmental Liaison Service (NGLS), New York and Geneva.

Görg, C., and Hirsch, J. (1998), 'Is International Democracy Possible?', *Review of International Political Economy*, vol. 5, no. 4, pp. 585-615.

Gough, J.W. (1950), *John Locke's Political Philosophy*, Oxford University Press, Oxford.

Gowan, P. (2001), 'The New Liberal Cosmopolitanism', *New Left Review*, second series, no. 11, September-October, pp. 1-14. Reprinted in D. Archibugi, ed. (2003), *Debating Cosmopolitics*, Verso, London.

Green, D.M. (2000), 'On Being European: The Character and Consequences of European Identity', in M.G. Cowles and M. Smith (eds.), *The State of the European Union, Volume 5: Risks, Reform, Resistance, and Revival*, Oxford University Press, Oxford.

Greenfeld, L. (1992), *Nationalism: Five Roads to Modernity*, Harvard University Press, Cambridge, Massachusetts.

Greven, M. T. and Pauly, L.W., eds (2000), *Democracy Beyond the State? The European Dilemma and the Emerging Global Order*, University of Toronto Press, Toronto.

Griffin, J. (1986), *Well-being: Its Meaning, Measurement, and Moral Importance*, Clarendon Press, Oxford.

Grimond, J. (2001), 'Civil Society', *EIU The World in 2002*, no. 16, London.

Gueniffey, P. (1993), *Le Nombre et la raison: la Révolution Française et les élections*, Éditions de L'École des Hautes Études en Sciences Sociales, Paris.

Habermas, J. (2001a), *The Postnational Constellation*, Polity Press, Cambridge.

Habermas, J., (2001b), 'So, Why does Europe Need a Constitution?', *European Union Institute*, available at: www.iue.it/RSC/EU/Reform02(uk).pdf.

Habermas, J., Cronin, C., and de Greiff, P., eds. (1998), *The Inclusion of the Other: Studies in Political Theory*, MIT Press, Cambridge, Massachusetts, and Polity Press, Cambridge.

Hall, J.A. (1996), *International Orders*, Poliy Press, Cambridge.

Hall, J.A. (2000), 'Globalization and Nationalism', *Thesis 11*, no. 63, pp. 63-79.

Hall, J.A., and Lindholm, C. (1999), *Is America Breaking Apart?*, Princeton University Press, Princeton.

Hall, P.A. (1999), 'The Political Economy of Europe in an Age of Interdependence', in H. Kitschelt, P. Lange, G. Marks, and J.D. Stephens (eds.), *Continuity and Change in Contemporary Capitalism*, Cambridge University Press, Cambridge.

Hamel, P., Lustiger-Thaler, H., Pieterse, J.N., and Roseneil, S. (2001a), 'Introduction: The Shifting Global Frames of Collective Action', in P. Hamel, H. Lustiger-Thaler, J.N. Pieterse, and S. Roseneil (eds.), *Globalization and Social Movements*, Palgrave, Houndmills.

Hamel, P., Lustiger-Thaler, H., Pieterse, J.N., and Roseneil, S., eds. (2001b), *Globalization and Social Movements*, Palgrave, Houndmills.

Hamilton, A., Jay, J., and Madison, J. (1955[1788]), *The Federalist*, Encyclopædia Britannica, Chicago.

Hampson, F.O., and Daudelin, J., eds. (2001), *Madness in the Multitude: Human Security and World Disorder*, Oxford University Press, Toronto.

Hampson, F.O., Hillmer, N., and Molot, M.A. eds. (2001), *Canada Among Nations: The Axworthy Legacy*, Oxford University Press, Toronto.

Hannerz, U. (1996), *Transnational Connections: Culture, People, Places*, Routledge, London.

Hansen, H.B., and Twaddle, M., eds. (1998), *Developing Uganda*, James Currey, Oxford.

Harker, J.H. (2001), 'Human Security in Sudan: The Report of a Canadian Assessment Mission', Centre for Foreign Policy Studies, Halifax.

Harling, P., and Mandler, P. (1993), 'From "Fiscal-Military" State to "Laissez-Faire" State, 1760-1850', *Journal of British Studies*, vol. 32, January, pp. 44-70.

Hauser, E. (1999), 'Ugandan Relations with Western Donors in the 1990s: What Impact on Democratization?', *Journal of Modern African Studies*, vol. 37, no. 4, December, pp. 621-41.

Hawthorn, G. (2000), 'Running the World through Windows', *New Left Review*, second series, no. 5, September-October, pp. 101-10. Reprinted in D. Archibugi (ed.), *Debating Cosmopolitics*, Verso, London..

Hayek, F.A. von (1976), *Law, Legislation and Liberty: The Mirage of Social Justice*, University of Chicago Press, Chicago.

Haynes, J. (2001), *Democracy in the Developing World: Africa, Asia, Latin America and the Middle East*, Polity Press, Cambridge.

Heater, D. (1996), *World Citizenship and Government*, Macmillan, Basingstoke.

Heater, D. (2002), *World Citizenship: Cosmopolitan Thinking and Its Opponents*, Continuum, London.

Held, D. (1992), 'Democracy: From City States to a Cosmopolitan Order', *Political Studies* vol. 40, pp. 10-39.

Held, D. (1995), *Democracy and the Global Order: From the Modern State to Cosmopolitan Government*, Stanford University Press, Stanford.

Held, D. (1997), *Models of Democracy*, 2nd edn., Polity Press, Cambridge.

Held, D. (1998), 'Democracy and Globalization', in D. Archibugi, D. Held, and M. Köhler (eds.), *Re-imagining Political Community: Studies in Cosmopolitan Democracy*, Polity Press, Cambridge.

Held, D. (1999), 'The Transformation of Political Community', in I. Shapiro and C. Hacker-Cordón (eds.), *Democracy's Edges*, Cambridge: Cambridge University Press.

Held, D. (2000), 'The Changing Contours of Political Community: Rethinking Democracy in the Context of Globalization', in B. Holden (ed.), *Global Democracy: Key Debates*, Routledge, London.

Held, D. (2002), 'Law of States, Law of Peoples: Three Models of Sovereignty', *Legal Theory*, vol. 8, pp. 1-44.

Held, D., and Koenig-Archibugi, M., eds. (2003), *Taming Globalization: Frontiers of Governance*, Polity Press, Cambridge.

Held, D., and McGrew, A., eds. (2002), *Governing Globalization*, Polity Press, Cambridge.

Held, D., McGrew, A., Goldblatt, D., and Perraton, J. (1999), *Global Transformations: Politics, Economics and Culture*, Stanford University Press, Stanford.

Herdegen, M. (1998), 'Price Stability and Budgetary Restraints in the Economic and Monetary Union: The Law as Guardian of Economic Wisdom', *Common Market Law Review*, vol. 35, pp. 9-32.

Hewson, M., and Sinclair, T.J. (1999), 'The Emergence of Global Governance Theory', in M. Hewson and T. Sinclair (eds.), *Approaches to Global Governance Theory*, State University of New York Press, Albany.

Heyzer, N., Riker, J.V., and Quizon, A.B., eds. (1995), *Government-NGO Relations in Asia: Prospects and Challenges for People-Centred Development*, Macmillan, London.

Hill, C. (1972), *The World Turned Upside Down: Radical Ideas During the English Revolution*, Viking Press, New York.

Hilton, B. (1977), *Corn, Cash, Commerce: The Economic Policies of the Tory Governments 1815-1830*, Oxford University Press, Oxford.

Hirst, P., and Thompson, G. (1999), *Globalization in Question*, Polity Press, Cambridge.

Hix, S., and Lord, C. (1997), *Political Parties in the European Union*, Macmillan, Houndmills.

Hobbes, T. (1960 ed.), *Leviathan*, Basil Blackwell, Oxford.

Hobbes, T. (1968 [1651]), C.B. Macpherson (ed.), *Leviathan*, Penguin, Middlesex.

Holden, B., ed. (2000), *Global Democracy: Key Debates*, Routledge, London.

Holmes, M., ed. (1996), *The Eurosceptical Reader*, St. Martin's Press, New York.

Holmes, S. (1988), 'Precommitment and the Paradox of Democracy', in J. Elster and R. Slagstad (eds.), *Constitutionalism and Democracy: Studies in Rationality and Social Change*, Cambridge University Press, Cambridge.

Holmgren, T., and Kasekende, L. (2000) 'Uganda', in S. Devarajan, D. Dollar, and T. Holmgren (eds.), *Aid and Reform in Africa: Lessons from Ten Case Studies*, International Bank for Reconstruction and Development, Washington D.C.

Holzner, B. (2002), 'The Ambivalent Quest for Transparency', inaugural lecture as Distinguished Service Professor, University of Pittsburgh.

Hont, I. (1994), 'The Permanent Crisis of a Divided Mankind: "Contemporary Crisis of the Nation State" in Historical Perspective', *Political Studies*, vol. 42, pp. 166-231.

Horne, A. (1988), *Harold MacMillan. Volume One: 1894-1956*, Viking, New York.

Hubert, D. (2000), 'The Landmine Ban: a Case Study in Humanitarian Advocacy', *Occasional Paper No. 42*, Watson Institute, Providence.

Hulme, D., and Edwards, M., eds. (1997), *NGOs, States and Donors: Too Close for Comfort?*, Macmillan, London.

Human Rights Watch (1999), 'Hostile to Democracy: The Movement System and Political Repression in Uganda', Human Rights Watch, New York.

Hutchings, K. (1999), *International Political Theory*, Sage, London.

Hutchings, K., and Dannreuther, R., eds. (1999), *Cosmopolitan Citizenship*, Macmillan, Houndmills.

ICISS (2001), 'The Responsibility to Protect', December, IDRC, Ottawa.

IFAD (2001), *Rural Poverty Report 2001: The Challenge of Ending Rural Poverty*, Oxford University Press, Oxford.

Ignatieff, M. (2000), *The Rights Revolution*, Anansi, Toronto.

Jackson, R. (1999), 'Sovereignty in World Politics: A Galance at the Conceptual and Historical Landscape', *Political Studies*, vol. 47 (Special Issue), pp. 431-56..

Jenkins, R. (2002) 'The Emergence of the Governance Agenda', in V. Desai and R.B. Potter (eds.), *The Companion to Development Studies*, Arnold, London.

Johnson, C. (2000), *Blowback: The Causes and Consequences of the American Empire*, Broadway Books, New York.

Jones, G.S. (1983), 'Rethinking Chartism', in G.S. Jones (ed.), *Languages of Class: Studies in English Working Class History 1832-1982*, Cambridge University Press, Cambridge.

Jones, P. (1994), *Rights*, Macmillan, London.

Joyce, P. (1991), *Visions of the People: Industrial England and the Question of Class 1848-1914*, Cambridge University Press, Cambridge.

Judt, T. (1996), *A Grand Illusion? An Essay on Europe*, Hill and Wang, New York.

Kaldor, M. (1990), *The Imaginary War*, Blackwell, Oxford.

Kaldor, M. (1998), 'Reconceptualizing Organized Violence', in D. Archibugi, D. Held, and M. Köhler (eds.), *Re-imagining Political Community: Studies in Cosmopolitan Democracy*, Polity Press, Cambridge.

Kaldor, M. (1999), *New and Old Wars*, Polity Press, Cambridge.

Kaldor, M. (2001), 'A Decade of Humanitarian Intervention: The Role of Global Civil Society', in H. Anheier, M. Glasius, and M. Kaldor (eds.), *Global Civil Society*, Oxford University Press, Oxford.

Kant. I. (1991 [1795]), 'Towards Perpetual Peace. A Philosophical Project', in H. Reiss (ed.), *Kant: Political Writings*, 2nd ed., Cambridge University Press, Cambridge.

Kasfir, N. (2000), '"No-Party Democracy" in Uganda', *Journal of Democracy*, vol. 9, no. 2, pp. 49-63.

Kasfir, N., ed. (1998), *Civil Society and Democracy in Africa: Critical Perspectives*, Frank Cass, London.

Kassimir, R. (1998), 'Uganda: The Catholic Church and State Reconstruction', in L.A. Villalón and P.A. Huxtable Villalon (eds.), *The African State at a Critical Juncture*, Lynne Rienner, Boulder, Colorado.

Kaus, M. (1991), *The End of Equality*, Basic Books, New York.

Keal, P., ed. (1992), *Ethics and Foreign Policy*, Allen and Unwin, Sydney.

Keating, M. (2001), *Plurinational Democracy: Stateless Naitons in a Post-Sovereignty Era*, Oxford University Press, Oxford and New York.

Keck, M., and Sikkink, K. (1998), *Activists Beyond Borders: Transnational Advocacy Networks in International Politics*, Cornell University Press, Ithaca.

Kelsen, H. (1920), *Das Problem der Souvernität und die Theorie des Völkerrechts. Beitrag zu einer reinen Rechtslehre*, Mohr, Tübingen.

Kelsen, H. (1944), *Peace through Law*, University of North Carolina Press, Chapel Hill.

Keohane, N.O. (1980), *Philosophy and the State in France: The Renaissance to the Enlightenment*, Princeton University Press, Princeton.

Keohane, R.O. (1998), 'International Institutions: Can Interdependence Work?', *Foreign Policy*, Issue 110, pp. 82-96.

Keohane, R.O. (2001), 'Governance in a Partially Globalized World', *American Political Science Review*, vol. 95, no.1, pp. 1-13.

Keohane, R.O. (2003), 'Global Governance and Democratic Accountability', in D. Held and M. Koenig-Archibugi (eds.), *Taming Globalization: Frontiers of Governance*, Polity Press, Cambridge.

Keohane, R.O., and Hoffmann, S. (1990), 'Conclusions: Community Politics and Institutional Change', in W. Wallace (ed.), *The Dynamics of European Integration*, Pinter Publishers for the Royal Institute of International Affairs, London.

Keohane, R.O., and Milner, H., eds. (1996), *Internationalization and Domestic Politics*, Cambridge University Press, New York.

Khadiagala, G.M., and Lyons, T., eds. (2001), *African Foreign Policies: Power and Process*, Lynne Rienner, Boulder, Colorado.

Khadiagala, L.S. (2001), 'The Failure of Popular Justice in Uganda: Local Councils and Women's Property Rights', *Development and Change*, vol. 32, no. 1, January, pp. 55-76.

Khagram, S., Riker, J.V., and Sikkink, K. (2002), 'From Santiago to Seattle: Transnational Advocacy Groups Restructuring World Politics', in S. Khagram, J.V. Riker, and K. Sikkink (eds.), *Restructuring World Politics: Transnational Social Movements, Networks, and Norms*, University of Minnesota Press, Minneapolis and London.

Khagram, S., Riker, J.V., and Sikkink, K., eds. (2002), *Restructuring World Politics: Transnational Social Movements, Networks and Norms*, University of Minnesota Press, Minneapolis and London.

Kidder, T.G. (2002), 'Networks in Transnational Labor Organizing', in S. Khagram, J.V. Riker, and K. Sikkink (eds.), *Restructuring World Politics: Transnational Social Movements, Networks, and Norms*, University of Minnesota Press, Minneapolis and London.

Kincaid, A.D., and Portes, A. (1994), *Comparative National Development: Society and Economy in the New Global Order*, University of North Carolina Press, Chapel Hill.

Kitschelt, H., Lange, P., Marks, G., and Stephens, J.D., eds. (1999), *Continuity and Change in Contemporary Capitalism*, Cambridge University Press, Cambridge.

Klausen, J. (1998), *War and Welfare: Europe and the United States, 1945 to the Present*, Palgrave, Houndmills.

Klausen, J. and Tilly, L.A., eds. (1997b), *European Integration in Social and Historical Perspective: 1850 to the Present*, Rowman and Littlefield, Lanham.

Klausen, J., and Tilly, L.A. (1997a), 'European Integration in a Social and Historical Perspective', in J. Klausen and L.A. Tilly (eds.), *European Integration in Social and Historical Perspective: 1850 to the Present*, Rowman and Littlefield, Lanham.

Klein, N. (2000), *No Logo: Taking Aim at the Brand Bullies*, Flamingo, London.

Knight, B., Chigudu, H., and Tandon, R. (2002), *Reviving Democracy: Citizens at the Heart of Governance*, Earthscan for Commonwealth Foundation, London.

Knox, T.M., and Pelczynski, Z.A. (1967), *Hegel's Political Writings*, Clarendon Press, Oxford.

Kobrin, S.J. (1999), 'Back to the Future: Neomedievalism and the Postmodern Digital World Economy', in A Prakash and J.A. Hart (eds.), *Globalization and Governance*, Routledge, London.

Koenig-Archibugi, M. (2002), 'Mapping Global Governance', in D. Held and T. McGrew (eds.), *Governing Globalization*, Polity Press, Cambridge.

Köhler, M. (1998), 'From the National to the Cosmopolitan Public Sphere', in D. Archibugi, D. Held, and M. Köhler (eds.), *Re-imagining Political Community: Studies in Cosmopolitan Democracy*, Polity Press, Cambridge.

Korzeniewicz, R.P., and Smith, W.C. (2001), 'Protest and Collaboration: Transnational Civil Society Networks and the Politics of Summitry and Free Trade in the Americas', paper 51, North-South Center, University of Miami.

Krasner, S.D. (1999), *Sovereignty: Organized Hypocrisy*, Princeton University Press, Princeton.

Kurth , J. (1993), 'A Tale of Four Countries: Parallel Politics in Southern Europe, 1815-1990', in J. Kurth and J. Petras (eds.), *Mediterranean Paradoxes: Politics and Social Structure in Southern Europe*, Berg Publishers, Providence.

Kurzman, C. (1998), 'Waves of Democratization', *Studies in Comparative International Development*, vol. 33, pp. 37-59.

Kwass, Michael (2000*), Privilege and the Politics of Taxation in Eighteenth-Century France: Liberté Égalité Fraternité*, Cambridge University Press, Cambridge.

Kymlicka, W. (1995), *Multicultural Citizenship*, Oxford University Press, Oxford.

Kymlicka, W. (1999), 'Citizenship in an Era of Globalization', in I. Shapiro and C. Hacker-Cordón (eds.), *Democracy's Edge*, Cambridge University Press, Cambridge.

Landau, A. (2001), *Redrawing the Global Economy: Elements of Integration and Fragmentation*, Palgrave, Houndmills.

Langley, D. (1996), *The Americas in the Age of Revolution, 1750-1850*, Yale University Press, New Haven.

Langseth, P, Munene, J., and Katorobo, J., eds. (1995), *Uganda: Landmarks in Rebuilding a Nation*, Fountain, Kampala.

Latham, R. (1999), 'Politics in a Floating World: Toward a Critique of Global Governance', in M. Hewson and T. Sinclair (ed.)., *Approaches to Global Governance Theory*, State University of New York Press, Albany.

Leino, P. (2001), 'The ECB and Its Legitimacy', *Jean Monnet Center Working Papers*, Harvard University, Cambridge, USA.

Lemarchand, R. (2001), 'Foreign Policy Making in the Great Lakes Region', in G.M. Khadiagala and T. Lyons (eds.), *African Foreign Policies: Power and Process*, Lynne Rienner, Boulder.

Lewis, D., and Wallace, T., eds. (2000), *New Roles and Relevance: Development NGOs and the Challenge of Change*, Kumarian, West Hartford.

Lind, M. (1995), *The Next American Nation: The New Nationalism and the Fourth American Revolution*, The Free Press, New York.

Lindberg, S., and Sverrison, A., eds. (1997), *Social Movements in Development*, Macmillan, London.

Linebaugh, P., and Rediker, M. (2000), *The Many-Headed Hydra: Sailors, Slaves Commoners, and the Hidden History of the Revolutionary Atlantic*, Beacon Press, Boston.

Linklater, A. (1992), 'What is a Good International Citizen?', in P. Keal (ed.), *Ethics and Foreign Policy*, Allen and Unwin, Sydney.

Linklater, A. (1998), *The Transformation of Political Community*, Polity Press, Cambridge.

Linz, J. (2000[1975]), *Totalitarian and Authoritarian Regimes*, Lynne Rienner, Boulder, Colorado.

Linz, J., and Stepan, A. (1996), *Problems of Democratic Transition and Consolidation: Southern Europe, South America, and Post-Communist Europe*, The Johns Hopkins University Press, Baltimore.

Lipset, S., and Schneider, W. (1983), *The Confidence Gap*, Johns Hopkins University Press, Baltimore.

Lipsey, R.G., Schwanen, D., and Wonnacott, R.J. (1994), *NAFTA: What's In, What's Out, What's Next*, C.D. Howe Institute, Toronto.

Locke, J. (1952), *The Second Treatise of Government*, Liberal Arts Press, New York.

Loomis, C. (1997), *Radical Democracy*, Cornell University Press, Ithaca.

Lundestad, G. (1986), 'Empire by Invitation? The United States and Western Europe, 1945-1952', *Journal of Peace Research*, vol. 23, no. 3, pp. 263-77.

MacCormick, N. (1996)',What Place for Nationalism in the Modern World?', in S. Caney, D. George, and P. Jones (eds.), *National Rights, International Obligations*, Westview Press, Boulder.

MacCormick, N. (1999), *Questioning Sovereignty: Law, State, and Nation in the European Commonwealth*, Oxford University Press, Oxford.

Macdonald, L. (1996), *Supporting Civil Society: The Political Role of NGOs in Central America*, Macmillan, London.

MacLean, S.J., and Shaw, T.M. (2001), 'Canada and New "Global" Strategic Alliances: Prospects for Human Security at the Start of the Twenty-First Century', *Canadian Foreign Policy*, vol. 8, no. 3, Spring, pp. 17-36.

Majone, G. (1997), 'Regulatory Legitimacy', in G. Majone (ed.), *From the Positive to the Regulatory State: Causes and Consequences of Changes in the Mode of Government*, Institutio Juan March de Estudios e Investigaciones Working Paper, Madrid.

Majone, G. (1998), 'Europe's "Democratic Deficit": The Question of Standards', *European Law Journal, vol.* 4, pp. 5-28.

Majone, G., ed. (1996), *Regulating Europe*. Routledge: London.

Makhan, V.S. (2002), *Economic Recovery in Africa: The Paradox of Financial Flows*, Palgrave Macmillan, London.

Makova, S. (2000), 'Decentralization for Good Governance and Development: Uganda's Experience', *Development Policy Review*, vol. 18, no. 1, March, pp. 73-94.

Makumbe, J. (1998), 'Is there a Civil Society in Africa?', *International Affairs*, vol. 74, no. 2, April, pp. 305-317.

Malcolm, N. (1994), 'Sense on Sovereignty', in M. Holmes (ed.), *The Eurosceptic Reader*, MacMillan, London.

Mann, M. (1993a), 'Nation-States in Europe and Other Continents: Diversifying, Developing, Not Dying', *Daedalus*, vol. 122, pp. 115-140.

Mann, M. (1993b), *The Sources of Social Power, Volume II: The Rise of Classes and Nation-States, 1760-1914*, Cambridge University Press, Cambridge.

Manning, S., (1999), 'Introduction', *Journal of World-System Research*, vol. 5 ('Special Issue on Globalization'), no. 2, pp. 137-41.

Marchetti, R. (2002), *Consequentialist Cosmopolitanism*, paper presented at the Global Studies Association Conference, July 22-4, University of Surrey, Roehampton.

Markoff, J. (1996), *Waves of Democracy: Social Movements and Political Change*, Pine Forge Press, Thousand Oaks.

Markoff, J. (1999a), 'Our Common European Home – But Who Owns the House?', in D. Smith and S. Wright (eds.), *Whose Europe? The Turn Towards Democracy*, Blackwell/Sociological Review, Oxford.

Markoff, J. (1999b), 'Where and When Was Democracy Invented?', *Comparative Study of Society and History*, vol. 41, no. 4, pp. 660-90.

Markoff, J. (2001), 'The Internet and Electronic Communications', in M.K. Cayton and P.W. Williams (eds.), *Encyclopedia of American Cultural and Intellectual History*, Scribner's, New York, vol. 3. pp. 387-395.

Markoff, J. (forthcoming), 'Margins, Centers, and Democracy: The Paradigmatic History of Women's Suffrage', *Signs: Journal of Women in Culture and Society*.

Markoff, J., and Montecinos, V. (1993), 'The Ubiquitous Rise of Economists', *Journal of Public Policy*, vol. 13, pp. 37-68.

Marks, G. (1997), 'A Third Lens', in J. Klausen and L.A. Tilly (eds.), *European Integration in Social and Historical Perspective: 1850 to the Present*, Rowman and Littlefield, Lanham.

Martinussen, J. (1997), *Society, State and Market: A Guide to Competing Theories of Development*, Zed, London.

Mashaw, J. (1997), *Greed, Chaos, and Governance: Using Public Choice to Improve Public Law*, Yale University Press, New Haven.

Mason, A. (2000), *Community, Solidarity and Belonging: Levels of Community and their Normative Significance*, Cambridge University Press, Cambridge.

Masson, J.M., and McCarty, S. (1995), *When Elephants Weep*, Delacorte Press, New York.

Mbabazi, P.K., and Shaw, T.M. (2000), 'NGOs and Peace-Building in the Great Lakes Region of Africa: States, Civil Societies and Companies in the New Millennium', in D. Lewis and T. Wallace (eds.), *New Roles and Relevance: Development NGOs and the Challenge of Change*, Kumarian, West Hartford.

Mbabazi, P.K., MacLean, S.J., and Shaw, T.M. (2002), 'Governance and Reconstruction in Africa at the Start of the New Millennium: Challenges for Policy Communities/Coalitions', *Global Networks*, vol. 2, no. 1, January, pp. 31-47.

McAdam, D., Tarrow, S., and Tilly, C. (2001), *Dynamics of Contention*, Cambridge University Press, New York.

McGee, R. (2000), 'Meeting the International Poverty Targets in Uganda', *Development Policy Review*, vol. 18, no. 1, March, pp. 85-106.

McGrew, A. (2000), *Transnational Democracy: Theories and Prospects*, text available at: www.polity.co.uk/global/mcgrew.htm.

McGrew, A. (2002), 'Transnational Democracy', in A. Carter and G. Stokes (eds.), *Democratic Theory Today,* Polity Press, Cambridge.

McGrew, A., ed. (1997), *The Transformation of Democracy?*, Open University, Milton Keynes.

McKinney, J.A. (2000), *Created from NAFTA: The Structure, Function, and Significance of the Treaty's Related Institutions*, M.E. Sharpe, Armonk.

McMichael, P. (2001), 'Can We Interpret the Anti-Globalisation Movement in Polanyian Terms', presented at the symposium 'Globalisation and Its Discontents: Re-Embedding the Economy in the Twenty-First Century', Trent University, Peterborough, Ontario, Canada.

McNamara, K. (1998), *The Currency of Ideas: Monetary Politics in the European Union*, Cornell University Press, Ithaca.

McNeill, W.H. (1963), *The Rise of the West*, University of Chicago Press, Chicago.

McNeill, W.H. (1987), *Polyethnicity and National Unity in World History*, University of Toronto Press, Toronto.

McRoberts, K. (1997), *Misconceiving Canada: The Struggle for National Unity*, Oxford University Press, Toronto.

Melucci, A. (1989), *Nomads of the Present: Social Movements and Individual Needs in Contemporary Society*, Temple University Press, Philadelphia.

Mendolsohn, M., and Wolfe, R. (2000), 'Probing the Aftermyth of Seattle: Canadian Public Opinion on International Trade, 1980-2000', *School of Policy Studies Working Paper No. 12*, Queen's University, Kingston, December.

Messner, D., and Nuscheler, F. (2002), 'World Politics – Structures and Trends', in P. Kennedy, D. Messner, and F. Nuscheler (eds.), *Global Trends and Global Governance*, Pluto Press, London and Sterling.

Mijumbi, P.B. (2001), 'Uganda's External Debt and the HIPC Initiative', *Canadian Journal of Development Studies*, vol. 22, no. 2, pp. 495-525.

Mill, J.S. (1975), 'Of Nationality, as Connected with Representative Government', *Considerations on Representative Government*, in J.S. Mill, *Three Essays*, Oxford University Press, Oxford.

Miller, C. (1997), 'Sir Frederick Goes to London: Money, Militia and Gentlemanly Capitalists', in C. Coates (ed.), *Imperial Canada, 1867-1917*, Centre for Canadian Studies, Edinburgh.

Miller, D. (1995), *On Nationality*: Oxford University Press, Oxford.

Miller, D. (2000), *Citizenship and National Identity*, Polity Press, Cambridge.

Milward, A. (1992), *The European Rescue of the Nation-State*, University of California Press, Berkeley.

232 *Transnational Democracy in Critical and Comparative Perspective*

Mittelman, J.H. (2000), *The Globalization Syndrome: Transformation and Resistance*, Princeton University Press, Princeton.
Mkandawire, T. (2001), 'Thinking about Developmental States in Africa', *Cambridge Journal of Economics*, vol. 25, pp. 289-313.
Montecinos, V., and Markoff, J. (2001), 'From the Power of Economic Ideas to the Power of Economists', in M.A. Centeno and F. Lopez-Alves (eds.), *The Other Mirror: Grand Theory Through the Lens of Latin America*, Princeton University Press, Princeton.
Moore, M. (2001), 'Globalization, Cosmopolitanism, and Minority Nationalism', in M. Keating and J. McGarry (eds.), *Minority Nationalism and the Changing International Order*, Oxford University Press, Oxford.
Moran, M. (2002), 'Review Essay: Understanding the Regulatory State', *British Journal of Political Science*, vol. 32, pp. 391-413.
Moravcsik, A. (2002), 'In Defence of the Democratic Deficit: Reassessing Legitimacy in the European Union', *Journal of Common Market Studies, vol.* 40, no. 4, pp. 603-624.
Morgan, E. (1988), *Inventing the People: The Rise of Popular Sovereignty in England and America*, Norton, New York.
Mugaju, J., and Olaka-Onyango, J., eds. (2000), *No-Party Democracy in Uganda: Myths and Realities*, Fountain, Kampala.
Munck, R., and Gills, B. (2002), 'Preface', *The Annals of the American Academy of Political and Social Science*, vol. 581 (Special issue: 'Globalization and Democracy'), pp. 8-9.
Murphy, C.N., ed. (2001), *Egalitarian Politics in the Age of Globalization,* Palgrave, London.
Murray, C. (1998), *What It Means to Be a Libertarian*, Broadway Books, New York.
Museveni, Y.K. (1997), *Sowing the Mustard Seed: The Struggle for Freedom and Democracy in Uganda*, Macmillan, London.
National Post (2002), 'Yukon court narrows definition of harassment', February 1.
Nayyar, D. (2002), 'The Existing System and the Missing Institutions', in D. Nayyar (ed.), *Governing Globalization: Issues and Institutions*, Oxford University Press, Oxford.
Nelson, P. (1995), *The World Bank and NGOs: The Limits of Apolitical Development*, Macmillan, London.
Nelson, P. (2002a), 'Agendas, Accountability, and Legitimacy Among Transnational Networks Lobbying the World Bank', in S. Khagram, J.V. Riker, and K. Sikkink (eds.), *Restructuring World Politics: Transnational Social Movements, Networks, and Norms*, University of Minnesota Press, Minneapolis and London.
Nelson, P. (2002b), 'The World Bank and NGOs', in V. Desai and R.B. Potter (eds.), *The Companion to Development Studies*, Arnold, London.
Nevitte, N. (1996), *The Decline of Deference*, Broadview Press, Peterborough.
Newman, S. (2000), 'Globalization and Democracy', in M.T. Greven and L.W. Pauly (eds.), *Democracy Beyond the State? The European Dilemma and the Emerging Global Order*, Rowman and Littlefield, Lanham.
Nimtz, A. (2002), 'Marx and Engels: The Prototypical Transnational Actors', in S. Khagram, J.V. Riker, and K. Sikkink (eds.), *Restructuring World Politics: Transnational Social Movements, Networks, and Norms*, University of Minnesota Press, Minneapolis and London.
Norris, P. (2002), 'Global Governance and Cosmoplitan Citizens', in J.S. Nye and E.C. Kamarck (eds.), *Governance.com: Governance in the Information Age*, Brookings, Washington.
Norris, P., ed. (1999), *Critical Citizens: Global Support for Democratic Governance*, Oxford University Press, Oxford.

Nsouli, S., and Le Gall, F., eds. (2001), 'Globalization and Africa', *Finance and Development*, vol. 38, no. 4, December, pp. 2-36.

Nye, Jr., J.S., and Donahue, J.D., eds. (2000), *Governance in a Globalizing World*, Brookings Institution Press, Washington DC.

Nye, Jr., J.S., Zelikow, P., and King, D. (1997), *Why People Don't Trust Government*, Harvard University Press, Cambridge, Massachusetts.

O'Brien, R., Goetz, A.M., Scholte, J.A., and Williams, M. (2000), *Contesting Global Governance: Multilateral Economic Institutions and Global Social Movements*, Cambridge University Press, Cambridge.

O'Donnell, G., and Schmitter, P. (1986), *Transitions from Authoritarian Rule: Tentative Conclusions About Uncertain Democracies*, Johns Hopkins University Press, Baltimore.

O'Rourke, K.H., and Williamson, J.G. (1999), *Globalization and History: The Evolution of a Nineteenth-Century Atlantic Economy*, The MIT Press, Cambridge and London.

Offe, C. (2000), 'The Democratic Welfare State in an Integrating Europe', in M. T. Greven and L.W. Pauly (eds.), *Democracy Beyond the State? The European Dilemma and the Emerging Global Order*, University of Toronto Press, Toronto.

Offer, A. (1989), *The First World War: An Agrarian Interpretation*, Oxford University Press, Oxford.

Okin, S.M. (1981), 'Liberty and Welfare: Some Issues in Human Rights Theory', in J.R. Pennock and J.W. Chapman (eds.), *NOMOS XXIII: Human Rights*, New York University Press, New York, pp. 232-56.

Orianne, P. (1973), 'Difficulties in Co-operation Between Local Authorities and Ways of Solving Them', *Local and Regional Authorities in Europe, Study No. 6*, September 1973, Council of Europe, Strasbourg.

Ostry, S. (1990), *Governments and Corporations in a Shrinking World*, Council on Foreign Relations, New York.

Ostry, S. (1997), *The Post-Cold War Trading System: Who's on First?*, University of Chicago Press, Chicago.

Ougaard, M. and Higgott, R., eds. (2002), *Towards a Global Polity*, Routledge, London and New York.

Overbeek, H. (2002), 'Neoliberalism and the Regulation of Global Labor Mobility', *The Annals of the American Academy of Political and Social Science*, vol. 581 (Special issue: 'Globalization and Democracy'), pp. 74-90.

Paine, T. (1794), *Rights of Man*, Citadel Press, Secaucus, New Jersey.

Paine, T. (1985 [1791]), *The Declaration of the Rights of Man*, Eric Foner, ed., Penguin, Harmondsworth.

Palmer, R. (1953), 'Notes on the Use of the Word "Democracy", 1789-1799', *Political Science Quarterly*, vol. 68, pp. 203-226.

Parpart, J.L., and Shaw, T.M. (2002), 'African Development Debates and Prospects at the Turn of the Century', in P.J. McGowan and P. Nel (eds.), 2nd ed., *Power, Wealth and Global Equity: An International Relations Textbook for Africa*, Oxford University Press, Cape Town.

Patomaki, H., Teivainen, T., and Ronkko, M. (2002), *Global Democracy Initiatives: The Art of Possible*, Hakapaino, Helsinki.

Payne, A. (1999), 'Reframing the Global Politics of Development', *Journal of International Relations and Development*, vol. 2, no. 4, December, pp. 369-79.

Pearson, R., and Seyfang, G. (2001), 'New Hope or False Dawn? Voluntary Codes of Conduct, Labour Regulation and Social Policy in a Globalising World', *Global Social Policy*, vol. 1, no.1, April, pp. 25-35.

Perraton, J. (2000), 'Hirst and Thompson's "Global Myths and National Policies": A Reply', in B. Holden (ed.), *Global Democracy: Key Debates*, Routledge, London.

Pettit, P. (1997), *Republicanism: A Theory of Freedom and Government*, Oxford University Press, Oxford.

Pharr, S., and Putnam, R., eds. (2000), *Disaffected Democracies: What's Troubling the Trilateral Countries?*, Princeton University Press, Princeton.

Phillips, K. (1999), *The Cousins' Wars: Religion, Politics and the Triumph of Anglo-America*, Basic Books, New York.

Pianta, M. (2001), 'Parallel Summits of Global Civil Society', in H. Anheier, M. Glasius and M. Kaldor (eds.), *Global Civil Society*, Oxford University Press, Oxford.

Pianta, M. (2003), 'Democracy vs Globalisation: The Growth of Parallel Summits and Global Movements', in D. Archibugi (ed.), *Debating Cosmopolitics*, Verso, London.

Piven, F., and Cloward, R. (1997), *The Breaking of the American Social Compact*, The New Press, New York.

Pogge, T. (1992), 'Cosmopolitanism and Sovereignty', *Ethics*, vol. 103, no. 1, pp. 48-75.

Pogge, T. (1997), 'Creating Supra-National Institutions Democratically: Reflections on the European Union's Democratic Deficit', *Journal of Political Philosophy*, vol. 5, no. 2, pp. 163-182.

Pogge, T., ed. (2001), *Global Justice*, Blackwell, Oxford.

Prakash, A., and Hart, J.A., eds. (1999), *Globalization and Governance*, Routledge, London.

Price, V.C. (2001), 'Some Causes and Consequences of Fragmentation', in S.W. Arndt and H. Kierzkowski (eds.), *Fragmentation: New Production Patterns in the World Economy*, Oxford University Press, Oxford.

Prins, G., and Sellwood, E. (1998), 'Global Security Problems and the Challenge to Democratic Process', in D. Archibugi, D. Held, and M. Köhler (eds.), *Re-imagining Political Community: Studies in Cosmopolitan Democracy*, Polity Press, Cambridge.

Prokosch, M., and Raymond, L., eds. (2002), *The Global Activist's Manual*, Thunder's Mouth Press, New York.

Przeworski, A. (1997), 'Democratization Revisited', *Items*, vol. 51, no. 1, pp. 6-11.

Przeworski, A., Alvarez, M., Cheibub, J., and Limongi, F. (2000), *Democracy and Development: Well-Being in the World, 1950-1990*, Cambridge University Press, Cambridge.

Quadir, F., MacLean, S.J., and Shaw, T.M. (2001), 'Pluralisms and the Changing Global Political Economy: Ethnicities in Crises of Governance in Asia and Africa', in F. Quadir, S.J. MacLean, and T.M. Shaw (eds.), *Crises of Governance in Asia and Africa*, Ashgate, Aldershot.

Rabkin, J. (1999), *Why Sovereignty Matters*, American Enterprise Institute, Washington.

Rawls, J. (1991), *Political Liberalism*, Columbia University Press, New York.

Rawls, J. (1999), *The Law of Peoples*, Harvard University Press, Cambridge, Massachusetts.

Raz, J., and Margalit, A. (1994), 'National Self-Determination', in J. Raz (ed.), *Ethics in the Public Domain : Essays in the Morality of Law and Politics*, Clarendon, Oxford.

Reinikka, R., and Collier, P., eds. (2001), *Uganda's Recovery:The Role of Farms, Firms and Government*, World Bank, Washington.

Rice, A.E., and Ritchie, C. (1995), 'Relationship Between International Non-Governmental Organizations and the United Nations: A Research and Policy Report', *Transnational Associations*, vol. 47, no. 5, pp. 254-65.

Riley, P. (1979), *The Political Writings of Leibniz*, Cambridge University Press, Cambridge.

Robertson, R. (1992), *Globalization: Social Theory and Global Culture*, Sage, London.

Rogister, J. (1995), *Louis XV and the Parlement of Paris, 1737-1755*, Cambridge University Press, Cambridge.

Rose, R., Mishler, W., and Haerpfer, C. (1998), *Democracy and Its Alternatives: Understanding Post-Communist Societies*. Johns Hopkins University Press, Baltimore.

Rosenau, J.N. (1997), *Along the Domestic-Foreign Frontier. Exploring Governance in a Turbulent World*, Cambridge University Press, Cambridge.

Rosenau, J.N. (1998), 'Governance and Democracy in a Globalizing World', in D. Archibugi, D. Held, and M. Köhler (eds.), *Re-imagining Political Community: Studies in Cosmopolitan Democracy*, Polity Press, Cambridge.

Rousseau, J-J. (1967), *Discourse on the Origin of Inequality*, L.G. Crocker (ed.), Simon and Schuster, New York.

Rousseau, J-J. (1981 [1756]), 'Judgement of Saint-Pierre's Project for Perpetual Peace', in S. Hoffman and D.P. Fidler (eds.), *Rousseau on International Relations*, Clarendon Press, Oxford.

Rowat, C. (1999), 'Comment on Berman and McNamara', *Foreign Affairs*, vol. 78, no. 4, July/August, p. 152.

Rubio-Marin, R. (2000), *Immigration as a Democratic Challenge*, Cambridge University Press, Cambridge.

Rueschemeyer, D., Stephens, E.H., and Stephens, J.D. (1992), *Capitalist Development and Democracy*, Polity Press, Cambridge.

Rugman, A.M., Kirton, J., and Soloway, J.A. (1997), 'Canadian Corporate Strategy in a North American Region', *The American Review of Canadian Studies*, Summer.

Rupesinghe, K., ed. (1989), *Conflict Resolution in Uganda*, James Currey, London.

Russell, P. (1992), *Constitutional Odyssey*, University of Toronto Press, Toronto.

Russett, B. (1993), *Grasping the Democratic Peace*, Princeton University Press, Princeton.

Russett, B., and Oneal, J. (2001), *Triangulating Peace: Democracy, Interdependence, and International Organizations*, Norton, New York.

Sáenz Peña, R. (1915), *Escritos y Discursos, vol. 2: La Presidencia*, Jacobo Peuser, Buenos Aires.

Salskov-Iversen, D., Hansen, H.K., and Bisley, S. (2000), 'Governmentality, Globalization and Local Practice: Transformations of a Hegemonic Discourse', *Alternatives*, vol. 25, no. 2, April/June, pp. 183-222.

Sandbrook, R. (2000), *Closing the Circle: Democratization and Development in Africa*, Between the Lines, Toronto.

Sandholtz, W. (1999), 'Globalization and the Evolution of Rules', in A. Prakash and J.A. Hart (eds.), *Globalization and Governance*, Routledge, London.

Sassen, S. (1994), *Cities in a World Economy*, Pine Forge Press, Thousand Oaks.

Saward, M. (1998), *The Terms of Democracy*, Polity Press, Cambridge.

Saward, M. (2000), 'A Critique of Held', in B. Holden (ed.), *Global Democracy: Key Debates*, Routledge, London.

Saward, M. (2001), 'Reconstructing Democracy: Current Thinking and New Directions', *Government and Opposition*, vol. 36, pp. 559-81.

Schaeffer, R. (1997), *Understanding Globalization: The Social Consequences of Political, Economic, and Environmental Change*, Rowman and Littlefield, Lanham.

Schaeper, T., and Schaeper, K. (1998), 'Cowboys and Gentlemen: Rhodes Scholars', *Oxford and the Creation of an American Elite*, Berg, Leamington Spa.

Scharpf, F.W. (1999), *Governing in Europe*, Clarendon Press, Oxford.

Schechter, M.G., ed. (1999), *The Revival of Civil Society: Global and Comparative Perspectives*, Palgrave, London.

Schmitter, P. (1999), 'The Future of Democracy: Could It Be a Matter of Scale?', *Social Research* vol. 66, no. 3, pp. 933-59.

Schmitter, P. (2000), *How to Democratize the European Union...and Why Bother?* Rowan and Littlefield, Lanham.

Schmitter, P., and O'Donnell, G. (1986), *Transitions from Authoritarian Rule: Tentative Conclusions about Uncertain Democracies*, The Johns Hopkins University Press, Baltimore and London.

Schmitz, H.P. (1999), 'Transnational Activism and Political Change in Kenya and Uganda', in T. Risse-Kappen, S.C. Ropp, and K. Sikkink (eds.), *The Power of Human Rights: International Norms and Domestic Change*, Cambridge University Press, Cambridge.

Schoenbrod, D. (1993), *Power Without Responsibility*, Yale University Press, New Haven.

Schoenbrod, D. (1999), 'Delegation and Democracy: A Reply to my Critics', *Cardoza Law Review*, vol. 20, pp. 731-66.

Scholte, Jan Aart (2002a), 'Civil Society and Democracy in Global Governance', *Global Governance*, vol. 8, pp. 281-304.

Scholte, Jan Aart (2002b), 'Governing Global Finance', in D. Held and A. McGrew (eds.), *Governing Globalization: Power, Authority and Global Governance*, Polity Press, Cambridge.

Schuck, P.H. (2000), *The Limits of the Law: Essays on Democratic Governance*, Westview Press, Boulder, Colorado.

Schudson, M. (1998), *The Good Citizen: A History of American Civic Life*, Harvard University Press, Cambridge, Massachusetts.

Schumpeter, J. (1976 [1942]), *Capitalism, Socialism, and Democracy*, Allen and Unwin, London.

Scully, R. (2000), 'Democracy, Legitimacy, and the European Parliament', in M.G. Cowles and M. Smith (eds.), *The State of the European Union, Volume 5: Risks, Reform, Resistance, and Revival*, Oxford University Press, Oxford.

Seckinelgin, H. (2002), 'Time to Stop and Think: HIV/AIDS, Global Civil Society, and People's Politics', in H. Anheier, M. Glasius, and M. Kaldor (eds.), *Global Civil Society*, Oxford University Press, Oxford.

Sell, S.K. (2000), 'Structures, Agents and Institutions: Private Corporate Power and the Globalization of Intellectual Property Rights', in R.A. Higgott, G.R.D. Underhill, and A. Bieler (eds.), *Non-State Actors and Authority in the Global System*, Routledge, New York.

Shapiro, I., and Hacker-Cordón, C., eds. (1999), *Democracy's Edges*, Cambridge Universtity Press, New York.

Shaw, J. (1999), 'Postnational Constitutionalism in the European Union', *Journal of European Public Policy*, vol. 6, pp. 479-97.

Shaw, T.M. (1997), 'Prospects for a "New" Political Economy of Development in the Twenty-First Century', *Canadian Journal of Development Studies*, vol. 18, no. 3, pp. 375-92.

Shaw, T.M. (1999), 'Foreword: Global/Local: States, Companies and Civil Societies at the End of the Twentieth Century', in K. Stiles (ed.), *Global Institutions and Local Empowerment: Competing Theoretical Perspectives*, Macmillan, London.

Shaw, T.M. (2002), 'Peace-building Partnerships and Human Security', in V. Desai and R.B. Potter (eds.), *The Companion to Development Studies*, Arnold, London.

Shaw, T.M. (2003), 'Africa', in M. Hawkesworth and M. Kogan (eds.), *Routledge Encyclopedia of Government and Politics*, 2nd ed., Routledge, London.

Shaw, T.M. and Nyang'oro, J.E. (2000), 'African Renaissance in the New Millennium? From Anarchy to Emerging Markets?', in R. Stubbs and G.R.D. Underhill (eds.), *Political Economy and the Changing Global Order*, 2nd ed., Oxford University Press, Toronto.

Siedentop, L. (2000), *Democracy in Europe*, Penguin Books, London.

Sigurdson, R. (1999), 'Canada as a Multi-National Federation: Promises and Problems', paper presented at the Atlantic Provinces Political Studies Association Conference, Sackville, N.B., October.

Sikkink, K. (2002), 'Restructuring World Politics: The Limits and Asymmetries of Soft Power', in S. Khagram, J.V. Riker, and K. Sikkink (eds.), *Restructuring World Politics: Transnational Social Movements, Networks, and Norms*, University of Minnesota Press, Minneapolis and London.

Sikkink, K., and Smith, J. (2002), 'Infrastructures for Change: Transnational Organizations, 1953-1993', in S. Khagram, J. Riker, and K. Sikkink (eds.), *Restructuring World Politics: Transnational Social Movements, Networks, and Norms*, University of Minnesota Press, Minneapolis and London.

Silver, B. (2003), *Forces of Labor: Workers' Movements and Globalization Since 1870*, Cambridge University Press, New York.

Sklair, L. (1991), *Sociology of the Global System*, The Johns Hopkins University Press, 1991.

Sklair, L. (2002), 'Democracy and the Transnational Capitalist Class', *The Annals of the American Academy of Political and Social Science*, vol. 581, pp.144-157.

Smillie, I., and Helmich, H, eds. (1999), *Stakeholders: Government-NGO Partnerships for Development*, Earthscan, London.

Smillie, I., Gberie, L., and Hazelton, R. (2000), 'The Heart of the Matter: Sierra Leone, Diamonds and Human Security', Partnership Africa Canada, Ottawa.

Smith, Jackie (1995), 'Transnational Political Processes and the Human Rights Movement', in *Research in Social Movements, Conflicts, and Change*, vol. 18, pp. 185-219.

Smith, Jackie (1997), 'Characteristics of the Modern Transnational Social Movement Sector', in Jackie Smith, C. Chatfield, and R. Pagnucco (eds.), *Transnational Social Movements and Global Politics: Solidarity Beyond the State*, Syracuse University Press, Syracuse.

Smith, Jackie (2000), 'Social Movements, International Institutions and Local Empowerment', in K. Stiles (ed.), *Global Institutions and Local Empowerment: Competing Theoretical Perspectives*, Macmillan, London.

Smith, Jackie (forthcoming a), 'Globalization and Social Movements: Exploring Connections Between Global Integration and Political Mobilization', in J. Bandy and Jackie Smith (eds.), *Coalitions Across Borders: Negotiating Difference and Unity in Transnational Struggles Against Neoliberalism*, Rowman and Littlefield, Lanham.

Smith, Jackie (forthcoming b), 'Transnational Processes and Movements', in D. Snow, S. Soule, and H. Kriese (eds.), *The Blackwell Companion to Social Movements*, Blackwell, London.

Smith, Jackie, Chatfield, C., and Pagnucco, R., eds. (1997), *Transnational Social Movements and Global Politics: Solidarity Beyond the State*, Syracuse University Press, Syracuse.

Smith, Julie (2001), 'The European Parliament and Democracy in the European Union', in R. Axtmann (ed.), *Balancing Democracy*, Continuum, London.

Smith, P.H. (1993), 'Decision Rules and Governance', in P.H. Smith (ed.), *The Challenge of Integration: Europe and the Americas*, University of Miami, New Brunswick, Florida.

Sohrabi, N. (1995), 'Historicizing Revolutions: Constitutional Revolutions in the Ottoman Empire, Iran, and Russia, 1905-1908', *American Journal of Sociology*, vol. 100, pp. 1383-1447.

Soros, G. (1987), The *Alchemy of Finance: Reading the Mind of the Market*, Simon and Schuster, New York.

Soros, G. (2000), *Open Society: Reforming Global Capitalism*, Public Affairs, New York.

Soros, G. (2002), *On Globalization*, Public Affairs, New York.

Spiro, P.J. (1995), 'New Global Communities: Nongovernmental Organizations in International Decision-Making Institutions', *The Washington Quarterly,* vol. 18, no. 1, pp. 45-56.

Spruyt, H. (1994), *The Sovereign State and Its Competitors*, Princeton University Press, Princeton.

Stiglitz, J. (2002), *Globalization and its Discontents*, Allen Lane, London.

Stiles, K., ed. (1999), *Global Institutions and Local Empowerment: Competing Theoretical Perspectives*, Macmillan, London.

Stone, A. (1994), 'What is a Supranational Constitution? An Essay in International Relations Theory', *The Review of Politics*, vol. 56, pp. 441-74.

Stone, B. (1981), *The Parlement of Paris, 1774-1789*, University of North Carolina Press, Chapel Hill.

Stone, B. (1986), *The French Parlements and the Crisis of the Old Regime*, University of North Carolina Press, Chapel Hill.

Stone, B. (1994), *The Genesis of the French Revolution: A Global-Historical Interpretation*, Cambridge University Press, Cambridge.

Strange, S. (1996), *The Retreat of the State: The Diffusion of Power in the World Economy*, Cambridge University Press, Cambridge.

Strikwerda, C. (1997), 'Reinterpreting the History of European Integration: Business, Labor, and Social Citizenship in Twentieth-Century Europe', in J. Klausen and L.A. Tilly (eds.), *European Integration in Social and Historical Perspective: 1850 to the Present*, Rowman and Littlefield, Lanham.

Sunday Monitor, February 3, 2002.

Swann, J. (1995), *Politics and the Parlement of Paris Under Louis XV, 1754-1774*, Cambridge University Press, Cambridge.

Tamir, Y. (1993), *Liberal Nationalism*, Princeton University Press, Princeton.

Tarrow, S. (2001), 'Transnational Politics: Contention and Institutions in International Politics', *Annual Reviews of Political Science*, vol. 4, pp. 1-20.

Taylor, C. (1989), *Sources of the Self*, Harvard University Press, Cambridge.

Taylor, C. (1991), *The Malaise of Modernity*, Anansi, Concord.

Te Brake, W. (1998), *Shaping History: Ordinary People in European Politics, 1500-1700*, University of California Press, Berkeley.

Telò, M., ed. (2001), *European Union and New Regionalism: Regional Actors and Global Governance in a Post-Hegemonic Era*, Ashgate, London.

Thaa, W. (2001), 'Lean Citizenship: The Fading Away of the Political in Transnational Democracy, *European Journal of International Relations*, vol. 7, no. 4, pp. 503-23.

The Economist (1999), 'The New Trade War', December 4.

The Globe and Mail (30 October 2001), p. A1.

The New Republic (2000), 'March Madness', May 1.

Thomas, C. (2000), *Global Governance, Development and Human Security*, Pluto, London.

Thompson, D.F. (1999), 'Democratic Theory and Global Society', *Journal of Political Philosophy*, vol. 7, no. 2, pp. 111-25.

Thompson, J. (1998), 'Community Identity and World Politics', in D. Archibugi, D. Held, and M. Kohler, eds., *Re-imagining Political Community: Studies in Cosmopolitan Democracy*, Polity Press, Cambridge.

Thucydides (1954), *The Peloponnesian War*, Penguin, Harmondsworth.

Tietmeyer, H. (1998), 'Financial and Monetary Integration: Benefits, Opportunites, and Pitfalls', *1998 Mais Lecture*, City University Business School, available at: www.eurocritic.demon.co.uk.

Tilly, C. (1985), 'War Making and State Making as Organized Crime', in P.B. Evans, D. Rueschemeyer, and T. Skocpol (eds.), *Bringing the State Back In*, Cambridge University Press, Cambridge.

Tilly, C. (1992), *Coercion, Capital, and European States, AD 990-1990*, Basil Blackwell, Cambridge.

Tilly, C. (1995a), 'Globalization Threatens Labor's Rights', *International Labor and Working-Class History*, no. 47, pp. 1-23.

Tilly, C. (1995b), *Popular Contention in Britain*, Harvard University Press, Cambridge, Massachusetts.

Tilly, C. (1997), 'Parliamentarization of Popular Contention in Great Britain, 1758-1834', in C. Tilly (ed.), *Roads From Past to Future*, Rowman and Littlefield, Lanham.

Torpey, J. (1999), *The Invention of the Passport: Surveillance, Citizenship and the State*, Cambridge University Press, New York.

Tripp, A.M. (2000), *Women and Politics in Uganda*, James Currey, Oxford.

Tsebelis, G., and Garrett, G. (2001), 'The Institutional Foundations of Intergovernmentalism and Supranationalism in the European Union', *International Organization*, vol. 55, no. 2, Spring, pp. 357-90.

Tuck, R. (1979), *Natural Rights Theories*, Cambridge University Press, Cambridge.

Tuck, R. (1993), *Philosophy and Government 1572-1651*, Cambridge University Press, Cambridge.

Tully, J. (1994), 'Diversity Gambit Declined', in C. Cook (ed.), *Constitutional Predicament: Canada After the Referendum of 1992*, McGill-Queen's University Press, Montreal and Kingston.

Tully, J. (1995), *Strange Multiplicity: Constitutionalism in an Age of Diversity*, Cambridge University Press, Cambridge.

Tully, J. (2000), *The Unattained Yet Attainable Democracy*, Programme d'études sur le Québec, McGill University, Montréal.

Tully, J. (2001), 'Introduction', in A. Gagnon and J. Tully (eds)., *Multinational Democracies*, Cambridge University Press, Cambridge.

UN Office of the Under-Secretary General for Political and General Assembly Affairs and Secretariat Services (1990), 'Directory of Departments and Offices of the UN Secretariat, UN Programmes, Specialized agencies and Other Intergovernmental Organizations Dealing with Non-governmental Organizations', United Nations, New York; also in *Transnational Associations*, no. 5, 1990, pp. 292-302.

UN Secretary General (1998), 'Arrangements and Practices for the Interaction of Non-Governmental Organizations in All Activities of the United Nations System', UN General Assembly A/53/170, 10 July.

UNCTAD (2000), *Least Developed Countries 2000 Report: Aid, Private Flows and External Debt: The Challenge of Financing Development in the LDCs*, available at: http://r0.unctad.org/en/pub/ps11dc00.en.htm.

UNDP (1994), *Human Development Report 1994*, Oxford University Press, New York.

UNDP (1998), *Human Development Report on Uganda*, UNDP, Kampala.

UNDP (2000a), *Poverty Report 2000: Overcoming Human Poverty*, Oxford University Press, New York.

UNDP (2000b), *Uganda Human Development Report 2000*, UNDP, Kampala.

UNDP (2002), *Human Development Report 2002*, Oxford University Press, New York.

UNDP (2002), *The Quality of Democracy: Human Development Report*, Oxford University Press, Oxford.

UNU (2002), 'The Peace and Governance Programme: At the Interface of Ideas and Policy', *Work in Progress*, vol. 16, no. 3, Summer, pp. 1-36.

Urbinati, N. (2003), 'Can Cosmopolitical Democracy Be Democratic?', in D. Archibugi (ed.), *Debating Cosmopolitics*, Verso, London.

Van Creveld, M. (1999), *The Rise and Decline of the State*, Cambridge University Press, Cambridge.

Van Rooy, A. (1998), *Civil Society and the Aid Industry: The Politics and Promise*, Earthscan, London.

Van Rooy, A. (2001), 'Civil Society and the Axworthy Legacy', in F.O.Hampson, N. Hillmer, and M.A. Molot (eds.), *Canada Among Nations: The Axworthy Legacy*, Oxford University Press, Oxford.

Van Rooy, A. (2002) 'Strengthening Civil Society in Developing Countries', in V. Desai and R.B. Potter (eds.), *The Companion to Development Studies*, Arnold, London.

Villalon, L.A. and Huxtable, P.A., eds. (1998), *The African State at a Critical Juncture: Between Disintegration and Reconfiguration*, Lynne Rienner, Boulder.

Wade, R. (1996), 'Globalization and Its Limits: Reports on the Death of the National Economy are Greatly Exaggerated', in S. Berger and R. Dore (eds.), *National Diversity and Global Capitalism*, Cornell University Press, Ithaca.

Wade, R., and Veneroso, F. (1998), 'The Gathering World Slump and the Battle over Capital Controls', *New Left Review*, vol. 231, pp. 13-42.

Waldron, J. (1988), *The Right to Private Property*, Oxford University Press, Oxford.

Waldron, J. (1995), 'The Cosmopolitan Alternative', in W. Kymlicka (ed.), *The Rights of Minority Cultures*, Oxford University Press, Oxford.

Waldron, J. (1999), *Law and Disagreement*, Oxford University Press, Oxford.

Wallerstein, I. (1991), *Unthinking Social Science: The Limits of Nineteenth-Century Paradigms*, Polity Press, Cambridge.

Walt, S. (1998/9), 'The Ties that Fray: Why Europe and America are Drifting Apart', *The National Interest*, vol. 54, pp. 3-11.

Wapner, P. (1995), *Environmental Activism and World Civil Politics*, State University of New York Press, Buffalo.

Waters, M. (1990), *Ethnic Options*, University of California Press, Berkeley.

Weber, E. (1976), *Peasants into Frenchmen: The Modernization of Rural France, 1870-1914*, Stanford University Press, Stanford.

Weinstock, D.M. (2001), 'Prospects for Transnational Citizenship', *Ethics and International Affairs*, vol 15, no. 2, pp. 53-66.

Weintraub, S. (1997), *NAFTA at Three. A Progress Report*, Center for Strategic and International Studies, Washington.

Weiss, L. (1997), 'Globalization and the Myth of the Powerless State', *New Left Review*, no. 225, pp. 3-27.

Weiss, L. (1998), *The Myth of the Powerless State*, Cornell University Press, Ithaca.

Weiss, T.G. (2000), 'Governance, Good Governance and Global Governance', *Third World Quarterly*, vol. 21, no. 5, pp. 795-814.

Weiss, T.G., and Gordenker, L., eds. (1996), *NGOs, the UN and Global Governance*, Lynne Rienner, Boulder.

Wendt, A. (1999), 'A Comment on Held's Cosmopolitanism', in I. Shapiro and C. Hacker-Cordón (eds.), *Democracy's Edges*, Cambridge University Press, New York.

Willett, S., ed. (2001), 'Structural Conflict in the New Global Disorder: Insecurity and Development', *IDS Bulletin*, vol. 32, no. 2, April, pp. 1-106.

Willetts, P. (2001), 'Transnational Actors and International Organizations in Global Politics', in J. Baylis and S. Smith (eds.), *The Globalization of World Politics*, 2nd ed., Oxford University Press, Oxford.

Williams M. (1998), *Voice, Trust and Memory*, Princeton University Press, Princeton.

Williams, M. (2001), 'Toleration, Canadian-Style: Reflections of a Yankee-Canadian', in R. Beiner and W. Norman (eds.), *Canadian Political Philosophy*, Oxford University Press, Toronto, 216-31.

Williamson, J.G. (1996), 'Globalization, Convergence, and History', *The Journal of Economic History*, vol. 56, no. 2, June, pp. 277-303.

Wolf, K.D. (1999), 'The New Raison d'Etat as a Problem for Democracy in World Society', *European Journal of International Relations*, vol. 5, pp. 333-63.

Wolfe, A. (1998), *One Nation, After All*, Viking, New York.

Woloch, I. (1994), *The New Regime: Transformations of the French Civic Order, 1789-1820s*, W.W. Norton, New York.

Woodhouse, A.S.P. (1938), 'Introduction', in A.S.P Woodhouse (ed.), *Puritanism and Liberty*, J.M. Dent and Sons, London.

Woods, N. (2002), 'Global Governance and the Role of Institutions', in D. Held and A. McGrew (eds.), *Governing Globalization: Power, Authority and Global Governance*, Polity Press, Cambridge.

World Bank Group (1999), 'Overview of World Bank NGO Collaboration', Washington, available: www.WorldBank.com.

World Trade Organization (1998), 'Relations with NGOs', available at: www.wto.org/english/forums_e/ngo_e/intro_e.htm.

You, J.-I. (2002), 'The Bretton Woods Institutions: Evolution, Reform, and Change', in D. Nayyar (ed.), *Governing Globalization: Issues and Institutions*, Oxford University Press, Oxford.

Young, I.M. (1990), *Justice and the Politics of Difference*, Princeton University Press, Princeton.

Young, I.M. (2000), *Inclusion and Democracy*, Oxford University Press, Oxford.

Zagorin, P. (2000), 'Hobbes without Grotius', *History of Political Thought,* vol. 21, no. 1, Spring, pp. 16-40.

Zakaria, F. (1997), 'The Rise of Illiberal Democracy', *Foreign Affairs*, vol. 76, no. 6, November/December, pp. 22-43.

Zolo, D. (1994), *Democracy and Complexity*, Penn State University Press, College Park.

Zolo, D. (1997), *Cosmopolis: Prospects for World Government*, Polity Press, Cambridge.

Zoubir, Y. (1995), 'Stalled Democratization of an Authoritarian Regime: The Case of Algeria', *Democratization*, vol. 2, no. 2, Summer, pp. 109-39.

Zürn, M. (2000), 'Democratic Governance Beyond the Nation-State: The EU and Other International Institutions', *European Journal of International Relations*, vol. 6, no. 2, pp. 183-221.

Websites

www.allavida.org
www.attac.org
www.commonwealthfoundation.com
www.copenhagencentre.org
www.cpsu.org.uk
www.dfa.gov.za/events/afrinit
www.dfait-maeci.gc.ca/foreignp/humansecurity
www.g8.gc.ca
www.unglobalcompact.org
www.gdnet.org
www.hrw.org/reports/2001/uganda
www.humanrightsinitiative.org
www.ids.ac.uk
www.ifg.org
www.jubilee2000uk.org
www.nologo.org
www.oneworld.net
www.oup.com/uk/best.textbooks/politics/globalization2e
www.polity.co.uk/global
www.sas.ac.uk/commonwealthstudies
www.udn.or.ug

Index